Introducing English Studies

D1446739

Online resources to accompany this book are available at: https://www.bloomsbury.com/cw/introducing-english-studies. Please type the URL in your web browser and follow the instructions to access the Companion Website.

Introducing English Studies

**Tonya Krouse and
Tamara F. O'Callaghan**

BLOOMSBURY ACADEMIC
LONDON • NEW YORK • OXFORD • NEW DELHI • SYDNEY

BLOOMSBURY ACADEMIC
Bloomsbury Publishing Plc
50 Bedford Square, London, WC1B 3DP, UK
1385 Broadway, New York, NY 10018, USA

BLOOMSBURY, BLOOMSBURY ACADEMIC and the Diana logo are trademarks of
Bloomsbury Publishing Plc

First published in Great Britain 2020

Cover design: Eleanor Rose
Cover image © Getty Images

A catalogue record for this book is available from the British Library.

A catalog record for this book is available from the Library of Congress.

ISBN: HB: 978-1-3500-5541-4
PB: 978-1-3500-5540-7
ePDF: 978-1-3500-5543-8
eBook: 978-1-3500-5542-1

Typeset by Newgen KnowledgeWorks Pvt. Ltd., Chennai, India

To find out more about our authors and books visit www.bloomsbury.com
and sign up for our newsletters.

Contents

Acknowledgments

In the fall of 2008, Danny Miller, then the chair of the Department of English at Northern Kentucky University, assembled an ad hoc committee to undertake what then seemed a gargantuan task: to complete a dramatic overhaul of the major in English, something that had not been achieved in more than twenty years. The goal of this committee was to revise the curriculum of the major in English to reflect the strengths of the department's faculty across the fields of the discipline and to showcase for students the dynamic, multifaceted discipline of English Studies in the twenty-first century. This work resulted in a new course, Introduction to English Studies, a core course that every English major would take.

The department agreed that such a course must not only introduce students to literary studies. It valued the diversity of English Studies as a discipline, and it wanted the course to show students this diversity and reveal to them the ways in which an English degree would facilitate their personal and professional goals beyond the appreciation and study of literature. The department agreed that the multiple sections of this course should address common student learning outcomes, and, toward that end, the department sought a common textbook to assign, since we knew that bringing guest speakers in for each of the fields would not ultimately be sustainable in the long term. Such a textbook did not exist.

We, Tonya Krouse and Tamara F. O'Callaghan, worked together to create the course despite the challenges. This endeavor, which forced us to learn about fields outside of our specialization in the discipline and to create compelling assignments for students across tracks in our major, constitutes the origin of this textbook. We would like to take this opportunity to express our gratitude to those without whom the writing of this textbook would not have been possible.

First, we must thank the Northern Kentucky Faculty Senate Benefits Committee, Provost Sue Ott Rowlands, and the Northern Kentucky University Board of Regents for granting us generous support for this project. Awards of a sabbatical (Tonya Krouse) and summer fellowship (Tamara F. O'Callaghan) gave us time to draft more than half of the textbook manuscript. Additionally, a project grant (Tonya Krouse and Tamara F. O'Callaghan) allowed us to hire three undergraduate students, who gained invaluable professional experience in English Studies through this experience, to assist with proofreading, copyediting, revision, and composition of the textbook's glossary. Without this generous institutional support, we would not have been able to bring this project to completion.

We also recognize the ways in which the students in our initial Introduction to English Studies courses influenced the textbook that we have written. Each English major in the course taught us what students value in our discipline and what students find inaccessible. Our students challenged our approaches, encouraged our experiments, and gave constructive feedback from fall 2010 to spring 2017, when the writing of this textbook commenced. Their contributions cannot be underestimated. In addition, the students in Tamara F. O'Callaghan's section of Introduction to English Studies in Spring 2018 read four draft chapters and case studies from the textbook and provided honest and helpful feedback on our writing and pedagogical approach.

The most important student contributions to this project, however, must be credited to Danielle Heiert, Enrica Jackson, and Rachel Sizemore, who worked tirelessly as our editorial assistants in the summer of 2018. Their diligent work, creative thinking, and bravery in challenging our decisions made all the difference in the textbook that we produced. We initially sought funding to hire them thinking that they would be the greatest beneficiaries of our doing so. We were wrong. We gained far more from their work than we can properly express in these acknowledgments.

We also appreciate the support that we have received from our colleagues. Within our department, Janel Bloch, Jennifer Cellio, Kelly Moffett, and Peter Schiff generously suggested readings and assignments when we first struggled to design the core course and, in doing so, helped us to recognize the need for a textbook. Our former department chair Jonathan Cullick, who encouraged our development of the Introduction to English Studies course, and our current department chair John Alberti, who offered us resources for the completion of the textbook manuscript, deserve special thanks. We are grateful to Vicki Cioffe and Debbie Hollon at our university's Copy Center; they graciously and efficiently printed multiple copies of the textbook in draft form, inspiring us with encouraging words each time we picked up the copies. We also appreciate colleagues both within and outside our institution who supported the spirit of the project, read excerpts of the manuscript and gave feedback, or who gave advice. Tonya would especially like to give thanks to Jan Stirm, Meg Cotter-Lynch, Andrea Gazzaniga, Renea Frey, Caleb Pendygraft, and Tamara Cady. Tamara would especially like to give thanks to Carol Percy, Andrea Harbin, Catherine Carter, Carol Ryan, Brandi Neal, Stephanie Klatzke, Wendy Knepper, Chris Palmer, Kathy Elrick, and Heather Bovaird. Both of us also feel particularly indebted to David Avital at Bloomsbury for his unbridled enthusiasm, steady encouragement, and patient shepherding of this textbook to completion.

Last, no book project comes to fruition without personal support. We thank Shawn Mummert and Scott Molnar for their wit, wisdom, and kindness throughout the writing of this book.

Choosing English: An Introduction

If you are reading this textbook, you likely have declared an English major or minor, or you are seriously considering doing so. You might have entered university knowing that you would major or minor in English Studies or one of its many more focused areas. If that is not the case, you might be adding an English major or minor to your existing academic plan, or you might be considering changing your major or minor from something else, such as business, nursing, something in the social sciences like psychology or sociology, or something in science, technology, engineering, or math (often referred to as STEM). Choosing a major or minor means that you select a **discipline**, or an academic area of inquiry, and often within that discipline you focus on a **field** or an area of specialization within that discipline. All majors and minors reflect the broader values of an academic discipline, and many also connect to more focused disciplinary fields.

Why might students choose to pursue training in English Studies? What might they expect to discover through that training? These questions drive each chapter of *Introducing English Studies*, which aims to familiarize students with the core components of advanced engagement with English as a discipline: **language** study; textual **analysis** and **interpretation**; the creation of literary, persuasive, and professional pieces of writing; theoretical frameworks in the discipline; **pedagogical** approaches to the discipline; and technological interventions and the future of the discipline. By offering a panoramic overview of the different fields of English Studies, this textbook highlights connections between those fields and showcases debates that shape English Studies as it evolves in the twenty-first century.

As students peruse the table of contents, they may wonder how their own interests in the discipline connect to the many fields that this book represents. Why is it important to understand **rhetoric** if I want to pursue creative writing? Why, if I am interested in writing in professional settings, should I understand literature as an **art** and cultural artifact? A fundamental **argument** of this textbook is that before individuals can specialize in distinct fields of the discipline, as they might do in pursuing graduate degrees, they benefit from understanding general information about each of the fields and learning how the different fields intersect. As English Studies evolves, ideas about what counts in the discipline change, and this textbook aims to prepare students to engage with the evolving discipline long after graduation. Beyond that, *Introducing English Studies* acknowledges the ways that people and their motivations change over time, and by offering a broad introduction to the discipline, this textbook anticipates the ways in which its readers' interests and investments may grow and change with time and experience.

Furthermore, as students begin reading, they may wonder how to resolve conflicts that they perceive between the values, preoccupations, and methods of the different fields of the discipline, or why it is important to bother to do so. This textbook suggests that the work that individuals do to understand the conflicts between fields helps individuals to articulate the core values on which the fields agree. For example, while literature, rhetoric and composition, and creative writing differ significantly on key issues, they all have similar respect for the power of language as a tool for **argumentation**, self-expression, **communication**, and creativity. As students trace the common values of the fields of English Studies, they gain the necessary background to serve as ambassadors for the discipline with public audiences as well as to better understand their own academic and professional passions and purposes.

This textbook aims to provide students with a framework for thinking about their own place in the discipline of English Studies. It offers tools that students can use for selecting a complement of courses to complete their major or minor requirements, which will serve their future goals. Choosing English prepares students not only for the world of work but also for their futures as lifelong learners and engaged citizens. English Studies teaches students to interpret, write, create, and share their work with others.

Defining English Studies: Why Does English Studies Matter?

A prerequisite to choosing English Studies is understanding concretely what English Studies includes. A straightforward definition of the discipline might be the following: English Studies is a flexible, dynamic field that emphasizes both the interpretation of written **texts** and the skills of critical, creative, and professional written communication. To go further, it can also be useful to specify the discipline's most important fields, each of which has a chapter in this textbook: history of the English language; linguistics; literature; cinema, popular culture, and new media; rhetoric and composition; creative writing; professional writing and technical communication; critical theory; English education; and English Studies in the digital age. Taken together, the fields of English Studies offer students a rich and diverse framework for understanding:

1. Language, both today and historically;
2. Interpretation of texts;
3. **Composition** of texts in critical, creative, and professional contexts;
4. Pedagogies of interpretation and writing; and
5. Technologies for the production and analysis of texts.

By engaging with the discipline in these five ways, students become more effective thinkers and communicators.

English Studies, however, does not corner the market on promoting effective thinking and communicating. And the above definition does not answer the question: Why choose English Studies and not something else? To make their work in English Studies meaningful, students need to understand why the discipline has value and the purpose of a focused course of study in the discipline. Understanding what English Studies is constitutes a first step, but that step must be followed by a deep consideration of students' own motivations for engaging with the discipline.

This textbook seeks to make a case for both intrinsic and extrinsic motivations for studying English at the undergraduate level. The fields of English Studies have value both for their promotion of personal and intellectual enrichment and for their promotion of portable skills in language, writing, and interpretation. The enrichment that the discipline offers students is rooted in humanistic inquiry and the appreciation of the language arts, and this education has worth because it acknowledges the positive emotional, creative, psychological, and **aesthetic** benefits that deep engagement with language and literature can produce. A major or minor in English Studies not only prepares students for a career, but it also prepares them for the complexities of life beyond work, and it promotes aesthetic, intellectual, and creative pleasures as central to a meaningful life. The skills that the discipline offers students make them career-ready at graduation, and most students—who go into considerable debt in order to pursue their educations and who are very aware of the need to choose career paths with solid return on investment in terms of job opportunities—care deeply about acquiring these skills. As a discipline, English Studies provides significant intrinsic and extrinsic rewards for students, and by learning about each of the discipline's fields, students gain a deeper sense of their own motivations for pursuing this course of study.

What Are You Going to Do with English Studies?

The short answer to that question is, anything you want. The benefit of a background in English Studies is that strong interpretive and communication skills are essential for all twenty-first-century careers, and majoring or minoring in English or one of its fields emphasizes those skills. Depending on the courses that you select for your program of study, combining your major(s) and/or minor(s), you can position yourself to excel in careers in the fields of:

- Law
- Human Resources
- Teaching
- Writing (creative or professional)
- Editing
- Politics
- Medicine or Health Professions
- Publishing
- **Social Media** or other **Journalism** or Public Relations Fields
- Technology
- Business

The benefit of a major or minor in English Studies is that it can assist you throughout your evolution as a professional, and it is not connected to one limited career path. Rather, English Studies can serve your goals as they evolve over a lifetime and as they combine with your evolving interests, talents, and skills. A major or minor in English Studies is "evergreen"—it remains alive, vibrant, and practical even if your career path takes a new direction.

How Does This Book Introduce English Studies, and How Should I Use It?

Introducing English Studies aims to do just that: to introduce you to the full breadth and scope of the discipline of English. The goal is to give a beginning major or minor, or someone who thinks they might choose a major or minor in English Studies, a comprehensive picture of each of the important fields of the discipline. This broad knowledge will assist them not only in planning the courses that they will take as a university student but also in determining how they can possibly use what they learn beyond their bachelor's degree—whether that means applying to graduate or professional school, pursuing a professional career after graduation, or beginning a career in teaching.

Beyond that, this textbook seeks to treat the different fields of English Studies fairly and judiciously, offering **commentary** that situates each field within larger conversations about the discipline. It aims to acknowledge the links between fields, and it seeks to draw attention to the different objectives and different problem-solving approaches of the fields. It is not the goal of this textbook to offer a judgment-free or "neutral" accounting of each field, which is, frankly, both impossible and impossibly dry reading. Instead, *Introducing English Studies* attempts in each chapter to excite students about the study of each field by pointing to important controversies, offering **context**, and making judgments about essential information for novices in the discipline. Individual instructors who use this textbook will offer their own perspectives, supplement these chapters with their own outside readings, or bring in outside speakers to give additional insight into the fields of the discipline, and they may offer contradictory points of view to what students read here. The biggest takeaway for students should be that English Studies is a living, breathing entity, and although its practitioners sometimes disagree, it is in negotiating those disagreements that we confirm the bonds between us and adapt for new problems, questions, and interpretive possibilities. By the time that students finish reading these chapters, they should have their own opinions about the discipline and feel equipped to enter these debates themselves.

As a foundation for that outcome, students should familiarize themselves with the parts of this textbook. Begin by paying close attention to the *key questions* of each chapter and the answers that the textbook offers to them. They provide students with a roadmap for thinking about each of the fields in the discipline and about how those fields connect to English Studies as a whole. While students may not be equally interested in all of the fields, as practitioners of English Studies, they might be asked questions related to one or more of them, and they should be able to answer key questions about each field. This textbook will teach students how to do that. Students should also pay attention to the *terms in bold*, for which definitions are provided in the glossary at the back of this book. By understanding the terms and phrases that English Studies practitioners think are important, you can yourself participate in conversations that are important in the discipline. At the end of each chapter, the textbook points students to *further reading* that they might do to learn more about the chapter's field. In the interest of providing students with all of the information they might need to access these sources without privileging one particular style for all English Majors, the textbook does not use the most common **citation styles** for undergraduates in English Studies: Modern Language Association (MLA Style) and American Psychological Association (APA Style). Students should not use the further reading citations as a model for their own citations unless instructed to do so by their professors. Finally, each chapter also includes *case studies. Case studies* in *Introducing English Studies* offer a model for how to approach a specific topic or example using an approach that is compatible with the field of English Studies to which the case study is linked. Then, they offer different ways that you can practice doing similar work with topics or examples with which you have a deeper familiarity. Your instructor might assign some of these to you, or you might be left to explore these case studies on your own. Each of the case studies gives exercises for students that will help them to understand a different field of the discipline, and if you are having trouble "getting" a particular field, the case study exercises will help you to make sense of it.

Making the Case for English Studies

English Studies excites its practitioners because it marries a love of language with a desire to interpret and to create. Unlike many majors or minors that students might choose, English Studies teaches skills that are transferrable across many different career paths, and it encourages students to hone their creative capacity even as they prepare for the world of work. English Studies gives students flexible skills for a variety of futures: it does not require them to know their futures before they meet them. It also gives them tools for lifelong learning: it does not see college as the end of intellectual life.

In the chapters that follow, students will learn about language, history, interpretation, writing, teaching, and technology. By addressing these various perspectives within the discipline of English Studies, *Introducing English Studies* makes an argument for the inclusivity of English Studies as a discipline. Instead of understanding English as a collection of fractured fields that compete for primacy within academic departments, this textbook considers it essential to integrate the different fields into one cohesive whole. Undergraduates typically come to English Studies with diverse backgrounds, motivations, goals, and ideals, and it is essential for the discipline to respond to that diversity with one coherent, if complex, message. This textbook seeks to provide its readers with just that.

1

History of the English Language

The English **language** has an immense wealth of vocabulary to which we are constantly adding as new **words** are created in response to cultural developments in such areas as technology, politics, social media, journalism, and music. Some words are used for a limited period of time, and others become part of our permanent vocabulary. Each year, members of the American Dialect Society (ADS), an organization founded in 1889 to study the English language particularly in North America, nominate and then select by vote the word or **phrase** that has been particularly prominent over the past year. Examples of words that have been chosen recently include *dumpster fire, #blacklivesmatter, hashtag, google, app, tweet, plutoed, subprime, bailout, truthiness, metrosexual, WMD,* and *9/11.* At first glance, these words may not seem to have much in common, or we may not understand why they would be grouped together. However, a quick scan of the words listed above reveals their association with significant cultural preoccupations in the early twenty-first century, including war, terrorism, economic crises, technological developments, social media, racial tensions, political challenges, scientific revision, and gendered stereotypes. The yearly nominations and their connection to specific historic events at national and global levels demonstrate how language change is normal, ongoing, and even entertaining. Perhaps more importantly, these words also reveal how we can better understand the significance of written and spoken English by intentionally examining the English language and its historical development.

Although few students come to the English major with a knowledge of the History of the English Language (HEL) and its importance for English Studies, most students are aware that words have power and that they, as savvy users of English, need to differentiate between informal and formal

registers of the language, especially in their **academic writing**. As a field of the broader discipline of English Studies, HEL can give students the tools to understand how language, at a fundamental level, grounds our ideas about interpretation and communication. At the heart of English Studies is language: language is not just a tool for writing text; it is the text's fundamental essence. This chapter will address how an understanding of the historical development of English as a language is foundational to English Studies.

Key Questions

1. What is History of the English Language, and why are we studying history and language in an English course?
2. Why does everyone else have an **accent**?
3. What do we mean by "good" and "bad" English, and who decides?
4. What are the conventions of HEL scholarship? What kinds of research and interpretation do HEL scholars do?
5. What is HEL in the twenty-first century? How does it connect to English Studies, more broadly conceived?

What Is History of the English Language, and Why Are We Studying History and Language in an English Course?

History of the English Language, or HEL (pronounced "hell") as it is jokingly called, provides an overview of the historical development of the English language and an introduction to **historical linguistics**. Whereas the field of linguistics in English Studies focuses primarily on language structure at a particular moment in time, HEL focuses on both the "internal" history of language—sounds, **inflection**, and word order—and the "external" history of language—the political, social, and intellectual forces that influence language—over time. By understanding something of the English language's history, we can better understand English's current and future changes as well as appreciate the power and politics of language in general. We can also become more sophisticated readers and writers of English: understanding this history of our language can help us to understand **dialect** in a regional novel, to create a fully developed character or concretely articulated image in our own fiction or poetry, or to communicate effectively in a workplace or community setting.

To begin, our understanding of this field can benefit from a brief overview of how English evolves over time. Although many mistakenly believe that English has its origins in Latin because Britain was once part of the Roman Empire, that is not true. We know that early Britain was inhabited by the Picts, Scots, and Celts who had their own language when Julius Caesar first crossed the English Channel from Gaul (present-day France) in 55 BCE. Despite Caesar's famous statement "*Veni, vidi, vici* [I came, I saw, I conquered]" upon arriving on British shores, it was not until Roman troops under Emperor Claudius invaded Britain in 43 CE that Britain actually came under Roman rule. The Romans subjugated the native inhabitants, destroying their communities and driving many of the survivors into Cornwall, Wales, and Scotland. Those who remained were enslaved and may have eventually intermarried, thereby losing their cultural and language **identity**. Latin was the language used by the Romans in Britain, but when the Romans withdrew in the fifth century, Latin did not leave the legacy we might expect. It simply did not take hold in Britain as it did in the Roman Empire elsewhere in continental Europe. This absence would have a significant impact on the development of the English language.

The Anglo-Saxons and Old English

The departure of the Romans left the Celtic people defenseless against the Picts and Scots, who almost immediately invaded from the north of Britain. Desperate, the Celts turned to their sometime trading partners, the Germanic tribes, for help. The Germanic tribes came from the northwestern coastline of continental Europe and consisted of the Angles, Saxons, Jutes, and Frisians, all of whom spoke closely related German dialects. They quickly drove the Picts and Scots back north. However, the Germanic tribes ultimately wanted Britain for themselves, so they also drove the Celts into Wales, Cornwall, and across the Channel into Brittany, France. The Germanic dialects spoken by the new conquerors became the basis for the English language, which is why English is a member of the Germanic language family along with German, Dutch, and Frisian. When **Old English** writings, such as the epic poem *Beowulf*, were first written down in the seventh, eighth, and ninth centuries, there was considerable regional variation in the language. We do not know much about this English in its earliest form because few written records survive.

When speakers of **Present-Day English** encounter Old English writing, they might mistake it for a foreign language because it has distinct features not found in English today. The Old English alphabet does not have the letters "v" or "z" but does have two unique ones, þ (thorn) and ð (eth), to represent the "th" combination of Present-Day English. The language is also characterized by non-rigid word order: inflectional endings on nouns, pronouns, adjectives, articles, and verbs indicate the grammatical function of words in a **sentence**, so word order does not contribute as significantly to meaning in Old English as it does in Present-Day English. Inflection also meant that end **rhyming** in poetry was extremely difficult to achieve, so **alliteration** was used instead.

We may think that English today does not inherit this feature of inflection from Old English, but it does. Just look at our pronouns. We have very different pronoun forms for the **subject**, object (direct or indirect), and **possessive**. Consider the following sentences:

Mary likes Bob.	*Bob likes Mary.*
She likes him.	*He likes her.*

In the sentences on the first line, the noun forms are the same where they are the subject or direct object of the sentence. However, change those nouns to pronouns, and we see something quite different. Those different pronoun forms are a holdover of the inflected forms in Old English.

We also see the legacy of Old English in some of our verbs. Old English had many verbs that indicated the past tense by a modification of the root vowel: what we now call **irregular verbs**, such as *sing-sang-sung*. Even some of our **regular verbs** indicate that they once used the vowel modification to indicate the past tense. The verb *melt-melted-melted* follows the regular verb pattern in Present-Day English, but look down the opening of a volcano and you see *molten* (not *melted*) lava. Since Old English seldom borrowed vocabulary from other languages, it relied on compounding to create new words. Therefore, *leohtfæt* ("light" + "fat") is translated as *lamp* and *dægred* ("day" + "red") as *dawn*.

The Vikings and Old Norse

By the eighth century, Viking raiders began to attack the Christian descendants of the Germanic tribes. These invaders spoke Old Norse and had settled into northern and eastern Britain by the mid-ninth century. England was even ruled by a Danish king, Canute, in the eleventh century. Therefore, we might expect Old Norse to have had a significant influence on the development of the English language, but it did not. Old Norse encouraged the loss of inflection in Old English. There was some borrowing of vocabulary from Old Norse, such as *wife, husband, happy, anger, awe, foot, leg,* and *freckles.* However, because Old English and Old Norse were likely mutually intelligible, the incorporation of numerous loanwords from Old Norse into Old English may not have been necessary. Why adopt a word from another language if you already have an equivalent?

The French and Middle English

If the Vikings had a limited influence on the development of the English language, the French had quite the opposite effect when they invaded England in 1066. A dispute over the English throne led to the Battle of Hastings between the two claimants, King Harold and William, Duke of Normandy. William was the victor, becoming William the Conqueror and William I of England, with the result that French became the language of the English court and the aristocracy. The English needed to learn enough Norman French to communicate, but they were only expected to learn more if they entered the professional classes. Because the Normans probably never exceeded more than two percent of the population in England, the English language persisted alongside Norman French. In the end, this allowed the English language to survive and thrive as **Middle English**, the English of the later Middle Ages.

This later medieval period marked a change in the grammar and vocabulary of English more extensive than at any time in history. Some changes were the direct result of the Norman Conquest, while others were already in progress but developed more rapidly under the Normans. The most significant grammatical change was the increased decay of inflection. The endings of nouns and adjectives marking distinction of number, **case,** and often **grammatical gender** altered in pronunciation and thus lost their distinctive form and usefulness. There is a similar change in verbs. The reduction of inflectional endings is result of (a) **phonetics** (changes in pronunciation) and (b) **analogy** (the tendency of language to follow familiar patterns). Middle English had two methods to indicate plural: –s or –es for the "strong" **declensions** and –en for the "weak." By 1200, –s was standard plural form in the north of England; two hundred years later, it was the standard plural form all over England, a change that may have been helped by –s plural ending in Norman French. As a result, we today pluralize "brother" as "brothers" rather than as the older form "brethren." This loss of inflection also encouraged the loss of grammatical gender.

The Norman invasion also introduced a large body of new vocabulary. Norman French was the language of the ruling class and, consequently, became the language of the law courts, of the military, and of culture. We can see this legacy in English today. Although the animal in the field may be a cow, pig, or sheep, that same animal served on a plate for dinner becomes *beef (boeuf)*, *pork (porc)*, and *mutton (mouton)*. Norman French spelling conventions were also borrowed. The scribes used "th" for the Old English thorn and eth; "uu" was introduced and ligatured as "w" as the name suggests; the scribes also introduced "v" and "z" as well as "ch," "sh," and "qu" as new letter combinations. The conquerors became the rulers of the English people, imposing the vocabulary and conventions of their language onto English.

The Printing Press and Standardization of Early Modern English

With the start of the English Renaissance in the fifteenth century, Middle English evolved into **Early Modern English**, lasting as such until the eighteenth century. The most significant development of the period was the invention of **movable type** and the introduction of the **printing press** in Germany in the mid-fifteenth century. William Caxton brought the printing press to England in 1476, setting up a shop in London. Within a century from that date, handwritten manuscripts are seldom seen and rarely used.

Before 1500, thirty-five thousand books were printed in Europe (mostly in Latin). By 1640, twenty thousand English titles were printed. Books became affordable. More importantly, books could be reproduced in unlimited quantities, thereby promoting a standard, uniform English language, spreading that language throughout England, and creating a demand for **literacy**. The middle class wanted books specifically in English rather than in Latin because they wanted to read but did not have the time or money for an education in Latin and Ancient Greek. The printing presses first came to London because of the city's commercial and political importance. As a result, the dialect of London became the standard for written English. As books were sold throughout England, people accepted London English as the one to know. In addition, English continued to be the language of choice for literary creation.

At the same time that the printing press was codifying written English and spelling was beginning to be standardized, a change in the pronunciation of **long vowels** began. The **Great Vowel Shift** started in the fourteenth century and did not finish until the eighteenth century. This change in vowel pronunciation helps us to understand why the Middle English of Geoffrey Chaucer is so difficult for students to read, but the Early Modern English of William Shakespeare is easier to decipher. Nevertheless, Shakespeare's English and its pronunciation is not that of Present-Day English. David Crystal, a British academic who works extensively on the English language, actively promotes **Original Pronunciation**—that is, the performance of texts in the original pronunciation of the English of the time. In 2004, he worked with the Globe Theatre in London to produce a highly successful performance of *Romeo and Juliet* in the original pronunciation of the play. For example, Crystal has demonstrated that *loins* and *lines* sounded very similar in the English of Shakespeare's time, making the words a pun and drawing a clear, but long missed, connection between the *loins* of the body and *lines* of families. Such reconstruction of English pronunciation allows us to hear effects in older texts that are lost when we read them with the pronunciation of Present-Day English.

The early modern period is also noteworthy for the artificial introduction of Latin-based words into the English language with the intention of making English a more "noble" language. Unlike the introduction of loanwords from past invaders, this vocabulary did not come from a conquering people. Instead, the educated borrowed from Latin to create new words in order to "improve" English. Not all these new words were successfully adopted, and it was the first time speakers actively debated over language use: was English enriched by new vocabulary or corrupted by unusable words? Those words that faced the greatest objections were called **inkhorn terms**, such as *anacephalize* (to recapitulate), *eximious* (excellent, distinguished, eminent), *fatigate* (to fatigue), and *illecebrous* (alluring, enticing, attractive). Those that faced objections but ultimately were accepted include *ingenious, capacity, mundane, celebrate, extol, dexterity, illustrate, superiority, fertile, contemplate, invigilate, pastoral, confidence, compendious, relinquish, frivolous, verbosity,* and *invidious.* Despite the seeming pretentiousness of this intentional introduction of new vocabulary, the result gives the English language breadth and diversity.

English in the United States

With global exploration in the seventeenth century, English begins its expansion as a colonizing and global language. It comes to the United States in the form of Early Modern English with the colonial settlers who initially land along the Atlantic coast from Maine to Georgia. With further migrations in the eighteenth and nineteenth centuries, American English along the Eastern seaboard developed into regional dialects that were influenced by other languages brought by additional waves of immigration from around the world. As the new population moved West, regional dialects merged, becoming broader and less distinct than those on the East coast. There is a perceived uniformity of American English, but that perception is wrong. Accent and dialect variation exists across the country, although we could argue that **Standard American English (SAE)** does exist as a uniform "broadcast standard" in national news media.

The standardization of American English was perhaps most desired by Noah Webster in the nineteenth century. As the United States sought to establish its own national identity in the years following the American Revolution, Webster helped to create an American English to support that identity. Both his *American Dictionary of the English Language,* first published in 1828, and his efforts at spelling reform significantly shaped American English for the future, making it distinct from British English. As a result, American English uses *honor, neighbor,* and *color* instead of *honour, neighbour,* and *colour* as well as *realize* and *analyze* rather than *realise* and *analyse.* American English also had to create new words over the years for animals (*chipmunk* and *racoon*), weather/geographic phenomena (*tornado* and *bayou*), and objects (*bleachers* and *soda pop*) that were unique to the United States. In fact, American English soon distinguished itself from its mother tongue in terms of vocabulary, pronunciation, and spelling.

The forced transportation of Africans as slaves to the United States in the seventeenth century was also significant for the development of **African American English (AAE)** or **African American Vernacular English (AAVE)**, often called **Ebonics** by nonlinguists. The exact origin of AAE is still being debated. Some scholars argue that it arose from the **creoles** spoken by victims of the **Transatlantic African slave trade**, which became less distinctive by the time of the American Revolution. Other scholars suggest that it emerged from the early British dialects of the American South. It has its own vocabulary and **syntax**. For example, AAE will use "ax" or "aks" in place of "ask." This form is not a mistake but a pronunciation variation known as **metathesis**, the switching of two sounds in a word. In fact, the AAE verb form can be found in early Old English; the sound switch to the more recognized standard form took place in the ninth century. Thus, the AAE forms of "ax" or "aks" are not inferior to the SAE "ask" and are, in fact, historically connected to it.

Half the countries in the world have **official languages** but not the United States. Legend states that English defeated German by only a single vote to become the official language of the United States in a 1795 debate in Congress, but this story is not true. What was argued at that congressional debate was a proposal to print federal laws in German as well as in English. A motion to adjourn failed by a single vote, and a month later, the translation proposal was voted down. Although English remains the standard language for government and law in the United States, it has no official status at the federal level. Thirty-two of the states have made English an official language at the state level: thirty states recognize English as their only official language; Hawaii and Alaska recognize English and specific native languages as official languages.

English Today

The extraordinary thing about English is that it continues to evolve and adapt. Approximately one thousand new words are formally added each year to the language, according to the *Oxford English Dictionary*, and that does not include the **slang** and new vocabulary that have yet to be formally accepted. American English, in all its varieties, is particularly influential on a global level, thanks to the influence of U.S. businesses, technology, cinema, music, and literature.

Why Does Everyone Else Have an Accent?

There are many stereotypes about accent in the United States: New Yorkers speak quickly; Southerners speak slowly; Minnesotans are "dutchified" (a regional English pronunciation influenced by German). We all notice other people's accents but never our own. As any HEL scholar will tell you, "Everyone has an accent ... even you." We generally perceive others as the ones with the accent because they do not sound like us. In fact, the challenge of accent is that we cannot hear it or define it until we have another accent to which to compare it. Accent may not initially appear to be present, but once it is, you cannot stop hearing it. Regional variations in accent and even dialect define you, whether you like it or not. For example, someone with a Southern accent will typically pronounce words ending in *-in*, *-en*, *-im*, and *-em* with the same vowel sound so that *pin* and *pen* will sound the same. And as a speaker of a Southern dialect, that person will likely refer to a soft drink as a *coke* rather than as a *soda* (Northeast coast) or *pop* (Midwest).

We all are highly aware of how the people around us use English, but we more rarely step back and think about our own language use, the relationship of language to our identities, and the power of language more generally. Traveling to or living in different parts of the country can heighten our awareness of dialect; mastering or teaching traditional grammatical rules can highlight the difference between our spoken and written language. We all speak a dialect, and we all have an accent. While all dialects and accents are considered equal linguistically, they are not equal socially: speakers often have biases for and against particular varieties of English (e.g., which varieties are "good" and which are "bad"; which are "ugly sounding"; and which are "cool sounding" or "smart sounding"). And many people worry that the internet, email, texting, and other new technologies are ruining English. HEL heightens your awareness of how the language all around you works, how beliefs about language work, and how intertwined language is with our identities.

For English Studies, accent and dialect are important to understanding literary works, films, or television shows. The use of accent and dialect can make a character more realistic, but it can also encourage stereotyping. How do you represent regional or cultural speech in written text if you are the writer or in a spoken text if you are an actor? How do you analyze it for a literary analysis if you are the reader? In fact, a close look at the representation of AAE in a television series, such as *Empire*, which premiered in 2005, illustrates that representing African Americans in the music industry requires the actors to speak AAE for realism. But compare that representation of AAE to the speech of the character of Carlton Banks in *The Fresh Prince of Bel Air*, a sitcom that ran from 1990 to 1996, and there is a significant difference. The Banks family uses SAE because the family is portrayed as upper class and well educated. AAE is more accepted on television and in movies today, but does it alienate audiences who judge AAE as inferior to SAE? Perhaps for now, but including AAE demonstrates a growing acceptance of African American culture.

When speakers of SAE are confronted with a variation of American English, such as AAE or English spoken with a foreign accent, they must decide if they are going to accept the variation and even participate in it. All too often, SAE speakers feel empowered to reject the variation and demand that the speaker embrace SAE or, alternatively, to relegate the variation to a negative or disempowered status. The linguist Rosina Lippi-Greene has argued that Disney animated movies teach children to judge accents that vary from SAE negatively. For example, in *The Lion King* (1994), Mufasa, the hero, speaks in SAE, while Scar, the villain, has a British accent, and his hyena compatriots speak in AAE or English with a Spanish accent. In fact, it seems that American audiences view the British-sounding villain as evil but intelligent; however, they view the comic minor characters who speak non-SAE as foolish and even stupid. Disney thus reinforces the stereotype that "happily ever after" is just for SAE speakers.

Rather than dividing regional and ethnic accents and dialects into "good" and "bad" English, we need to understand their origins and recognize the diversity of English across the United States and across the world.

What Do We Mean by "Good" and "Bad" English, and Who Decides?

Lots of people talk about "good" and "bad" English. Some even speak about a "standard" English. However, very few people consider who makes the rules about English and who implements them. Other languages have long-standing, formal institutions, known as language academies, to oversee a language and enforce decisions about grammar rules, language use, etc. Such institutions include L'Académie Française for French, Real Academia Española for Spanish, and Rat für deutsche Rechtschreibung for German. However, of the ten most spoken languages in the world, English is the only one without such a legislative body. English has, instead, evolved and continues to evolve without such intentional guidance and legislated restrictions. And English is not likely to create such an institution now.

Since this is the case, to whom do we turn for advice about the "rules" of English usage? For most of us, these authorities include parents, who first teach us English; teachers, who instruct us in formal grammar, spelling, and punctuation as part of our education; journalists and columnists who write about the English language; and editors of **dictionaries, lexicons, grammar books, usage guides**, and **style guides**. We may view some of these people as experts because of their education, training, and work, but many of them would deny that their role is to legislate English. A few journalists, such as *Atlantic Monthly* columnist Barbara Wallraff, do view their role as "policing" the English language, but most authorities want to instruct.

Dictionaries and lexicons are often considered absolute authorities on the English language—just consider the role of a dictionary when playing the board game Scrabble. However, such authority is relatively new; English dictionaries were originally just lists of "hard words" rather than comprehensive catalogues of the language. Even Webster's *American Dictionary of the English Language* was not intended so much as a language authority as a statement of American identity after the winning of the American Revolution. In addition, there are usage guides that provide instructions on the conventionally accepted use of language and grammar, especially in relation to writing. A standard guide has been Henry Watson Fowler's *A Dictionary of Modern English Usage* (1926), which has undergone a number of revisions and new editions with new editors over the years. Such a guide explains the perceived "rules" of English at the time of publication, providing the history and application of each rule. Fowler's text has become a standard and particularly relevant for British and Commonwealth English. As a result, in 1998, Bryan Garner, a lawyer in the United States, wrote *A Dictionary of Modern American English Usage* to address conventions of American English. It has been revised and expanded to become *Garner's Modern Usage* (2016).

Many of these so-called authorities would also deny that there is such a thing as "good" and "bad" English, only a stable language that is constantly changing. For example, students have often been taught not to begin a sentence with *and* or *but* in formal writing. Even today, many grammar guides, both online and in print, discourage starting a sentence with either word as though it is a grammar rule when, in fact, it is not. From the Anglo-Saxon period to the present day, and in a wide variety of texts, including the Bible, writers and translators often begin sentences with *and* or *but*. In fact, this textbook, including this chapter, does too. Even the English usage guides by Fowler and Garner find such sentences acceptable. It is just a matter of stylistic preference.

Much of this discussion rests on the distinction between **prescriptivism** and **descriptivism** in language: that is, the *prescribing* of rules for English usage versus the *describing* of how English is actually used. HEL scholars generally see themselves as descriptivists: they are interested in how English is used and evolving. Nevertheless, there are instances when prescriptivist rules are the guiding principle in English. In 2014, a class-action lawsuit about overtime pay for a group of truck drivers in Maine depended on the lack of an **Oxford** (or **serial**) **comma** in the state law of Maine. The Oxford comma is the inclusion of a comma before "and" in a list of three or more items. The drivers sued their employer, Oakhurst Dairy, for unpaid overtime and lost wages. A provision in the state law regarding overtime work stated that the following activities did not qualify for overtime pay:

The canning, processing, preserving, freezing, drying, marketing, storing, packing for shipment and distribution of:

(1) *Agricultural produce;*
(2) *Meat and fish products; and*
(3) *Perishable foods.*

The absence of a comma between "shipment" and "and" allowed the drivers to argue that the "packing for shipment and distribution" was a single activity (packing), not two separate activities (packing and distributing). Since the drivers distributed but did not pack the Dairy's products, they claimed that they were owed overtime pay. The court found in favor of the drivers, and Oakhurst Dairy was suddenly responsible for millions of dollars in back pay. The company appealed the decision but, in February 2018, lost the appeal and agreed to pay the drivers $5 million. In the meantime, the Maine Legislature corrected the problem in the language of the law, a revision that included replacing all the commas with semicolons and adding a semicolon before the troublesome "and." However, even though most style guides in the United States require the Oxford comma, the *Associated Press Stylebook*, which governs American newspapers, is much more ambivalent about it, recommending it only be used to avoid confusion.

As the historical development of the language demonstrates and what these examples show is that English has been—and continues to be—a flexible language that continually changes based on its everyday usage. This means that writers and speakers of English must make difficult choices about their language use in order to assure that what they say communicates not only what they mean but also the tone and authority that they intend. Research in HEL can help us to understand the stakes of those judgments.

What Are the Conventions of HEL Scholarship? What Kinds of Research and Interpretation Do HEL Scholars Do?

HEL scholars have traditionally focused on the language of literary texts. Such a focus is not surprising given the fact that HEL is taught in English departments and has its origins as a scholarly field in the nineteenth century, a period that valued literature above other writing. Although we might be more familiar with a literary studies approach to literature, one in which we may examine the development of images, themes, characters, plot devices, or poetics in poetry, drama, or fiction, the HEL scholar would be interested in the grammar, lexical or syntactic innovation, dialect, slang, or **jargon** in the text, be it literary or something else. For example, a HEL analysis of William Shakespeare's *Hamlet* might focus on the use of *thou* and *you* in terms of character relationships or the social and emotional factors in the play. Or the HEL scholar might explore new words in the English language that are introduced by Shakespeare. Another approach would be to examine dialect in a regional novel and consider the appropriateness of the dialect to the characters—and even the author—who use it. For example, how does an author of a story set in the mountains of West Virginia ensure that the characters' dialect accurately reflects the complexity of Appalachian English rather than a caricature of "hillbilly" speech?

Recent approaches in HEL scholarship have moved away from focusing only on literary texts. Slang or jargon in a specific community or occupation is often the subject of research. HEL scholars are also curious about recent loanwords from other languages and the constant challenges to punctuation and grammar rules. There is also considerable interest in language and technology. Technology places demands of various kinds on language, including limits on the length of communication that can be sent through social media networks like texting and Twitter, calls for new and increasingly specialized vocabularies in the fields of science and engineering, and requirements that the language of technology be accessible to more global and linguistically diverse communities. While these kinds of demands can be seen to impoverish English by limiting or reducing its use, they can also spur innovative and creative language use.

Although HEL scholars often examine old texts and **archival materials** in order to trace language change, they also use **online linguistic corpora** just as linguists do. They simply ask different questions of the electronic data. They are not so interested in a snapshot of English at a specific moment in time but rather its evolution over a period of time.

What Is HEL in the Twenty-First Century? How Does Its Connect to English Studies, More Broadly Conceived?

Although there will always be considerable interest in the early development of the English language, practitioners in the field of HEL are currently intrigued by the influence of social media and activism on the development of English. Let's consider the word *woke*. It has its origins in AAE where the verb *awake* is often expressed as *woke* as in "I was sleeping, but now I am woke." The word took on the more figurative meaning of being well-informed or aware in the early 1960s. That meaning has narrowed to more specifically an awareness of social and racial justice, thanks primarily to Erykah Badu's 2008 song "Master Teacher" with its steady refrain of "I stay woke." Thus, the word *woke* became the phrase *stay woke* with which many African Americans identified as an expression of their self-awareness of injustice and racial struggle. It evolved yet again with the 2014 shooting of Michael Brown in Ferguson, Missouri. The phrase *stay woke* became the hashtag *#StayWoke* as social media activists called for justice.

As *woke* and *stay woke* have been accepted into mainstream English, the meaning has broadened. Any activism on social media may be described as "woke twitter," expanding to include political activism and social justice beyond the African American community. Significantly, in June 2017, this figurative use of *woke* was included for the first time in the *Oxford English Dictionary* with the definition "Originally: well-informed, up-to-date. Now chiefly: alert to racial or social discrimination and injustice." In addition, the dictionary made a public appeal for citations of *woke* that predate the earliest citation found by the editors: the word in a glossary of African American slang in the 1962 *New York Times* article "If you're woke, you dig it" by novelist William Melvin Kelly. In this article, Kelly addresses the appropriation of African American slang by white social activists, a concern that continues today. Although *woke* is now more broadly accepted in the English language, it becomes so at a price. As the meaning has narrowed from *awake* to a social justice movement, the word *woke* has been increasingly embraced by an online white community seeking to recognize their own social consciousness. The result can be viewed as the appropriation rather than support of African American racial justice.

As the preceding example shows, HEL does not merely focus on dusty tomes locked in an **archive** but connects to the language that we use every day and the way that it informs our understanding of the world in which we live. In this way, HEL's concerns connect to concerns that drive other fields in the discipline of English Studies.

Further Reading

Adams, Michael. *Slang: The People's Poetry*. New York: Oxford University Press, 2009.
   Examines slang in American English, focusing on its inventiveness.

Bailey, Richard W. *Images of English: A Cultural History of the Language*. Ann Arbor: University of Michigan Press, 1991.
   Offers a cultural overview of the history of the English language.

Blake, N. F. *A History of the English Language*. New York: New York University Press, 1996.

Offers a standard general history of the English language.

Coleman, Julie. *The Life of Slang*. New York: Oxford University Press, 2012.
Examines slang from Old English to today's English.

Crystal, David. *The Cambridge Encyclopedia of the English Language*. 2nd ed.
New York: Cambridge University Press, 2003.
Presents an accessible encyclopedia on the English language.

Crystal, David. *The Stories of English*. New York: Overlook Press, 2005.
Offers an accessible introduction to the history of the English language.

Crystal, David. *Txtng: The Gr8 Db8*. New York: Oxford University Press, 2008.
Explores the impact of technology on the English language.

Fought, Carmen. *Chicano English in Context*. New York: Palgrave
Macmillan, 2003.
Offers a comprehensive study of Chicano English.

Hodson, Jane. *Dialect in Film & Literature*. New York: Palgrave
Macmillan, 2014.
Examines dialect representation in both film and literature.

Lippi-Green, Rosina. *English with an Accent: Language, Ideology, and
Discrimination in the United States*. 2nd ed. New York: Routledge, 2011.
Examines how accent in American English contributes to discrimination in
the United States.

Mufwene, Salikoko S., John R. Rickford, Guy Bailey, and John
Baugh, eds. *African American English: Structure, History and Use*.
New York: Routledge, 1998.
Provides a comprehensive overview of AAE.

Rickford, John R., and Russell J. Rickford. *Spoken Soul: The Story of Black
English*. New York: Wiley, 2000.
Explores AAE, from its origins to its social impact.

Smith, K. Aaron, and Susan M. Kim. *This Language, A River: A History of
English*. Peterborough: Broadview Press, 2018.
Introduces the history of the English language, recognizing multiple
varieties of the language in both current and historical contexts.

Wolfram, Walt, and Natalie Schilling-Estes. *American English: Dialects and
Variation*. 2nd ed. Malden: Blackwell, 2005.
Examines language variation in American English, including regional,
ethnic, and gender-based differences.

In this Case Study, we examine how new words are created in the English language, focusing on Shakespeare's traditional position as the author who introduces more new words than anyone else to English and the unique vocabulary pool now offered by rap artists. We then offer engagement activities that you can use to help you better understand the process of word formation in English, its impact on the language, and its connection to the History of the English Language.

Do Hip-Hop Artists Have a Larger and More Unique Vocabulary in English than Shakespeare?

One of the facts you may have heard when you first encountered Shakespeare was that Shakespeare introduced the most **neologisms**, or new words, into the English language, including such examples as *new-fangled*, *pageantry*, *eyeball*, *bedazzled*, and *assassination*. But how are such new words created in English? And how does a word get absorbed into our culture? Is it really true that Shakespeare has introduced the most words?

How Do We Create New Words in English?

A search of the online *Oxford English Dictionary* indicates that Shakespeare first introduced well over a thousand of the words listed in the dictionary. It may be that many, if not all, of these words circulated verbally before Shakespeare, but, at the very least, he is the first writer to have written down these words and had them eventually published (and survive) in print, a significant contribution.

English, like all languages, has a variety of techniques for forming new words. Certainly, we sometimes invent new words spontaneously, but there are actually formal processes for creating new vocabulary:

Compounding: word formed by the combination of two words to create a new one—*hashtag*

Prefixing: word formed by attaching a prefix to the head of an existing word—*retweet*

Suffixing: word formed by attaching a suffix to the end of an existing word—*impactful (impact + -ful)*

Alphabetism: word formed from the initials of a phrase, which must be spelled out—*BFF (Best Friends Forever)*

Acronymy: word formed from the initials of a phrase, which can be pronounced—*AIDS (Acquired Immune Deficiency Syndrome)*

Clipping: word formed by losing an element next to its root—***zine*** (shortening of *magazine*)

Backformation: word formed by removing either a prefix or suffix from an existing word—*Net* (for *internet*)

Blending: word formed by the joining of two or more words; at least one of the words is clipped—*smog (smoke + fog)*

Shifting: word formed by shifting from one lexical category to another—*gift* (noun → verb)

Calque: word formed by the word-for-word translation of a foreign word into English—*earworm* (from German *ohrwurm*)

Of all English writers, William Shakespeare is generally acknowledged to be one of the most prolific creators of neologisms in English.

Activities for Critical and Creative Engagement

1. *Access the* Oxford English Dictionary *online via your university's or public library's website. Select the "Sources" option on the* OED *homepage to explore the top thousand authors and works quoted in the* OED. *Select an author to see what words they contributed to the dictionary. What words surprise you? Are they standard now or still relatively unfamiliar? Briefly explain your results.*

2. *In the movie* Mean Girls *(Mark Waters; 2004), Gretchen Weiners tries to force everybody to use the word "fetch" to mean "cool" or "awesome." Periodically she will say that something is "so fetch." At a certain point, the "Queen Bee" character, Regina George, finally has had enough and states, "Stop trying to make fetch happen. It is never going to happen." Using three different techniques for creating new words in English, create three new words. Write definitions for each of them. Use them in a sentence or line of poetry that could be included as an example for your definition. Make an argument why they should be accepted and not relegated to the status of inkhorn terms (hint: go back and reread the section in this chapter on inkhorn terms).*

Hip-Hop's Large Vocabulary

Is it really true that Shakespeare has contributed the most words to the English language or has influenced English in the late twentieth and early twenty-first centuries? Matt Daniels asked this question but was also interested in how hip-hop has changed the language that we use today. Daniels, a hip-hop lexicographer and data visualist, first conducted a study in 2014 to determine which hip-hop artists had the largest unique vocabulary. Once Daniels eliminated the common words for each artist and author, he produced an interactive data visualization of the results (http://poly-graph.co/vocabulary.html). He began by examining the first thirty-five thousand words from the lyrics of eighty-five rappers. He also included the first five thousand words from the plays of William Shakespeare and the first thirty-five thousand words from the works of Herman Melville. The reduced data pool for Shakespeare has been a major criticism of the project. Given the fact that Melville, author of the classic novel *Moby-Dick* (1851), introduced a substantial vocabulary pool of whaling terminology to English, it is not surprising that his contribution is significant, but do we care about words relating to whaling? Perhaps the unique vocabulary from rap is more meaningful for us as twenty-first-century readers of lyrics and listeners of music.

The East coast rapper, Aesop Rock, has the largest vocabulary of the artists analyzed, followed by Wu-Tang Clan and its individual members: GZA, RZA, Ghostface Killah, and the Wu (as a collective). Since the initial study was done in 2014, some rappers you may expect to be included, such as Kendrick Lamar, are not, although they may be added if Daniels continues to update the study. Even hip-hop fans may not know the music of the most prolific contributors of unique words, but the data visualization makes it clear that, surprisingly, the most popular rappers in 2014 are generally in the bottom 20 percent. What do you think this result says about language creativity in hip-hop? Are more popular rappers less creative in their lyrics? Or does a larger, more unique vocabulary make a rapper less marketable to a wide audience? Is it a question of audience taste in music? Ultimately, we need to ask if hip-hop truly rewards creativity. Daniels's study seems to suggest that bigger is not necessarily better. However, it is important that we do not accept the data visualization at face value but critique the results in order to be sure that our interpretation is accurate.

Activities for Critical Engagement

3. *Review Daniels's data visualization (http://poly-graph.co/vocabulary.html) and determine what he could have done to improve the accuracy of his study. Is his data pool for the works of literary authors and the lyrics of hip-hop artists sufficient? Which other artists and/or authors should he include or remove? Does the study group words appropriately? For example,* pimp, pimps, pimping, *and* pimpin *are counted as four separate words. Should they be? Explain your rationale.*

4. *Check out the* Urban Dictionary *for slang available online (https://www.urbandictionary.com/). Selecting lyrics for two rappers found on the data visualization, look up two words that you believe are unique. What are the definitions for these words? Are these words truly unique, or are they accepted into the language of rap culture or popular culture more generally?*

5. *Select a hip-hop artist who falls to the left or middle of the data visualization. What does their position reveal about them? Check out some of their lyrics to see why they may have ended up in their position. Are their lyrics more readable and/or understandable than the lyrics of the artists to the right? What advice would you give these artists to raise their position? What three words would you recommend they substitute for specific words in their lyrics in order to make their language pool more unique? And does that substitution make the lyrics more (or less) appealing?*

How Does English Studies Help Us to Understand the Evolution of the English Language?

As this case study demonstrates, English as a language is not static but constantly changes. We can learn a lot about the origins of English by studying its structure and vocabulary in historical context. Although traditional resources for examining language development in English, such as the *Oxford English Dictionary*, often privilege literary language, sources for new word creation in popular English, such as music lyrics and social media, can provide new perspectives on English language development and its impact.

2

Linguistics

For native speakers of English, speaking the **language** seems both effortless and intuitive. However, a close look at any human language, spoken or written, reveals that language is an extremely sophisticated system. Linguistics, the study of spoken and written language, is the field of English Studies that explores issues relating to language and the brain. As English majors, language is, at the most basic level, what you study. You may analyze **sounds**, **words**, and **sentences** for their meaning in a literary work, and you also examine them for their rhetorical effect and ability to communicate in all forms of writing and speech. Even though you probably have had no formal training in Linguistics, you understand the importance of the English language and the judgments that people make every day about how to use it. Learning about Linguistics will heighten your awareness of how the English language works.

Linguists are interested in both spoken and written language. They prefer to describe language as it is, has been, or will be rather than to regulate it according to what language authorities believe it should be. In other words, they are **descriptivists** rather than **prescriptivists**. For example, many people think that technology and social media are ruining the English language. **Alphabetisms**, such as *BFF*, *b4*, and *fyi*, have crept into written English beyond texting and Twitter. The noun *friend* has become a verb (with its opposite *unfriend*) thanks to Facebook. Linguists do not judge such developments in English but instead explore and analyze these sorts of changes: they believe that these changes reflect language evolving in response to our increased fascination with and dependence on new technologies. Linguists study language—any language, not just English—as a system that includes **phonology** (sound), **morphology** (word formation), **syntax** (**phrase**, **clause**, and sentence structure), and **semantics** (meaning). In fact, phonology, morphology, syntax, and semantics together form the

grammar of language—that is, its structure and rules. However, linguists do not limit their explorations to grammar but also include **discourse**, which Linguistics defines as continuous text (written or spoken) longer than a single sentence. This chapter will explore how Linguistics helps us to understand the structure of the English language in speech and writing, and how linguistic methods can enhance our understanding of the texts we consume (read) and produce (write).

Key Questions

1. What different approaches do linguists take to language? Why are we studying the "science" of language in an English course?
2. What are the differences between spoken and written English? Why do we need to be so concerned with the "sounds" of English?
3. How does Linguistics relate to philology, which focuses on the historical development of the English language particularly in relation to literary works?
4. What are the conventions of linguistic scholarship? What kinds of research and interpretation do linguistic scholars do?
5. What is Linguistics in the twenty-first century? How does it connect to English Studies more broadly conceived?

What Different Approaches Do Linguists Take to Language? Why Are We studying the "Science" of Language in an English Course?

Linguistics is the science of language and what it is about humans that makes us able to learn and communicate using language. Language is one of our most distinctive skills as humans, it is one of our most misunderstood skills, and it is often the cause of heated conflict. Not surprisingly, disciplines including sociology, anthropology, psychology, neuroscience, and computer science all influence Linguistics. Linguists draw on these diverse areas of knowledge in order to understand not only the factors that influence how language comes into being but also the many diverse impacts that language has both on individuals and on society and culture.

There are three main branches: theoretical linguistics, descriptive linguistics, and applied linguistics.

Theoretical Linguistics

Theoretical linguistics is concerned with developing models of linguistic knowledge and theory. It includes **semiotics**, the study of signs and symbols as elements of communicative behavior, as well as **structuralism**, the study of how elements of language relate to one another. The Swiss linguist, Ferdinand de Saussure, promoted the nonhistorical approach to Linguistics, which dominated the field throughout the twentieth century. In fact, theoretical approaches in Linguistics have provided the foundation for contemporary critical theory. In particular, Saussure's work on semiotics and **structuralist linguistics** encouraged the examination of the structure of literary texts, the linguistic elements of the text, and how these structures convey meaning. Thus, Linguistics can help us better to understand both critical theory and interpretive approaches to literature.

Descriptive Linguistics

Descriptive linguistics examines how language is actually used by members of a speech community. This branch includes **historical linguistics**, the study of how language changes over time. The approach resulted from the discovery at the end of the eighteenth century of a relationship among English, European languages, and Sanskrit, an ancient language in India. For example, the initial consonant "f" in English corresponds to the initial consonant "p" in Latin, Greek, French, Spanish, and Sanskrit in the words for *father*:

father—pater—pater—pére—padre—pitar

Since the sounds of the letters "f" and "p" are very close, linguists hypothesized that these languages are related to one another and must have developed from a common ancestral language. Historical linguistics dominated the discipline until the end of the nineteenth century. Not surprisingly, the History of the English Language (HEL) developed directly out of historical linguistics to become a field of English Studies.

Descriptive linguistics also includes **sociolinguistics**, which explores the relationship between language and culture. For example, sociolinguists are very interested in the "English Only" movement in the United States and the efforts to make English the "official" language of the country because language is so integral to national **identity**. Language, in fact, constructs identity as much as it reflects it. In her study of high school students in suburban Detroit, the sociolinguist Penelope Eckert demonstrated that teenagers speak more like their friends with whom they share social practices than like others of their own social **class**. Eckert found that there were three adolescent social groups at the high school: the Jocks, who actively engaged in school life; the Burnouts, who did not; and the In-betweens, who fell between the two dominant groups. Each group consisted of individuals from different social backgrounds and created its own culture through a shared linguistic community rather than through a common social class. Building on Eckert's research, the sociolinguist Mary Bucholtz added a fourth adolescent group, the Nerds, who have their own social and linguistic behaviors in opposition to the other three. They typically speak an excessively formal English in order to differentiate themselves from the other groups. In such a way, language contributes significantly to the construction of adolescent identity.

The controversial **Sapir-Whorf hypothesis**, which argues that the structure of a language determines or greatly influences cognition and behavior in the culture in which it is spoken, also falls under sociolinguistics. This theory of linguistic relativity was the basis for the storyline of the film *Arrival* (Denis Villeneuve; 2016). Once Louise Banks, the linguist trying to communicate with the aliens who have arrived on earth, learns that their written language is circular in construction, she begins to see time as circular, just as the aliens do. In other words, the language you speak influences the way you perceive the world. Linguists generally do not accept the strong version of the hypothesis that all human thoughts and actions are bound by the restraints of language; they do, however, agree that the weaker version, which states that language shapes to some extent both our language and behavior, may be true.

Applied Linguistics

Applied linguistics identifies, investigates, and provides solutions to language-related real-life problems. Early interest in the field focused on using "scientific methods" to improve the teaching of foreign languages, including the teaching of English to non-native speakers. Over the years, this branch has become much more **interdisciplinary**. Researchers interested in the role of the human brain with respect to language, including the effects of a stroke or brain hemorrhage on speech, language processing, and language acquisition, practice **neurolinguistics**. **Psycholinguistics** is primarily concerned with the psychological and neurobiological study of language production and comprehension. Eye tracking in reading in order to analyze the visual processing of written text is a current significant research area in this field. One of the more recently developed branches of Linguistics is **ecolinguistics**, which addresses the ecological context and consequences of language in order to explore the role of language in the life-sustaining interactions of humans, other species, and the physical environment.

In addition to language learning, applied linguistics includes **biolinguistics**, the study of biology and the evolution of language; **clinical linguistics**, the application of Linguistics to speech-language pathology; **computational linguistics**, the study of statistical modeling of language from a computational perspective as well as the study of computational approaches to linguistic questions; **evolutionary linguistics**, the study of the emergence of language through human evolution; and **forensic linguistics**, the application of Linguistics to forensics. What real-life problems do applied linguistics address? They vary. For example, a forensic linguist may study the language of legal texts, ransom demands, suicide notes, death-row statements, emergency calls, and even social media statements. In 1987, a series of bomb threats were made by telephone to the Pan American counter in the Los Angeles airport. A baggage handler was accused of making the calls and jailed. The linguist William Labov was then asked to listen to tapes of the telephone calls in order to confirm that the identity of the caller as the baggage handler. However, Labov immediately recognized the speaker on the tapes as someone from the Boston region, while the baggage handler was clearly innocent because he had a New York **accent**. As a result, the case was thrown out of court, and the baggage handler freed. Linguistics can provide a language "fingerprint" of a speaker and, as a result, have real-world applications both in criminal investigation and legal proceedings.

Linguistics draws on multiple bodies of knowledge in order to examine language structure at every level and to evaluate language's influence. Linguistics does not necessarily require practitioners to know many different languages, although some linguists do. Instead, it emphasizes language acquisition, structure, variation, and influence on communication and understanding.

What Are the Differences between Spoken and Written English? Why Do We Need to Be So Concerned with the "Sounds" of English?

If you are a native English speaker, you will remember learning to write your letters, but do you actually remember learning to speak? Probably not. Speaking comes naturally to humans, starting with babbling at six months of age. If you spend any time around small children, you will notice that they make "mistakes" when they first speak. For example, a toddler may tell you, "I *goed* to zoo" or "I *seed* a monkey." An adult will likely correct the child in an effort to teach standard English. However, despite a general belief that we teach children oral language, they, in fact, learn this language on their own because we, as human beings, are wired to speak. Those perceived "mistakes" in early speech are examples of the child listening carefully to the speech around them and applying the patterns they hear. Since adding a final "d" to a verb is the standard way to create the simple past tense in English, a child will initially apply this ending to all verbs before eventually learning that there are **irregular verbs**, such as *to go* and *to see*, in English that form the past tense differently. All children, unless they have a disability that affects speech, can learn to speak any language; they just start by speaking the language they hear around them.

Human beings are, however, not wired to write. Writing must be intentionally taught for us to learn it. For the English language, writing represents the sounds that we speak in graphic form using the twenty-six letters of the alphabet on their own or in combination. Although there are only about forty different sounds in spoken English, we use approximately two thousand letters and combinations of letters to represent these sounds in writing. As a result, learning to read English, especially for a non-native speaker of the language, can be challenging. Just consider the following example:

dough—through—cough—rough—bought—drought

Add to this list the British spelling *hiccough* (for *hiccup*) and the British words *slough* (pronounced as "ow" in "bow wow" or as "oo" in "sloo") and *lough* (pronounced as the Gaelic *loch*), and we see that *-ough* has ten possible pronunciations in English. Writing is also more formalized than speech. We will adjust our **register** and tone in both spoken and written English according to our **audience** and **rhetorical situation**. However, in English Studies, we revere the written word as essential to the literary tradition and often (mistakenly) respect it more than we do speech. We view **prose**, **poetry**, and **drama** as writing and, in a literature course, we can easily forget that a poem or play should be performed—that is, spoken aloud—to be fully appreciated. In fact, writing has many unique and formalized conventions to which we must adhere. For example, we rely on punctuation and, more importantly, the separation of words on the page in order to read the text silently to ourselves. We may think we hear this punctuation and word separation when an English speaker talks, but we really just hear a continuous sound that our brain has to separate into meaningful segments.

The foundation of Linguistics is grammar: phonology, morphology, syntax, and semantics. The study of language sound, including its production and reception, is phonology. Each distinctive sound in a language is a **phoneme**. In the words *tin* and *thin*, the initial consonant sounds of the letter "t" and the combined letters "th" sound different to us as speakers of American English, allowing us to distinguish between the two words. To represent the distinct sounds of these letters, we use the appropriate symbols from the **International Phonetic Alphabet (IPA)**, a system of phonetic symbols created to represent the sounds of all world languages. Therefore, the initial "t" sound of *tin* is represented as /t/, and the "th" sound of *thin* is represented as /θ/ (Greek character *theta*) using IPA. Understanding the formation of sound in English helps us to interpret literature, especially poetic devices used in poetry, as well as "hear" **dialect** in a novel, play, or film. It also allows us to appreciate the impact of political **rhetoric** or help a child with a speech impediment.

As we all know, sound sequences create words. The study of word structure is called morphology, a term that you may find highly technical sounding and even perplexing. But it is important to understand that morphology does not just analyze whole words; it also analyzes the smallest units of meaning in a word known as **morphemes**. In English, words are comprised of free morphemes—those morphemes that have meaning on their own— and bound morphemes—those morphemes that cannot have meaning on their own. Take, for example, the word *unfaithfulness*. It is comprised of four morphemes: the free morpheme *faith*, which can stand on its own as a noun; the bound morpheme *–ful*, which turns the noun into an adjective; the bound morpheme *–ness*, which turns the adjective back into a noun; and the bound morpheme *un-*, which negates the new noun.

Syntax is the study of the rules governing the way words are combined to form phrases, clauses, and sentences. In other words, when we talk about syntax, we are talking about grammar. We know, for example, that words cannot appear in any order in English. We also know that words have certain functions in a sentence. Consider the following jumbled collection of words:

saw lunchtime friend restaurant I my a at and

We immediately recognize that the words convey no meaning ordered this way. We also recognize that we can organize these words according to parts of speech or **lexical categories**: verb, nouns, pronouns, preposition, article, and coordinating conjunction. Once we have determined their lexical categories, we know how they may function in a sentence: **subject**, verb, **direct object**, and **prepositional phrase**. Now we can begin to group them into phrases and clauses (*at lunchtime*) or leave them on their own or in combination (*saw, my friend and I, a restaurant*) before ordering them into a simple sentence: *My friend and I saw a restaurant at lunchtime*. We can also make the sentence more complex by adding a clause: *My friend and I saw a restaurant at lunchtime when we were walking down the street.* Linguists study the ways in which words are combined to create well-formed phrases, clauses, and **sentences** as well as how these elements are combined to form more complex sentences. English grammar is a hierarchy in which words must be combined into phrases and then clauses before they can be combined into sentences.

Although we may be challenged by phonology, morphology, and syntax in the English language, they are all systematic and predictable. But, as any linguist will tell you, such is not the case in semantics, the study of meaning in language. Simply put, meaning in English constantly shifts. It is not predictable because it generally depends on **context**. Linguists emphasize the role of **cognition** in understanding meaning. For example, words have meaning that is embedded in our minds; this meaning relates to syntax and discourse; and this meaning is influenced by context, be it cognitive, linguistic, or experiential. Consider the person who delivers your mail. When you hear someone refer to a "mail carrier," you probably do not think of a dictionary definition of the phrase but rather of your neighborhood mail carrier. As an English speaker, you are unlikely to think the person said "male carrier" because "male" makes little sense linguistically. And whether you think of a man or a woman as the mail carrier will partly depend on your own experience with such postal workers. Is your local mail carrier male or female? This context is also strongly influenced by the phrase itself. Thanks to recent efforts to use gender-neutral terms for jobs that employ both men and women, our mail is delivered by a mail carrier rather than by a mailman, and a meeting is held by a chair or chairperson rather than by a chairman. Such efforts demonstrate the role that language can play in breaking down prescribed gender roles and encouraging greater inclusiveness. Context is not static, and shifts in cultural perspective can influence context significantly.

Linguists are not solely interested in grammar but also in how language is used, especially in discourse. **Discourse analysis** is the study of such text in a sociopolitical context. Deborah Tannen, a linguist who specializes in discourse analysis, studies the expression of interpersonal relationships in conversation, particularly in relation to gender and culture. She has explored conversational style and power shifts between family members in the home and between men and women in the workplace in order to determine who gets heard and why. For example, women communicate in a style that encourages social bonding and emotional connections, whereas men prefer to exchange information without emotion. When women and men talk to each other, the result often leads to miscommunication and misunderstanding. Many readers of Tannen's work have praised its ability to save their relationships, but some linguists believe that Tannen overgeneralizes at times. However, understanding such communication differences in discourse can help a creative writer develop female and male characters and voices that are realistic and convincing, or it can help a writer in the workplace to craft more sensitive communications with colleagues.

Speakers in a conversation have systems, such as **intonation**, **pausing**, and phrasing, to signal taking turns in a dialogue. In addition, **discourse markers**, those little words like *well, oh, like, uh, so, but*, and *and*, break speech into parts and, at times, connect those parts. **Speech Act Theory** argues that all verbal utterances perform speech acts—that speech is action, not just talking. For example, only when the minister states at the end of the wedding service, "I now pronounce you husband and wife," is the couple officially married; only when a judge proclaims at the end of a trial, "The defendant is not guilty," does the individual go free.

Speech acts can be direct or indirect. Imagine you and a friend are walking down a street at lunchtime and see a restaurant. You turn to your friend and say to them, "Let's stop and eat lunch at this restaurant." That utterance is direct and clear. Now consider the following sign that you may encounter when you first enter the restaurant:

**Our Staff Will Be Pleased
To Seat You**

The text on the sign is indirect because it does not explicitly ask you to do anything; it tells you that a restaurant employee would be happy to escort you to an available table. Although we often use indirect speech acts in English to be polite, the approach can be somewhat manipulative. Even though the restaurant appears to be offering you a service, the sign also makes clear that you had better not sit yourself at a table without consulting with their staff first. Thus, language wields power by what it states both explicitly and implicitly.

How Does Linguistics Relate to Philology, Which Focuses on the Historical Development of the English Language Particularly in Relation to Literary Works?

Although historical linguistics was the focus of the nineteenth century, attention shifted in the early twentieth century to the fact that not only does language change but also language structure is systematic and governed by regular rules and principles. This study of how languages work is called general linguistics, a movement led by Saussure. Linguists came to focus more on the study of grammar—in the technical sense of the term, the organization of the sound system of a language and the internal structure of its words and sentences. By the 1920s, the program of structural linguistics, inspired in large part by the ideas of Saussure, was developing sophisticated methods of grammatical analysis. This period also saw an intensified scholarly study of languages that had never been written down.

Yet, as we know, historical linguistics did not go away. One development was **philology**, the study of language in oral and written historical sources. Philologists combine Linguistics with literary criticism and history, primarily studying literary texts in order to explore the development and meaning of language over time. Both linguists and philologists use similar approaches to the analysis of language: **synchrony** and **diachrony**. Synchronic analysis examines language at a specific point of time, usually the present, without taking history into account. For example, we might be interested in how texting is influencing the structure of written English, so we would look at the language at a specific moment in time. Diachronic analysis focuses on the development and evolution of language throughout history. For example, we might be interested in English as it is spoken in Appalachia, but we would need to consider its change over a period of time. Saussure placed an emphasis on synchronic analysis as essential to linguistic study. As Linguistics expanded to include structuralism and syntax, this emphasis has only increased.

Not surprisingly, philologists generally view themselves as scholars in the field of HEL rather than that of Linguistics. This textbook, consequently, has separate chapters on Linguistics and HEL. Literary studies has been traditionally organized along historical periods. Given the fact that HEL falls under historical linguistics, there is a clear affinity between it and literary studies. Linguistics, with its highly interdisciplinary approach, is more difficult to pin down; it can serve a number of disciplines and even stand alone as its own department.

What Are the Conventions of Linguistic Scholarship? What Kinds of Research and Interpretation Do Linguistic Scholars Do?

Linguistic scholarship often seems more aligned with the social sciences than with the humanities, since it may involve statistical analysis and the production of graphs as well as follow American Psychological Association (APA), rather than Modern Language Association (MLA), style. Since linguists are so interested in how language is used today, **field research** (the collection of data outside a library or laboratory) is common. For example, the study of language acquisition employs both **qualitative** and **quantitative methods** but has a common concern with describing and understanding language use and/or processes of language teaching/learning in classrooms at any level. Consequently, research may include collecting data from human subjects, such as students and teachers. Field research often requires that a Linguistics scholar apply to their university for formal permission to conduct research with human subjects. The United States Department of Health and Human Services defines a human research subject as a living individual from whom a research investigator obtains data through interaction with that individual. A linguist conducting such research must ensure that the individuals involved participate voluntarily and are treated ethically. Such considerations are also important for research in rhetoric and composition, English education, and professional writing and technical communication since these fields of English Studies often require similar data collection from human subjects.

With advances in technology and the collection, storage, and manipulation of **big data** in electronic form, linguists can now confirm that what they think about the English language is true more quickly, more easily, and more accurately than they could before computers by using large bodies or **corpora** of text stored in electronic databases. These linguistic corpora are very large and available online. For example, at the time of writing this textbook, the Corpus of Contemporary American English (COCA) contains over 500 million words from spoken American English, fiction, popular magazines, newspapers, and academic texts from 1990 to 2017; the Corpus of Historical American English (COHA) contains around 400 million words from a variety of genres from 1810 to 2009; the Wikipedia Corpus contains almost 2 billion words from all *Wikipedia* entries up to 2014; and the British National Corpus contains 100 million words from spoken British English, fiction, popular magazines, newspapers, and academic texts from the 1980s to 1993. We must keep in mind that, despite their size, such corpora are representational of the varieties of English rather than comprehensive. They allow linguists to test a hypothesis by searching for patterns in and influences on the English language through statistical analysis. You could use COHA and COCA to examine if an English grammar rule, such as never splitting an infinitive, is currently being followed or if practitioners of the language no longer consider it important. You could also determine when and where the rule first began to be relaxed. And you could explore the adherence to the grammar rule (or lack thereof) across the English-speaking world by using other corpora.

Corpus linguistics, as this applied approach to language study is called, has exploded in recent years thanks to the increased availability online of large samplings of real-world text from a variety of genres.

What Is Linguistics in the Twenty-First Century? How Does It Connect to English Studies More Broadly Conceived?

As the Linguistics Society of America (LSA) website states, today's linguists are interested in all aspects of language study but are particularly eager to understand the unconscious knowledge that humans have about language, how children acquire language, the structure of language in general and of particular languages, how languages vary, and how language influences the way in which we interact with each other and think about the world.

We can easily recognize the significance of Linguistics for the study of English grammar, but we may not be so familiar with its importance for **close reading**. Close reading allows us to focus on significant patterns in a text in order to develop a deeper, more precise understanding of the text's form and meaning. Searching for patterns in language is one way to achieve it. However, analyzing a text stylistically is unlike doing a literary analysis as it needs to be much more objective. With **stylistics**, we aim to explain how the words of a text create the feelings and responses that we get when we read them. When beginning a stylistic analysis, start with your initial response to the text. Then, as you analyze the language of the text, you can determine if your initial interpretation is valid. Sometimes the text's linguistic structure will not support your interpretation, in which case you may have to reconsider your initial response. Take, for example, the sign in a restaurant that reads as follows:

Please Be Seated

Our initial observations about the text would include the following:

- The statement is a command.
- The verb is in the imperative form.
- The imperative is tempered by the adverb *please* to add polite emphasis or urgency.

- An uppercase letter begins every word for emphasis.
- There is no punctuation.
- The instructions are brief and clear.
- The statement is easily comprehended.

Now that we have broken down the components of the sign's text, we are ready to write an analysis of the sign and its purpose. We can now structure a convincing argument that the sign's goal is to politely instruct us, as potential customers, to perform an action that will result in our dining in the restaurant.

Because stylistics is so precise and so focused on language, it is a useful method for interpreting literary texts. Consider the first two lines of William Butler Yeats's poem "The Second Coming" (1920):

Turning and turning in the widening gyre
The falcon cannot hear the falconer;

By pulling apart the linguistic structure of these two lines, we discover the following:

- The lines do not rhyme.
- The lines use assonance with the repetition of long vowel sounds.
- There is no punctuation at the end of line 1.
- The second line is iambic pentameter: / ᴜ ' / ᴜ ' / ᴜ ' / ᴜ ' / ᴜ ' /
- The first line is pentameter but with a meter pattern of spondee, iamb, pyrhhic, iamb (the -*en* of *widening* is elided in Anglo-Irish spoken English), and iamb: / ' ᴜ / ᴜ ' / ᴜ ᴜ / ᴜ ' / ᴜ ' /
- The stress falls on the long vowel sounds in line 1.
- The word *turning* is the first word of the line 1 and repeats in that line.
- Three verb forms end with –*ing* in line 1.
- The letter *g* occurs four times in line 1: three times as a long *g* sound at the end of the multisyllabic words and once as a harsh, staccato *g* sound at the opening of the single-syllable word that ends the line.
- Two noun forms of *falcon* appear in line 2.

We can now write an analysis of these lines that discusses the language in detail, relating it to the poem as a whole and the poet's presentation of the major themes and characters. This analysis would focus on such features as rhythm, meter, sound, and meaning in order to validate our reading of the lines and poem. A stylistic analysis does not just support the interpretation of a literary work; it strengthens it, often highlighting features of the text that could be missed. Such a close reading of language and its function in a text has broad applications across English Studies. Fundamentally, all fields of English Studies are interested in language and how writers use language in a wide variety of texts.

Further Reading

Bauer, Laurie, and Peter Trudgill, eds. *Language Myths*. New York: Penguin, 1999.
Discusses popular myths about language.

Bucholtz, Mary. *White Kids: Language, Race and Styles of Youth Identity*. Cambridge: Cambridge University Press, 2011.
Explores language and adolescent identity among California teenagers.

Crystal, David. *The Cambridge Encyclopedia of Language*. 3rd ed. New York: Cambridge University Press, 2019.
Provides an accessible and comprehensive encyclopedia on language and linguistics.

Crystal, David. *How English Works: How Babies Babble, Words Change Meaning, and Languages Live or Die*. New York: Overlook Press, 2007.
Explores the development of human language.

Curzan, Anne, and Michael Adams. *How English Works: A Linguistic Introduction*. 3rd ed. New York: Pearson Longman, 2012.
Introduces linguistics to English majors, especially those in English education.

Eckert, Penelope. *Jocks and Burnouts: Social Categories and Identity in the High Schools*. New York: Teachers College Press, 1989.
Explores language and adolescent identity among Detroit high school students.

Fromkin, Victoria, Robert Rodman, and Nina Hyams. *An Introduction to Language*. 11th ed. Boston: Cengage, 2019.
Provides a standard introduction to linguistics.

Harris, Randy Allen Harris. *The Linguistics Wars*. New York: Oxford University Press, 1995.
Presents the history of twentieth-century linguistics in the United States.

Hope, Jonathan, and Laura Wright. *Stylistics: A Practical Coursebook*. New York: Routledge, 1995.

Introduces the techniques of stylistic analysis.

Minkova, Donka, and Robert Stockwell. *English Words: History and Structure.* 2nd ed. New York: Cambridge University Press, 2009.
Examines English vocabulary in the context of introductory linguistics.

Paltridge, Brian. *Discourse Analysis: An Introduction.* 2nd ed. London: Bloomsbury, 2012.
Introduces the analysis of discourse as it relates to society, pragmatics, conversation, and grammar.

Pinker, Stephen. *The Language Instinct: How the Mind Creates Language.* New York: Harper Perennial Modern Classics, 2007.
Explores the development of the language and the human brain.

Robbins, R. H. *A Short History of Linguistics.* Longman Linguistics Library. 4th ed. New York: Routledge, 1997.
Presents a general, comprehensive history of linguistics.

Seargeant, Phil, and Bill Greenwell. *From Language to Creative Writing: An Introduction.* London: Bloomsbury, 2013.
Introduces the English language and linguistic creativity as they relate to the practice of creative writing.

Simpson, Paul. *Stylistics: A Resource Book for Students.* 2nd ed. Routledge, 2014.
Provides an accessible overview of stylistics and covers the major theories, concepts, and methods required for the investigation of language in literature.

Sotirova, Violeta, ed. *The Bloomsbury Companion to Stylistics.* New York: Bloomsbury, 2015.
Provides an overview of stylistics with essays on key areas of research written by leading scholars in the field.

Trask, R. L., and Bill Maublin. *Introducing Linguistics: A Graphic Guide.* 2nd ed. London: Icon Books, 2006.
Introduces linguistics in comic-book-style.

*In this Case Study, we examine **American Sign Language (ASL)**, a very real language with a distinct grammar and rich vocabulary, to explore how ASL differs structurally from English. We then offer engagement activities that you can use to help you better understand how ASL works grammatically, the choices someone signing using ASL has to make in order to interpret the spoken word, and the connection between ASL and Linguistics.*

American Sign Language: Can a Language Have No Sound?

Have you attended a rap or rock concert recently and seen a signer on stage with the singer and/or band? According to recent media reports, American Sign Language (ASL) interpreters are stealing the show at rap and rock concerts. Their videos online signing for music legends, such as Beyoncé, Snoop Dogg, Red Hot Chili Peppers, and the Black Keys, are attracting large audiences of both deaf and hearing viewers and even going viral. Thanks to the Americans with Disabilities Act (ADA) that was approved by Congress in 1990, ASL interpreters may be requested for public events. These ASL interpreters do not just translate the lyrics of the music; they also interpret them in order to engage deaf concertgoers more fully with the performance. Being deaf does not necessarily mean you hear no sound whatsoever, but the sound may not be distinct enough to allow you to hear the song lyrics. Given the volume of the typical concert, a deaf concertgoer can certainly feel the decibels even if they cannot hear the music.

Sign language, in general, consists of words or "signs" created by five standard building blocks:

- Handshape
- Movement
- Location
- Palm Orientation
- Non-Manual Signals (such as facial expressions)

ASL is a specific sign language used in the United States and parts of Canada. It is not universal but developed independently within the U.S. deaf community. Even in countries, such as the United States and Great Britain, where English is the common language of the hearing community, sign languages are not mutually intelligible. They differ in terms of grammar and vocabulary just as spoken languages do.

Just like English, ASL can have different accents and dialects. Accent is demonstrated by the distinct way a word/sign is formed. For example, regional accent in ASL is often revealed by the speed of signing (New Yorkers typically sign very quickly) or by the signer's hand/body position (Southerners often touch their lower face and chest a lot when signing). Dialect variation may be indicated by a variant signing technique for a specific word. ASL has many ways to sign "pizza" or "picnic," and the different signing choices can indicate whether an ASL signer is from the Northeast and Southeast in the United States. And African Americans may use **Black American Sign Language (BASL)**, also known as **Black Sign Variation (BSV)**. BASL is a variant of ASL that developed in the Southern United States as a result of segregation in schools that included schools for the Deaf community. Whereas users of ASL typically sign with one hand close to the body, users of BASL more frequently employ both hands to sign and use more signing space and body language.

Researchers are very interested in which side of the brain is used for ASL. The right hemisphere typically controls visual and spatial function, while the left hemisphere supports language. We may be surprised to learn that ASL signers use their brains just as English speakers do. In fact, damage to the left side of the brain results in same aphasias for deaf signers as for English speakers; damage to the right side of the brain does not appear to impact deaf individuals. So keep that in mind the next time you see someone signing with ASL at a music concert. They are expressing themselves and their experience as fully and as successfully as hearing individuals can do at the same event.

Let's think about what an absence of verbal cues means for a language. To what extent do we rely on facial expression and body language to convey meaning when we talk?

Activities for Critical Engagement

1. *Partner with at least three other students. Each student should have six slips of blank paper. Write a different noun on each slip, but do not let the other group members see what you write. Everyone should then place their completed slips into a bag or hat and select three slips from the bag or hat. One player gets the other group members to guess the noun using the rules for each round.*

   Round 1: Verbal Clues

Select a slip of paper and read the noun written on it. Do not let your group members see the word. You may state one word as a clue for your noun. If you utter an expletive, that counts as your one word. Once each group member gives one guess, you state another one-word clue. The winner then leads the next game.

How quickly did your group successfully guess the nouns? What sorts of verbal clues did you give? Words in the same category as the noun? The opposite of the noun? Something else? What was the most successful strategy?

2. *Round 2: Nonverbal Clues*

Select three new slips of paper. Choose one and read the noun, again not letting the other group members see the word. This round does not allow you to give a verbal clue. Instead, you must act out your noun without speaking. Once each group member gives one guess, you continue to act out your noun until someone successfully guesses the noun. The winner then leads the next game.

How quickly did your group successfully guess the nouns? What sorts of nonverbal clues did you give? What were particular challenges with this round?

3. *Which round was the easiest? Which was the hardest? Why? What is the difference between verbal and nonverbal communication? Which do we depend on more during our everyday lives? As hearing individuals, how do we typically combine the two strategies to our advantage?*

ASL is produced by the movement of hands, arms, torso, face, and head and perceived visually. It is neither a performance nor English "with hands." It also has a manual alphabet of twenty-six different handshapes that correspond to the English alphabet. Fingerspelling uses this manual alphabet to sign when no ASL word exists. ASL is just as expressive as spoken language and has a grammatical structure that includes phonology, morphology, and syntax. We know that phonology is the study of sound, so how could ASL possibly include phonology? Rather than being based on sound, ASL "phonemes"—that is, the smallest units of a sign—are spatial and temporal. The phonetic parameters include handshape, movement, signing space, and nonmanual signals. In terms of morphology, ASL includes the same lexical categories as a spoken language: nouns, adjectives, verbs, pronouns, and adverbs. However, articles and prepositions are not typically used. Forming words does not rely on adding prefixes and suffixes to word stems but rather by nesting a sign stem in a hand movement. ASL syntax follows a basic word order as follows: time–location–topic–action–question word. The topic can vary for emphasis, and articles and most prepositions are not used. Therefore, the following sentences can be transformed into ASL syntax as follows:

I am going to the store today.	TODAY ME GO STORE
	TODAY ME STORE GO
	TODAY STORE ME GO

By moving "store" to the topic position ahead of "me go" in the third example, emphasis is placed on the destination.

When will Kim go to the store?	KIM GO STORE WHEN?
	KIM STORE GO WHEN?
	STORE KIM GO WHEN?

With questions, the question word is always the last element signed in the sentence.

Activities for Critical Engagement

4. *Select a short poem or lyrics from a song. Rewrite a few lines or the entire text using the syntactical structure of ASL, a process known as ASL glossing. What words do you have to eliminate? What words do you have to reorder? What words or phrases were particularly challenging? Where do you think you may have to fingerspell? How accurate is your "translation"? Read it aloud to your group members and determine how quickly they can guess the poem or song.*

5. *Now review video clips showing ASL interpreters in action at a concert. You can find suitable clips at the textbook website, or you can search for examples online. We know that ASL uses hand, arm, torso, face, and head movements, but what other actions do the signers seem to include that help convey the music experience, particularly in terms of representing rhythm? What does the audience do that presents a similar*

representation? What do you and your friends do at a concert to express your enjoyment of the experience? Now reread your translation of the poem or song. If you knew how to use ASL, where specifically in the text would you choose to do more than translate? How would you do it?

How Does English Studies Help Us to Understand Structure and Meaning in Language?

This case study demonstrates how an understanding of structure in the English language can help us to explore the structure of any language (even a seemingly silent language) and its impact on both speakers and nonspeakers. Linguistic communication is often enhanced by body language and facial expression. For most of us, understanding spoken English involves the comprehension of both auditory expression and physical performance.

3

Literature

Often, students first become aware of the status of English Studies as an academic **discipline** through their encounters with Literature—imaginative writing in the form of **drama, poetry,** or **prose**—during their compulsory education. Looking back on English classes that they took in high school, they may recall reading classic works of Literature, such as William Shakespeare's *Romeo and Juliet* (written between 1591 and 1595) or F. Scott Fitzgerald's *The Great Gatsby* (1925), and then being asked to take tests or write **essays** demonstrating that they understood how to analyze Literature's formal structures and **figures of speech**, the development of characters, or the connection between themes in the Literature and important issues in history or in today's world. For this reason, they may assume that the study of Literature constitutes the totality of English Studies, that it is the discipline's most significant field, or that it is the field of the discipline with the longest history. These assumptions are not necessarily true. When we examine the evolution of English Studies, we discover that the study of Literature comprises only one approach within the larger discipline. Its significance to the larger discipline has changed over time, and the study of Literature as we have experienced it in school is a relatively recent development when compared with older fields like **rhetoric** or linguistics.

The oldest forms of Literature, poetry and drama, have existed for over two thousand years, and for a very long time, most people experienced them as performance-based **art**. They did not engage with them as written works to be studied in isolation but rather as entertainments to be experienced by large groups. The transcription of literary works facilitated their preservation, but it did not make those works accessible to the public, the vast majority of whom were not literate. Although the printing press was introduced to England by William Caxton in 1476, only later did printed **texts** become affordable and widely available to a reading public.

With that increasing availability, alongside greater **literacy**, not only poetry and drama but also **fiction** and **nonfiction** prose forms rose in popularity. By the nineteenth century, literary works became widely available—in **serial** forms published by periodicals and newspapers, for loan through subscription libraries like Mudie's Lending Library, which was founded by Charles Edward Mudie in 1842, or for purchase. This availability of printed literary texts changed the ways in which people engaged with Literature, making it more likely for people to experience it individually or in small groups such as the family as opposed to in large public forums. Furthermore, it encouraged the study of literary works, and Literature came to be seen as a serious endeavor that contributes to human enrichment. Ultimately, Literature became a respected academic field as a result of social, scientific, technological, and cultural advancements, including the following:

- Industrialization
- Increases of leisure time provided by electricity, transportation and **communication** innovations, and other modern conveniences
- Growing literacy rates and decreasing prices for books and periodicals
- Expansion of formal education to include rural, working-class, and middle-class men and women

Because growth of Literature as a field corresponded to the development of the modern university, it was perhaps the most dominant field of English Studies throughout the nineteenth and twentieth centuries. With the twentieth century, interventions of **movies**, radio, and **television** made Literature less popular for most people as a form of entertainment, but people continued to read for enrichment and edification, and a **knowledge** of Literature became an important marker of socioeconomic status. These changing attitudes about literary study transformed its stature as a field in the discipline.

Now, in the twenty-first century, students, scholars and teachers of Literature are compelled to answer tough questions about the value of Literature in people's everyday lives. They also must justify the place of Literature as a worthwhile object for scholarly inquiry, even though such scholarship does not directly contribute to solving the world's most pressing problems. As practitioners in the field of Literature, scholars have had to adapt to answer these challenges. Although other fields have increased in their importance to English Studies over the past one hundred years, Literature remains a robust field in the broader discipline.

This history serves as a backdrop to what you will learn in this chapter, which aims to break down the field of literary studies and to explore its central areas of inquiry as well as to situate it within the broader **context** of English Studies in the twenty-first century.

Key Questions

1. What counts as Literature, and why is Literature a worthy topic of study?
2. Who gets to decide questions of literary merit, or why are all written texts not considered Literature?
3. Once we have decided what Literature is, how do we organize it into categories?
4. What are the conventions of literary scholarship? What kinds of research and **interpretation** do literary scholars do?
5. What is literary studies in the twenty-first century? How does it connect to English Studies, more broadly conceived?

What Counts as Literature, and Why Is Literature a Worthy Topic of Study?

Many students are first attracted to English Studies because they enjoy reading in their free time, only to discover that the sorts of books that they most enjoy never appear on a course syllabus. This phenomenon has everything to do with the evolution of Literature as a field and with the establishment of English Studies as a discipline in general. For this reason, before we can answer the question, "What counts as Literature?" or begin to justify the enterprise of Literature's specialized study, we must think broadly about the purposes of higher education.

Originally, higher education was reserved for a wealthy elite, and academic study bore little relationship to establishing one's qualifications for employment. Rather, institutions of higher learning existed to discover, preserve, catalog, and understand significant artifacts of science, history, art, and culture. As institutions of higher learning began to reach wider audiences—including first middle-class and then working-class white men and then, later, women and people of color—the purpose of higher education evolves to emphasize its role in preparing people to enter the world of work. Disciplines, including but not limited to English Studies, needed to justify their value by creating formal **methodologies** for scholarship and establishing clear criteria for appropriate objects of study, criteria that often connect to the real-world value of what happens in classrooms, laboratories, and libraries. This process exerts dramatic influence on the study of Literature and the prominence of the field in the discipline.

Literature comes to be defined as creative works of drama, poetry, fiction, and nonfiction that display an awareness not only of **content** but also of form. Furthermore, these works seek to edify readers in some way, not just to entertain them. With this definition in place, practitioners argue that Literature reveals and gives individuals a path toward understanding their humanity. Literature tells stories that connect to people's day-to-day lives or to the lives of people whose circumstances differ from theirs, while at the same time emphasizing the beauty that **language** makes possible. Literature reflects the world that individuals inhabit, and it also amplifies and imagines that world in ways that enrich understanding. Often, people are introduced to Literature as a special kind of writing, which uses particular figures of speech and formal techniques to represent reality. Beyond that, advanced literary study shows that Literature can do more than hold a mirror up to people's personal experience: it can challenge their ideas about what it means to be human and help people to perceive ways of living and thinking that are different from their own. Literature does not just offer something with which an individual can identify. It also allows readers to imagine possibilities beyond their own limited perspectives.

The reasons that we should study and interpret Literature connect to a basic belief: Literature provides readers with insight into their own experiences and with alternative possibilities for how to live in the world. With this belief in mind, the study of Literature emphasizes the significance of asking questions, not the end result of arriving at definitive answers or final interpretations. Scholarly methods in the study of Literature provide a rigorous, critical framework for making sense of **narratives**, stories, rhythms, and **sounds** of language. Relating to a literary text may inspire our interest or curiosity, but relating is only a beginning: studying Literature means understanding what we read, making sense of it, and connecting it to broader and deeper contemplation about humanity. Finally, we should study Literature because doing so teaches the power and potential of human creativity.

Who Gets to Decide Questions of Literary Merit, or, Why Are All Written Texts Not Considered Literature?

Once we agree that Literature is worthy of study, we must ask ourselves who gets to decide what counts as Literature and who gets to make judgments about literary quality. Is all creative writing Literature? What makes a work creative? How do we measure the **value**, **impact**, originality, or success of creative works, and beyond what point do they achieve the status of Literature? Ultimately, our answers to these questions are not **objective** or universal: they are based on taste, preference, background, and many other factors. The **literary canon**, the group of texts that experts agree educated people should have read, grows out of decisions and judgments that readers make.

From the emergence of literary studies in the nineteenth century up until the 1960s, people commonly believed that works made their way into the canon because of their universal appeal, their timeless relevance, their unquestionable **aesthetic** quality, and their historical importance. However, radical social change in the middle of the twentieth century, which involved the expansion of higher education to include women, people of color, and the working classes, instigated debates about the criteria used for determining canonical status. Disputes arose about the canon's preoccupation with Literature written by and representing the experiences of upper-class white men, and many scholars tried to revise the canon to include a more diverse array of Literature to represent other kinds of identities and perspectives on the human experience.

While individuals might disagree about the literary merits of particular texts by particular **authors**, it is nevertheless the case that a fairly standard list of criteria exists for evaluating texts and deciding which deserve inclusion in the canon.

Here are some criteria for evaluating a text's literary merits:

1. *Literary texts have historical significance.* While "significance" is a **subjective** term, and while debates arise about what counts as significance, it is nonetheless the case that most critics agree that works of Literature should make a historical impact. Historical significance might connect to a work's influence on subsequent literary works, or it might connect to events, political movements, or philosophies prevalent during its own time. For example, a book like Herman Melville's *Moby-Dick* (1851), which was not acclaimed during Melville's own lifetime, meets the standard for historical significance because of the influence of this **novel** on Literature of the early part of the twentieth century and beyond. Conversely, a book like Harriet Beecher Stowe's *Uncle Tom's Cabin* (1852), which may not have as much aesthetic appeal to readers in the twenty-first century, holds historical significance because of its relevance in its own time and its representation of ideologies and effects of slavery in the United States leading up to the Civil War. These examples demonstrate how historical significance can shape a work's relative importance in the canon.

2. *Literary texts do more than tell a story or entertain, although they may also do those things: they attempt to use language in a way that produces beauty through its imagery, rhythms, and careful attention not only to content but also to style and form.* Again, the distinctions that we make on the basis of aesthetics are subjective, and they connect to a range of influences that affect individual readers differently. That said, critics do tend to agree that a work of Literature should have value that extends beyond the content that it represents. Thus, while a text might achieve popular acclaim and a wide readership, it might not meet the artistic standards of literary language. For example, when we compare a **fairy tale** like "Snow White," first published in the first edition of *Grimm's Fairy Tales* (1812), with an acclaimed literary work like Helen Oyeyemi's *Boy, Snow, Bird* (2014), we see that the original tale is not rooted in a literary tradition or invested in the same formal aesthetics that we associate with works of Literature, while Oyeyemi's novel is. When we consider popular texts—like a **folktale** or fairy tale, as in this example, but also like works of **genre fiction** (**science fiction, romance, the western, fantasy**, etc.) or other narrative texts that do not regard themselves as Literature—we may find them compelling or instructive, or we may recognize their cultural significance. However,

we do not typically regard their formal, aesthetic elements as intrinsic to their meaning or value.

3. *Literary texts connect to Literature that came before them.* While it is true that people might relate to or enjoy texts that tell an original **story**, Literature tends to trace a line back to other texts regarded as Literature. While telling a good story is important, most Literature does not exist in a vacuum. Rather, it alludes to other literary texts. For example, the film *Eternal Sunshine of the Spotless Mind* (Michel Gondry; 2004) finds its title in Alexander Pope's eighteenth-century poem *Eloisa to Abelard* (1717), which finds its origin in the letters between Peter Abelard and Heloise d'Argentuil (written in the twelfth century). Similarly, James Joyce's novel *Ulysses* (1922) takes its structure from Homer's *Odyssey* (composed in the late eighth century BCE), and one of its primary characters, Stephen Dedalus, whose name reminds readers of the skillful craftsman and artist from Ancient Greek mythology, has many characteristics in common with the title character of Shakespeare's **play** *Hamlet* (written between 1599 and 1602). Literature connects to Literature across history.

4. *Literary texts give insights into humanity, representing psychologies, experiences, and motivations that either reflect our own lives or allow us vicariously to understand things outside of our frame of reference.* For example, Shakespeare's *Hamlet* (written between 1599 and 1602) may at first seem very distant from much of its **audience**: most of us are not concerned with inheriting the throne of Denmark, and most of us do not have an uncle who married our mother after our father's untimely death. However, we may have experience with feeling paralyzed to take action, depression and suicidal thoughts, anxiety about a parent remarrying, or confusion about how to handle the loss of a parent. Basically, *Hamlet*'s value lies not just in its ability to entertain us but also in its ability to give us insights into the human condition. Literary works help us to think critically about emotions, motivations, and reactions.

Today, some scholars and critics might argue that debates about canon formation and what counts as Literature have been settled and no longer meaningfully shape the study of Literature. Others, however, would disagree, noting that as politics and social values change, our attitudes toward Literature change, too. Ultimately, how settled the canon seems to an individual may come down to how much it reflects their own **identity**, values, and education.

At the end of the day, readers decide what counts as Literature, though some readers' opinions count more than others. Professionals, such as authors, **literary agents, editors, publishers**, journalists, scholars, and teachers, make distinctions and value judgments about the literary merits of various texts. These distinctions and judgments ultimately shape what we understand as the canon of Literature.

Once We Have Decided What Literature Is, How Do We Organize It into Categories?

One of the jobs that scholars of Literature do is to group works of Literature in ways that assist their analysis. They usually do so in four ways: by historical period, by national tradition, by **genre**, and by identity. Such groupings can help readers to understand literary texts and help us to prioritize their value. Just as with the criteria for canonicity in the previous section, these categories to some extent overlap. For example, historical periods of Literature connect to the national traditions of Literature because what events matter historically in one national tradition do not necessarily matter in another.

In general, historical periods encourage readers to group authors and texts based upon the time during which the author lived and/or the time during which their works were published. These periods tend to connect to important historical events within the national tradition in which the work of Literature is also categorized. Students can find it instructive to compare the periodization of the British canon with the periodization of the American canon because doing so reveals the cultural differences between the two nations. Further, understanding the basics about the historical divisions that mark these two canons can help students to understand important features of the Literature that they contain.

The British Canon is often divided into the following periods:

- Medieval (500–1500)
- Early Modern (1500–1700)
- The Long Eighteenth Century (1688–1815)

- Romanticism (1785–1830)
- Victorian (1830–1901)
- Modernism (1890–1945)
- Contemporary (1945–present)

Perhaps not surprisingly, this version of literary history emphasizes the centrality of monarchy to British cultural and political life, and the start and end dates of literary periods often correspond to the reigns of kings and queens.

In contrast, the American canon is typically divided into periods that reflect its religious, democratic, and racial history. Its periods are sometimes organized as follows:

- Native American (up to 1600)
- Colonial and Early National (1600–1830)
- American Romanticism (1830–1870)
- **Realism** and Naturalism (1870–1910)
- Modernism (1910–1945)
- Contemporary (1945–present)

Comparing the American canon with the British one, we do see some correspondences, particularly as we move closer to the present day. Nonetheless, readers should understand that these literary periods help these national traditions to define their original literary contributions and to stake a claim for the unique qualities of the Literature that they produce.

It is important to emphasize that these periods of Literature, whether British or American, are not fixed, and scholars of Literature continue to debate where they should begin or end and even the usefulness of dividing Literature into periods at all. Literary history and the practices of historical reading are in flux in the twenty-first century. What had been a commonplace of the undergraduate English major curriculum, "traditional" **survey courses** in British and American Literature, now no longer fits into **core requirements** or even **elective** course offerings at some universities. Students may encounter discussions of the canon or of the periodization of Literature without ever having been taught what the canon is or what the traditional boundaries between literary periods are. Many scholars are also showing a revived interest in **deep reading** within a very narrow moment in literary history, such as one year, or in **transhistorical** reading across one or more periods. Finally, critics have called to question the tendency to divide Literature geographically, turning instead to **transnational** approaches to

Literature. All of these practices challenge the neat divisions that the above lists illustrate.

In other words, the above discussion of common ways of categorizing Literature by historical period is not intended to be exhaustive or comprehensive. Rather, it is an introduction to the ways in which scholars have traditionally understood Literature through historical periods. Perhaps more important than knowing the above dates, period names, and period characteristics is engaging with the questions that now guide ongoing debates about how to understand Literature as embedded in history:

- What is the relationship between texts written in different geographical locations in a given time period or across time periods?
- How do periods of Literature change as we get more distance from and perspective on the times in which they are written?
- In what ways does attention to **mass culture** and material culture in a given period influence our readings of the Literature of that period?
- Are there ways of reading historically that violate the temporal boundaries of conventional periodization?

These questions are, by definition, open-ended and produce many different answers depending on one's critical and theoretical investments. Further, they are complicated by the other methods that we use to categorize Literature.

For example, when we categorize Literature according to its genre, we attend to the formal characteristics of the writing through which the ideas in the text are expressed.

Genres of Literature

Poetry	• A written work that pays great attention to the sounds of language, in the forms of **rhyme**, **meter**, and other **poetic devices** like **alliteration**, **metaphor**, **simile**, and **imagery**. • Typical **poetic forms** include the **sonnet**, **lyric poetry**, the **ode**, or **free verse**.
Drama	• A **script** that is meant to be performed for an audience by actors, which includes stage directions and **dialogue**.
Fiction	• A **prose narrative** that tells an imagined story, with an emphasis on **exposition**, **narrative point-of-view**, **plot**, and **characterization**. • Typical fiction types include the **short story**, the novel, and the **graphic novel**.

Creative Nonfiction	• A prose narrative that tells a true story, using many of the stylistic techniques of fiction.
Cinema	• A visual narrative, much like drama, that is meant to be performed and recorded. • An emergent form of **cinema**, beyond feature-length productions and television series, is **video games**.

When we evaluate Literature by attending to genre, we might find similarities between texts that come from very different historical periods or very different national literary traditions. We also may discover something about how form influences the meaning of a text that might be obscured by more historically focused reading.

Another way of categorizing Literature is to focus on how various indexes of identity, either of the author or of the characters represented in a work of Literature, inform the work's interpretation.

Identities in Literature

Working-Class Literature	• Literature written by and about working-class people. • Explores the impact of socioeconomic **class** on rural and/or urban life.
Multicultural American Literature	• Literature written by and about culturally diverse populations in the United States. • Identities explored in Multicultural American Literature include African-American, Latinx, and Asian-American, among others.
Postcolonial Literature	• Literature written by and about culturally diverse populations that had formerly been colonized by Imperial powers. • Often refers to Literatures and populations connected to the British Empire. • Explores concepts such as **diaspora**, **hybridity**, split subjectivity, and the impact of colonialism and decolonization on individual identity.
Anglophone Literature	• Literature composed in English but written from cultural locations outside of the United Kingdom or the United States. • May intersect with postcolonial Literature but does not necessarily do so.

Identities in Literature

Decolonized Literature	• Literature by authors of color and non-Western ancestry. • Prioritizes nondominant historical, cultural, political, and social perspectives, making those perspectives central to analysis rather than "other" to standard, white European perspectives and methods of categorization. • Explores questions of class, **race**, and **gender**, making those questions central to literary analysis rather than regarding them as subordinate to aesthetics or as valuable only inasmuch as they inject diversity into an already existing literary canon.
Women's Literature	• Literature written by and about women. • Explores the impact of gender on identity. • May promote feminist political values but does not necessarily do so.
LGBTQ Literature	• Literature written by and about diverse sexual populations, including but not limited to lesbian, gay, bisexual, transgender, and queer.

These categories potentially offer new ways to read texts that might be very familiar to us in the historical canon of Literature. A good example of this is Kate Millett's foundational work of feminist **literary criticism**, *Sexual Politics* (1970). When Millett began her project, the author D. H. Lawrence was considered one of the most important authors of British modernism, and his novels were promoted as some of the greatest of the twentieth century. When Millett read his novels, such as *Lady Chatterley's Lover* (1928) and *Women in Love* (1920) focusing on how women were depicted in them, she revealed a weakness in Lawrence's techniques for characterization as well as, she argued, the misogyny of his fiction. Categorizing Literature in this way also may allow us to admit authors into the canon who historically may have been excluded on the basis of their race, ethnicity, **sexuality**, gender, or social class.

What becomes clear as we investigate the different approaches for categorizing Literature is that all of these categories are constructed by readers, and the categories that we use reflect our values. The ways in which readers fix the boundaries through which they organize Literature not only reflect what they see in the Literature that they study but also create the conditions for what they value while they read. Making distinctions between works of Literature based on periods, genres, cultural identity, or national tradition can both assist our interpretations and limit them.

What Are the Conventions of Literary Scholarship? What Kinds of Research and Interpretation Do Literary Scholars Do?

Many times, members of the general public and even our friends in other disciplines around the university do not really understand what it means to conduct literary scholarship. Everyone understands that chemists conduct experiments in labs, or that historians examine documents in **archives**, or that political scientists evaluate polling **data**, as just a few examples. But what do literary scholars do? Just read books? What is so special about that? Scholars of Literature do not "just" read books, although that is often the starting point for their work. In fact, there are a number of approaches that literary scholars take to their endeavors.

Close reading is probably a term that you have heard instructors use in assignments and in class but which you might not have ever seen defined. Close reading is a term and a practice that originates in the early part of the twentieth century and is associated with a methodology called **New Criticism**. The idea is this: the work of Literature, the text, should encompass all of the material that is necessary to understand it. A reader should not need to look outside—to the **biography** of the author or to historical information, for example—to understand the significance or meaning of a literary work. Instead, the New Critics argued, the key to interpreting Literature resided in a careful analysis of the formal elements of the work, in combination with the content that was communicated. While the New Critics espoused a very rigid methodology for close reading, which informs twenty-first-century methods, today we can think about close reading as an important starting point for any project of literary analysis. In general, close reading begins with looking at the formal elements of any literary work. Then, the reader moves to consider the work's contents. Finally, the reader thinks about how form and content mutually influence each other and create the context for discovering the meaning of the text as a whole.

Archival Research and **Materialist Approaches** ask scholars to work with **primary sources**: original, unedited materials that may include unpublished creative works as well as first-hand accounts connected to events, practices, or conditions informing a work of Literature. These handwritten, print, or digital sources often consist of diaries, letters, reports, financial records, memos, or even literary works in the author's own hand. Because of their uniqueness, such materials are held in archives, special collections, and other repositories around the world and do not circulate. Scholars are interested not only in interpreting these potentially unique texts but also in analyzing them as physical objects. The manuscript, printed page, and electronic book are all textual artifacts that can offer insight into the culture that created them. Such materialist approaches include the production, circulation, and reception of these texts as well as the histories of reading and authorship. Technology has allowed for the digitization of these unedited artifacts, making them widely available online. However, the **digital facsimile**, even if it is available, is sometimes insufficient, thereby requiring the scholar to travel to consult the original, physical text. Archival research and materialist approaches are, not surprisingly, time-consuming and demand that scholars have a special set of skills, such as the ability to read variations in handwriting across historical periods and to interpret the physical construction of an original document. The research process is similar to the work of a detective: a scholar will examine a single document or dig through vast quantities of documents in varying conditions of preservation in the hope of finding something relevant to a **research question**.

While all literary scholars typically consult **secondary sources**—that is, the critical interpretations made by other scholars—not all work with unedited primary sources. Yet literary studies benefits from such research because it often leads to the recovery and, in some cases, discovery of hitherto unknown literary works as well as to a fuller understanding of the historical and cultural contexts of literary production. Take, for example, *Le Morte d'Arthur* by Thomas Malory. This fifteenth-century retelling of the medieval legend of King Arthur and the knights of the Round Table is perhaps the best-known version of the story, but for almost 450 years, the only available text was the 1485 edition printed by Caxton, the man who introduced the printing press to England. Then, in 1934, a fifteenth-century manuscript of *Le Morte d'Arthur* was found by a librarian in Winchester College, an English boarding school for boys. Devoid of the heavy editing by Caxton, the manuscript predates the printed edition and is believed to be closer to Malory's original version of the story.

Theoretically oriented literary criticism approaches works of Literature through the lens of critical theory—which encompasses a range of disciplinary perspectives including linguistics, philosophy, sociology, political science, anthropology, psychology, and others. It became common in English Studies after the "turn to theory" in the 1960s, which is often symbolized by Roland Barthes's controversial essay "The Death of the Author" (1967). The 1980s and 1990s probably mark the high point for critical theory's dominance as a methodology in the study of Literature, and critical theory rose to that level of importance because it provided a way to think about the politics of literary works and the ways in which literary works replicate or construct cultural **ideologies** for their readers. Not all literary critics, however, responded positively to theoretical interventions in literary criticism. Some viewed the "turn to theory" as a distraction from the focused analysis of literary works. Additionally, some who at first embraced theoretical methodologies later have questioned whether theoretical approaches blocked critics from thinking about emotional and **affective** responses to literary texts. In the twenty-first century, critical theory remains influential in literary studies, but scholars and critics have become more conservative in its use than they were in the "high theory" heyday of the late twentieth century.

Basically, critical theory provides a framework through which to view a work of Literature, and by applying a theoretical approach, it becomes possible to produce new interpretations of a work. A reader begins with a question about a literary work, which evolves out of their close reading of it. Then, the reader turns to a theoretical approach to help pursue answers to that question. In the end, the reader integrates an analysis of the work of Literature with a theoretical model that analyzes similar questions. For example, a reader of Charles Dickens's *Great Expectations* (1860–1) may want to think about the way that the novel represents working-class life. A **Marxist** theoretical approach, which draws on writing from many disciplines and explicitly addresses issues connected to social class, not only today but also historically, may productively deepen the reader's analysis and broaden the reader's initial interpretation. The theory can provide a context for the reader's critical analysis of the literary work.

Digital scholarship uses **digital technologies** to enhance research in literary studies and to explore scholarly questions about Literature. It often involves transferring literary texts to a digital **medium** for the purpose of analysis as well as the creation of **digital tools** in order to conduct this analysis. Consequently, digital scholarship includes the building of large literary collections such as The William Blake Archive (http://www.blakearchive.org/), which curates online all of Blake's writings and artwork. Digital scholarship also includes the creation of digital analysis tools such as Voyant (http://voyant-tools.org/), which allows for the **text mining** of literary works. Literature is text, and according to digital scholarship, such text is pure data. Any data can be analyzed for patterns using the appropriate digital tool, a process that can shed light on the Literature in new and innovative ways. In addition, digital tools can examine **big data** easily and efficiently, thereby allowing for the analysis of large quantities of literary works. Scholars, such as Jerome McGann, argue that **computer-assisted textual analysis** can enhance close reading in literary studies, while more recently, scholars such as Franco Moretti argue that it encourages **distant reading**, a process that has the reader zooming out from the single work to find patterns in entire **corpora** of Literature. Despite their disparate views on the implications of digital tools, both scholars emphasize the perception of Literature as a **dataset** that is waiting to be **crunched** by the appropriate digital tool.

Cognitive approaches apply the principles of cognitive theory and science to Literature. Drawing primarily on **neuroscience** as well as on **evolutionary biology**, **psychology**, **artificial intelligence**, and linguistics, cognitive approaches seek to understand the human mind, especially in terms of memory and **empathy**, as it is represented in a literary work. Literary narrative is essentially a more focused version of the stories we tell in our lives. There is not much difference between Literature and thought: creative **cognition** is required for both. Cognitive approaches can help us understand how the mind produced a particular text in the past and, more importantly, how it creates meaning from such a text now. They also explore how we, as readers, respond to texts in terms of comprehension, emotion, and interpretation. Even though cognitive approaches to literary studies can help reveal the meaning of a literary text, it is important to note that the methodology of the field is still very much evolving.

Cognitive researchers, such as George Lakoff, have been particularly interested in metaphor production as central to the mind's ability to construct meaning. Cognitive (or Conceptual) Metaphor Theory argues that language is filled with metaphors—many of which are unconsciously overlooked by us and yet strongly influence our actions. For example, we typically use terminology associated with warfare during discussions about academic statements of argument: *targeting* an argument's *strategy*; *attacking* an argument's weak points; *defending* an argument; *winning* or *losing* an argument. However, arguments are just verbal discourse, not armed combat. Because we conceive of arguments in terms of this metaphor, we perform and describe them as such. However, we must not overgeneralize that meaning from limited linguistic evidence. There remains a need to establish consistent criteria for identifying such metaphors. Even though cognitive approaches to literary studies can help reveal the meaning of a literary text, it is important to note that the methodology of the field is still very much evolving.

What Is Literary Studies in the Twenty-First Century? How Does It Connect to English Studies, More Broadly conceived?

In the twenty-first century, literary studies is a field of English Studies that is in transition. Whereas throughout much of the twentieth century people viewed literary studies as synonymous with English, the discipline of English has now expanded to place a greater emphasis on writing skills and writing fields, including rhetoric and composition, creative writing, and professional writing and technical communication. Additionally, many scholars and students who might have once chosen to focus their attention on canonical literary texts now find themselves intrigued with the field-shaping possibilities of working on cinema, popular culture, and new media. Where does that leave literary studies? This is the question that many scholars and teachers of Literature are attempting to answer.

First, students should remember that there are deep connections between the critical thinking that close reading and interpretive analysis engender and the development of strong writing skills. Through the reading and study of literary texts, individuals strengthen their vocabularies, their **fluency** in the English language, and their ability not only to communicate their own points of view but also to listen to and understand the points of view of others. Literary studies in the twenty-first century emphasizes the connection between skilfull analysis and interpretation of literary texts and the real-world need for strong critical thinkers in the workforce.

Next, literary studies in the twenty-first century is committed to emphasizing the ways in which reading Literature increases our empathy for others and gives us insight into both our history and the issues that face us today. While most students of Literature will not go on to become professional critics or scholars, they will go on to be citizens and lifelong learners, and literary studies aims to promote the value of Literature to everyday people and to the communities in which they live. By opening ourselves to hearing the stories of people whose lives look different from our own, we become more compassionate and informed individuals.

Finally, literary studies today emphasizes the intrinsic value of creativity, art, contemplation, and reflection to living a rich life. Reading a work of Literature forces us to hit "pause" on the many things that encroach on our day-to-day lives. It allows us to create a space of privacy into which technology or the world of work cannot intervene. The sustained concentration that literary study requires allows us to slow down and to appreciate the beauty of Literature and the power of Literature to transport us.

There are many continuities between these three features of literary studies in the twenty-first century and the other fields of English Studies. Literary studies engenders an appreciation for creativity that is the cornerstone of creative writing as a field in the discipline. It also encourages a focus on **stylistics** in order to determine the relationship between the form and effect of language and linguistic style. The emphasis on strong communication skills that literary studies promotes connects both to rhetoric and composition and to professional writing and technical communication. The techniques of analysis that literary studies endorses inform the methodologies that English education emphasizes for students in the schools. In the end, literary studies exists in conversation with the other fields in English Studies, and its future is being shaped through those conversations.

Further Reading

Bérubé, Michael. *The Employment of English: Theory, Jobs, and the Future of Literary Studies.* New York: New York University Press, 1998.
Discusses the academic job market and the ways in which hiring practices in universities have impacted the study of Literature and literary scholarship.

Eagleton, Terry. *How to Read Literature.* New Haven: Yale University Press, 2013.
Offers practices for reading Literature for a nonacademic audience.

Felski, Rita. *Uses of Literature.* Malden: Blackwell, 2008.
Studies the reasons that people read and argues for the necessity in literary criticism to account for the historical and social dimensions of reading practices.

Guillory, John. *Cultural Capital: The Problem of Literary Canon Formation.* Chicago: University of Chicago Press, 1993.
Investigates canon formation and the politics of inclusion and exclusion that inform what counts as Literature.

Jay, Paul. *Global Matters: The Transnational Turn in Literary Studies.* Ithaca: Cornell University Press, 2010.
Explores the ways in which globalization impacts the study of Literature in the twenty-first century.

Ramsay, Stephen. *Reading Machines: Toward an Algorithmic Criticism.* Urbana: University of Illinois Press, 2011.
Examines how computers can be used as "reading machines" in order to open new possibilities for literary criticism.

In this Case Study, we examine how an author's literary reputation is established and how an author comes to enter the literary canon, issues of central significance in literary studies. We then offer engagement activities that you can use to help you better understand the process of canon formation and its connection to literary criticism.

I'm Not Dead Yet: Jean Rhys's Evolving Reputation in Literary Studies

At a basic level, the study of Literature involves the study of authors and their creations. But what makes someone who writes an author? And what makes an essay, poem, play, or work of fiction a canonical work of Literature? This case study uses a single author—Jean Rhys—to model how practitioners in literary studies come to answer these questions.

Who Was Jean Rhys?

The author that we know as Jean Rhys (1890–1979) was born Ella Gwendolyn Rees Williams on the Caribbean island of Dominica, which was a British colony until 1978. Rhys, whose father was a Welsh doctor and whose mother was a third-generation Creole of Scottish ancestry, lived in Dominica until the age of 16, when she immigrated to England. Rhys trained as an actress at the Royal Academy of Dramatic Art in London, worked as a chorus girl in a touring company, and experimented with making a living as a courtesan or "kept woman." Rhys went on to marry three times; one marriage ended in divorce, and Rhys was widowed twice.

Rhys's literary career began in 1924 when she met the English writer and editor Ford Madox Ford in Paris. Through his patronage she started publishing short stories. In 1927, she published her first book, *The Left Bank and Other Stories*, and she followed that with the publication of four novels: *Postures* (published in the United States as *Quartet*) (1928), *After Leaving Mr. Mackenzie* (1931), *Voyage in the Dark* (1934), and *Good Morning, Midnight* (1939). From this point, she faded into obscurity. Her novels went out of print, and many believed her to be dead.

In 1949, Selma Vaz Dias wanted to adapt the novel *Good Morning, Midnight* for theatrical production, and she needed Rhys's permission to do so. After placing **advertisements** in *The New Statesman* and *The Nation*, Dias discovered that Rhys had been living in a village in Devon in the United Kingdom. Only then, after twenty-seven years of silence, did Rhys publish her fifth and final novel, the masterpiece *Wide Sargasso Sea* (1966), a rewriting of Charlotte Brontë's classic *Jane Eyre* from the perspectives of Edward Rochester and "the madwoman in the attic"—Caribbean-born Bertha Antoinette Mason, Edward Rochester's first wife. Rhys published three additional short story collections, and her unfinished autobiography *Smile Please* was posthumously published in 1979.

Activity for Critical Engagement

1. *Select an author of your choosing and do research to find three different biographies of that author. These biographies may be short pieces of writing (brief biographies on websites or in encyclopedias), long pieces of writing (book-length works), or cinematic (television or film). Once you have looked at each of these biographies, compare the similarities and differences. Which of these biographies seems most legitimate, comprehensive, and authoritative? What makes you evaluate it as such? Do different biographies emphasize different things? Why? What is the impact of these different areas of emphasis? How does your perception of this author change based on the biographies that you have examined?*

What Is an Author?

Knowing about the historical person Jean Rhys—the life that she lived and the story of her literary achievements—gives readers information that can influence their understanding of her fiction. But what makes Jean Rhys an "author"? According to the theorist Michel Foucault in his essay "What Is an Author?" (1969), what makes someone an author is something he calls "the author function," a list of associations and characteristics that readers assign to a given writer's name. According to Foucault, the author function is important for the following reasons:

- By assigning a name to a group of texts, the author function demonstrates that texts and the ideas that they contain can be owned.
- Authorship is not as important for some texts as it is for others, which shows that texts to which we assign an author function hold a special place in our culture.
- The author function is not simply the attribution of the writer's real name to a text in the moment of writing or completion; it involves decisions about how the name will be recorded for publication, whether the "real name" of the author will be used or whether a pseudonym will be used, and determinations by readers about the character of the person who writes.
- The author function does not refer purely or simply to a real person, since the name of the author gives rise to many different selves, or interpretations of the author's identity, depending on the reader's analysis.

When we talk about the evolving reputation of any author, we are really talking about how the meanings that we assign to their author function change.

Activity for Critical Engagement

2. In "What Is an Author?" Foucault cites William Shakespeare as a good example that can help people to understand how the author function works. When you see that a play has been written by William Shakespeare, what information does that give you? Make a list of all the things that you expect to see when you read a work by William Shakespeare. Then, choose one of Shakespeare's plays that you have read. Are all of those things that you listed present in that play? Are there things present in the play that you do not find on the list? How do "author functions" both enable and limit our reading?

The Shifting Fortunes of Authors and Texts

When we talk about the evolving reputation of Jean Rhys, we are not really talking about the person that Jean Rhys was or about the books that she wrote: we are talking about how perceptions about Rhys and her works changed over time as a result of events, attitudes, and ideas that had little to do with Rhys herself. For example, when we talk about Rhys fading into obscurity, that is an external perception about Rhys based on the pause in her publication history between 1939 and 1966. Her real life went on during that period, but her life as an author seemed to be over. For this and other reasons, Rhys provides interesting insight into the ways in which critical reception shapes readers' understanding of what Literature matters, what we should pay attention to in the Literature that we read, and how the fortunes of particular texts and authors change over time.

The short stories and novels that make up Rhys's early career position assign her to the author function "minor modernist," a writer whose primary interest lies in her formal experimentation with narrative. Rhys's early novels develop a version of stream of consciousness, fragmented narrative that corresponds to that deployed by "major modernists" like Virginia Woolf in her novel *The Waves* (1931) or James Joyce in his novel *Ulysses* (1922). In this period, critics tended to regard her novel *Good Morning, Midnight* (1939) as her masterpiece, since it best reflected the characteristics often associated with modernist Literature as the period was defined. Rhys's place in the canon, however, was not assured by this version of her author function, and her books did not remain in print.

In the wake of second-wave **feminism**, Rhys is "rediscovered" in the 1970s and 1980s, and she acquires a new author function that sparks new interest in her works: woman writer. In this version of Rhys's early works, her formal experimentation is less important than her depiction of women on the margins of society who live and work without the protection of men. Additionally, with the publication of *Wide Sargasso Sea* (1966), Rhys establishes her direct engagement with a canon of women's Literature by drawing directly on Charlotte Bronte's classic novel *Jane Eyre* (1847) for **inspiration**. Establishing this author function for Rhys leads critics to look at her oeuvre with fresh eyes, and it helps them to connect Rhys's accomplishments to a feminist project of canon revision.

Finally, Rhys acquires a third author function in the 1990s with the rising interest in postcolonial approaches to Literature. In this version of Jean Rhys, her works matter because they express preoccupations with the impact of imperialism on subjectivities of the oppressed, intersections of race, class and gender, the harmful effects of colonial domination, and hybridity. Seen from this perspective, *Voyage in the Dark* (1934) and *Wide Sargasso Sea* (1966), which most explicitly address Rhys's own Caribbean origins and interrogate the ways in which her colonial upbringing influences her, rise in prominence. Consequently, Rhys's novels that had previously been held in higher esteem diminish in significance.

Activity for Critical Engagement

3. *When composing a work of literary criticism, a first step that many practitioners of literary studies take is to conduct a review of the interpretations about the work of Literature that they want to discuss. To begin, they use library databases to find books, articles, and electronic sources about their topic. Next, they might compile an annotated bibliography in which they cite those sources and provide a brief summary and analysis of what they have to say. Finally, they might compose a formal literature review, in which they summarize and synthesize the research that they have done, arriving at a general sense of the critical landscape about their topic and how their own ideas fit into it. Most scholarly journal articles include some review of the secondary criticism that reveals changing attitudes toward the work or author being discussed. Find a scholarly, peer-reviewed journal article about a work or author that interests you in a database such as the Modern Language Association International Bibliography, the primary database for cataloging articles and books for scholars of Literature. If your library does not subscribe to this database, ask your instructor or a librarian for a suitable alternative. Then, read the article. What assessment of secondary criticism does it offer? How does it describe changing attitudes, controversies, or analyses about this author or text, and what insights does this assessment offer to enhance your interpretation? What case does the article make about the place of this author or text in the canon of Literature through its assessment of prior criticism?*

How Does English Studies Help Us to Understand Canon Formation and the Literary Marketplace?

What is important about these shifting ideas about Rhys's place in the canon is that they directly connect to the corporate and critical apparatuses that structure the literary marketplace. The prominence of Rhys or of her works depends not on something inherent in the Literature that she has written but on shifting politics and areas of interest in the reception of that Literature. In this regard, Rhys offers a paradigmatic example of the ways in which practitioners of literary studies create the Literature that we read.

This may contradict some of our preconceived notions about how we identify a work of Literature—that it stands the test of time, that it has universal appeal, or that it demonstrates formal unity and particular stylistic achievement. Instead, we see that professionals in literary studies assign given works value based on interpretive judgments that can change over time and that might have the unfortunate result of limiting our ways of reading. By understanding the relationship between the literary marketplace and the Literature that we read, we can become more conscious of our own reading practices and more sophisticated in our interpretation of literary texts.

4

Cinema, Popular Culture, and New Media

Most people in their day-to-day lives have some engagement with one or more **texts** that could be categorized as Cinema, Popular Culture, or New Media. Each time we choose a **movie** from a **streaming service** to watch with family or friends, click on a **link** analyzing the latest celebrity scandal, or like a **meme** that somebody posts on **social media**, we consume Cinema, Popular Culture, or New Media texts. Still, prior to entering a university classroom, we might not have had much academic exposure to Cinema, Popular Culture, and New Media, so we may not be sure how to approach them appropriately in that **context**. Some questions we might ask include the following: When I analyze these sorts of texts, am I reading too much into them? Are Cinema, Popular Culture, and New Media topics worthy of academic inquiry? Are these really subjects that I can study? English Studies helps to answer these questions.

Because English Studies as a **discipline** is invested in **narrative** across **genres** and **communication** across a breadth of formats, English Studies has a deep investment in areas of inquiry connected to Cinema, Popular Culture, and New Media. Significantly, many of the writers that we might more commonly associate with the creation of literature have also worked as screenwriters (e.g., William Faulkner and Michael Chabon) and in Popular Culture and New Media outlets (e.g., Hunter S. Thompson and Roxane Gay).

As is the case with the field of rhetoric and composition, the field of Cinema, Popular Culture, and New Media in English Studies vies for territory with the discipline of **Communication Studies**. In contrast to practitioners in Communication Studies who focus on the technical production of Cinema, Popular Culture, and New Media texts and the impact of these texts on consumers, practitioners in English Studies focus more of their attention on the stories in Cinema, Popular Culture, and New Media and the methods for composing and interpreting those narratives. English Studies practitioners, like their colleagues in Communication Studies, are also interested in the possible application of critical theory to Cinema, Popular Culture, and New Media.

While not all English departments offer majors, minors, or focused coursework about Cinema, Popular Culture, and New Media, literature professors often draw on cinematic **adaptations** to help students to engage with course material. Professors of rhetoric and composition and professional and technical communication turn to the reportage of current events or to New Media formats like **blogs, wikis**, or social media to help students understand important issues in writing and its reception. In creative writing, authors may hone their **craft** in genres such as screenwriting or **video game narrative**. As English Studies attempts to define itself as central to citizens in the twenty-first century, it is essential to understand the influence of Cinema, Popular Culture, and New Media studies on the discipline.

This chapter aims to break down the field of Cinema, Popular Culture, and New Media and to explore its central areas of inquiry as well as to situate it within the broader context of English Studies in the twenty-first century.

Key Questions

1. Why are we studying Cinema, Popular Culture, and/or New Media in an English Course? How does evaluating narrative in these contexts change our understanding about what counts as a **story**, how stories are told, and who gets to tell stories for different **audiences**?
2. What is Cinema? What are Popular Culture and New Media? How do Cinema, Popular Culture, and New Media intersect? What is the relationship of these fields to more "traditional" fields in the discipline?
3. What theories are most central to discussions of Cinema, Popular Culture, and New Media in English Studies? How do these theories inform the sorts of approaches that English Studies practitioners take?
4. What are the conventions of scholarship for English Studies practitioners who examine Cinema, Popular Culture, and New

Media? What kinds of research and **interpretation** do Cinema, Popular Culture, and New Media scholars do?

5. What is Cinema Studies, Popular Culture Studies, and New Media Studies for the twenty-first century? How does it connect to the discipline of English Studies, more broadly conceived?

Why Are We Studying Cinema, Popular Culture, and/or New Media in an English Course? How Does Evaluating Narrative in These Contexts Change Our Understanding about What Counts as a Story, How Stories Are Told, and Who Gets to Tell Stories for Different Audiences?

At its foundation, English Studies is a discipline that values interpretation, critical analysis, and effective written communication. The study of Cinema, Popular Culture, and New Media encourages these activities, just as the study of literature did in the past and continues to do today. Fundamentally, these newer formats draw upon **storytelling traditions** that reach back not only to the **prose narratives** of **literary fiction** but also to **poetry** with its emphasis on visual images and sensory detail, to **drama** with its emphasis on **plot**, **dialogue**, and **setting**, to **visual narratives** in painting and sculpture, and to oral storytelling traditions. By understanding Cinema, Popular Culture, and New Media through the lenses of **language**, rhetorical communication, creative writing, and/or literary interpretation, English Studies practitioners connect the creation and reception of this diverse array of texts to other kinds of written communication.

There are three main benefits to integrating the study of Cinema, Popular Culture, and New Media into English Studies:

1. We learn how **recording** and **digital technologies** have changed storytelling practices in the twenty-first century. Stories in Cinema, Popular Culture, and New Media combine images, **words**, and sometimes **sounds** to create their narratives. Rather than focusing storytelling through the primary **medium** of written language, they expand the possibilities of storytelling using performance, music and **sound effects**, **animation**, **photographic images**, and **graphics** in concert with written language.

2. We acquire additional opportunities for creative composition. Whether alone or in collaboration with others, writers can use Cinema, Popular Culture, and New Media to tell stories and to represent identities, communities, experiences, and ideas that other formats do not as easily accommodate.

3. We expand potential audiences for both our critical and creative efforts. Cinema, Popular Culture, and New Media texts, as well as **commentary** about those texts, can reach audiences that might be excluded from or uninterested in **essays**, **short stories**, **novels**, **poems**, or **plays**, which we perhaps more commonly associate with English Studies.

These additional communication approaches, storytelling opportunities, and audiences contribute to the vibrancy of English Studies today.

What Is Cinema? What Are Popular Culture and New Media? How Do Cinema, Popular Culture, and New Media Intersect? What Is the Relationship of These Fields to More "Traditional" Fields in the Discipline?

Defining Cinema, Popular Culture, and New Media clarifies how these fields intersect and explains their collective relationship to more "traditional" fields in English Studies.

Cinema

Briefly, Cinema includes narrative productions, which may be fictional or factual in nature, that incorporate images, sound, and language in the service of telling a story. That definition, however, does not necessarily reveal how Cinema evolves as an art form, discuss the impact of changing technology on Cinema's evolution, or outline the most important concepts to understand for evaluating Cinema from an English Studies perspective. Consequently, it makes sense here to give a brief history of Cinema as it evolves, paying careful attention to how that history shapes the cinematic narratives that we consume and how we consume them.

In late nineteenth and early twentieth centuries, **motion pictures** or movies become a popular form of entertainment. The earliest films were black and white, silent, and accompanied by placards of dialogue or **description** interspersed between the film's moving images, which the audience would read. A live organist or pianist would accompany the images projected on the **screen**. These films were typically short by today's standards, fewer than thirty minutes. Patrons would pay about five cents—or a nickel—for admission to a **nickelodeon**, a simple, small, indoor location converted for the exhibition of Cinema.

In the 1920s, Cinema evolves from silent pictures to **talkies**, films in which the audience can hear the actors speak dialogue and a range of other sound effects and music accompanying the images on the screen. At this time, **movie theaters**, or large spaces with **stadium seating** where audiences would go to watch films, begin to replace nickelodeons. We call this period, from the introduction of **sound recording** to Cinema up until the widespread adoption of **television** in people's homes in the 1950s and 1960s, the **Golden Age of Cinema** or the **Golden Age of Hollywood**. Films were produced by major movie studios, and actors signed contracts that exclusively committed them to acting in pictures that those major studios produced. Popular genres of Cinema in this period include **film noir**, **screwball comedy**, **romantic comedy**, **the western**, and **the musical**. This Golden Age ends with the breakup of the **studio system**.

In the later twentieth century, new genres like **horror**, **science fiction**, and **melodrama** appear. Additionally, movies begin to be divided into two broad categories: those intended to appeal to a **mass audience** versus **arthouse Cinema**, which is intended to appeal to a narrower audience and includes foreign films and experimental productions. This distinction survives today. Think about the difference between blockbuster movies based on comic books, like the *X-Men* movie franchise (2000 to present), versus what we might call **Oscar movies**, such as *Moonlight* (Barry Jenkins; 2016) or *Call Me by Your Name* (Luca Guadagnino; 2017). Blockbusters are designed to appeal to a mass audience with broad entertainment value, while Oscar movies appeal to a more limited audience, focusing their attention more on exploring the artistic potential of Cinema as a medium. Cinema also evolves as television expands the possibilities of cinematic representation. Television tells different kinds of stories than movies do, both in terms of **content** and in terms of form. For this reason, it is useful to pause to talk about some of those primary distinguishing characteristics between movies and television:

Movies	Television
Typically involve a feature-length film of roughly 75–120 minutes that runs without interruption.	Television shows may be **serial** in nature, and their length varies depending on a variety of factors. Typically, situation comedies are scheduled for a half hour with **commercials**, and dramas are scheduled for an hour with commercials.
While films may have sequels or be part of franchises, they are generally intended to stand alone for consumption by an audience that may not be familiar with other films that are linked to it.	Television programs are usually consumed in the home, either on a television set or on a computer or other portable device.
Audience members often go to a theater to screen feature-length films, and they must buy a ticket to enter.	Serial television dramas are often preceded with scenes from the preceding **episode**, to remind audiences of where they are in the story that the show depicts. While television shows are not typically preceded by trailers, trailers have become more common for television with the advent of YouTube.com. Situation comedies typically are not set up in this way.
Films are often preceded by trailers or short promotional excerpts from films that have yet to be released. Trailers are often now screened on social media sites like YouTube.com.	Historically, **network television** has promoted upcoming programming on the television channel with commercials. Since the advent of **premium cable television** and television produced for streaming services, network, premium, and streaming television series may also be promoted with trailers, which appear online or which are featured on the premium channel or service that airs the show.

Films begin with the production company's logo and opening credits that announce names of starring actors, director, cinematographer, and other important people involved in the movie's production.	Television series begin in a variety of ways, often with a cold open followed by opening credits and theme music.
Films conclude with closing credits that list the names of every individual involved in the film and give credits for copyrighted material included in the film such as songs from the soundtrack.	Television series conclude with the logo of the production company responsible for the series.
Films are financed by production companies and investors. In addition, filmmakers may help to finance their productions by agreeing to engage in "product placement" or using a particular product in a prominent way during scenes of the film.	Television series on network and **basic cable television** are financed through commercials, which are interspersed between the scenes of the program. Series on premium cable television are financed through production companies and investors as well as by the channel itself that charges viewers a subscription fee. Television series also may use product placement for financing.

By the end of the twentieth century, the cost of going to a movie theater to see a movie in its initial release rises with three significant developments in Cinema:

1. the introduction of **cable television**, which gives viewers access to hundreds of channels, including premium channels like HBO and Showtime, as opposed to the limited network and local television options that existed before cable;
2. the decrease in the cost of purchasing a television set, which means that homes typically have more televisions in different rooms available for individuals in a household to watch; and
3. the introduction of **VCRs** into homes, giving people the ability to record programs or movies for later viewing, to rent movies from local or national **video rental businesses** at their convenience, or to purchase videos that they would like to watch more than once. Significantly, these changes impact the types of Cinema that audiences consume.

On the one hand, a subscriber to a premium movie channel or member of a video rental club might be more likely to try out a film that they would never have gone to see in a movie theater. This might include a mainstream movie of a genre that the viewer has not historically found appealing, a movie that might only have had a limited release in cities like New York or Los Angeles, or a pornographic film that a viewer might have been embarrassed to see in public. On the other hand, movie makers who want to attract an audience to movie theaters for box-office profit place greater emphasis on visual and auditory pyrotechnics such as special visual effects (which today might involve using **CGI** and **3-D** technologies) and innovations in sound recording (**Dolby Surround Sound**) to wow audiences and make it "worth" the price of admission. **Action films** and **comic book films** particularly address this need to bring large audiences to see Cinema on "the big screen." These developments also initiate the fragmentation of the audience for Cinema, beginning a decline in Cinema as a collectively experienced medium and transforming it into a medium experienced individually or by niche audiences with little in common with one another. Finally, these developments dramatically influence the production quality of films, the profit structure for cinematic productions, and the creative autonomy of those entering the film or television industries. In each of these ways, the landscape of Cinema in the late twentieth century anticipates the cinematic future of the twenty-first century, when viewers are more likely to stream Cinema on **personal computers**, **tablets**, or **smartphones** than to watch Cinema on either a movie screen or a television set.

Indeed, as we enter the twenty-first century, what we talk about when we discuss Cinema is often one of the following:

1. Feature-length fictional or factual productions that might first be released at **film festivals** and then distributed in **limited release,** independent from major studios (**independent films**), at theaters and in **wide release** through streaming services and for sale through **Blu-ray** or **DVD** for collectors, what we formerly might have called arthouse films.

2. Feature-length fictional or factual productions that are intended for wide release nationally and internationally, which are then distributed in further wide release through streaming services and for sale through Blu-ray and DVD for collectors, what we formerly might have called mass audience films.

3. Serial fictional or factual productions that might be first released on network television (typically twenty-two episodes per season), basic cable television (typically twelve to twenty-four episodes per season), premium cable television (typically twelve episodes per season), or a streaming service (typically twelve episodes per season), what we formerly might have called television. Shows may first be watched on a variety of devices (television, computer, tablet, smartphone) at a variety of times through **DVR** and streaming technology. Successful series may then be sold through Blu-Ray and DVD for collectors.

As with literature, Cinema evolves to include a range of genres and conventions through which to tell its stories, and it develops its own terminology for describing techniques and concepts that it finds central. However, having a basic vocabulary for thinking about some of the most central issues in Cinema can be helpful to any practitioner of English Studies, and that vocabulary does not directly mimic the vocabulary we use to discuss literature. Most importantly, students of English Studies should understand that the various cinematic genres that we encounter in either feature-length or serial formats emerge through the relationship among language (the **screenplay**), performance (a collaboration between director and actors), visual images (cinematography), and recorded sound (score, soundtrack, and sound effects).

Even though there may be similarities between literature, and most particularly the literary genre of drama, and Cinema, there are also significant differences. Sound, film, and digital recording technologies, as well as visual techniques (such as **point-of-view shots**, **close-ups**, **wide shots**, **panning**, and **jump cuts**), introduce additional narrative structures that make it irresponsible to reduce interpretation of a cinematic text's meaning to the words of its screenplay. In the end, Cinema is a medium that is performance-based, engages multiple senses, and comes into being through the collaboration of a team of trained technicians, artists, and writers. Even in English Studies, we would never study a film's screenplay in isolation as literature, even though we do study the **scripts** of plays, such as in the cases of **playwrights** such as William Shakespeare, Oscar Wilde, or Tennessee Williams. The story of a work of Cinema depends on sounds and images as much as it depends on words.

Popular Culture and New Media

Popular Culture and New Media are terms that we use to discuss the range of cultural products that involve a storytelling component. Popular Culture, for example, might include a range of **mass media** products including **advertisements**, articles in **print media** such as magazines and newspapers, **board games**, **comics**, **music videos**, and more. Still, Popular Culture is not limited to narrative products designed for **mass consumption**. Popular Culture may also include community-based forms of narrative that emerge locally and are not disseminated on a large scale.

New Media signals the shift away from what we would call Popular Culture toward the range of narrative products that emerge with advanced digital, **computing**, and **internet technology**, including social media, **video games** (designed for smartphone, tablet, **PC**, and **console**), apps, **websites**, blogs (web logs), **vlogs** (video logs), and more. Taken together, Popular Culture and New Media connect to narrative potential across a range of formats; they focus less on storytelling through lengthy **exposition** and more on storytelling through **telegraphic narrative** modes. They place value on cultural narratives that are objects of mass consumption as well as on narrative modes that exist for purposes of entertainment and community-building, which may or may not conform to high-brow **aesthetic** standards.

Popular Culture and New Media are important to English Studies because they directly connect our discipline's interest in storytelling to the world in which we live. Through Popular Culture and New Media, practitioners of English Studies discover a format through which to link the discipline's focus on **rhetoric**, narrative, and the conventions of effective writing to everyday topics and concerns. While it is possible to achieve the same thing across more traditional fields of the discipline, such as linguistics or literary studies, people often make the mistake of believing that the work of English Studies applies only to historical texts, **high culture**, or an educated elite. Studying Popular Culture and New Media from an English Studies perspective showcases how incorrect these views are. These fields tie to **folklore**, oral storytelling traditions, the great works of literature, and Cinema. Further, these new storytelling formats make it possible for people to engage more deeply with those high-culture texts that English Studies has traditionally emphasized. Popular Culture and New Media offer new lenses for interpretation as well as new creative opportunities for writers.

What Theories and Concepts Are Most Central to Discussions of Cinema, Popular Culture, and New Media in English Studies?

English Studies scholars engage a wide variety of theories and concepts in their approaches to Cinema, Popular Culture, and New Media, some of which might seem similar to theories and concepts that English Studies practitioners historically emphasized in their study of literary texts. Here are some key theories and concepts that beginners will find useful as they approach these types of texts and as they begin to have sophisticated conversations about them.

Five Key Theories and Concepts in Cinema Studies

Theories and concepts in Cinema Studies address not only the **creative process** and cinematic production but also the means for analyzing and interpreting cinematic texts. Drawing on ideas about performance, production, and direction from the world of theater (what theater scholars and practitioners refer to as **dramaturgy**) and on ideas about how to "read" cinematic texts adapted from the worlds of **literary criticism** and critical theory, the theories and concepts below facilitate scholarly **discourse** about Cinema.

Auteur Theory

Auteur Theory offers a useful starting point for practitioners of English studies who are interested in a deeper understanding of Cinema. *Auteur* is the French word for **author**, and when we use it in the context of Cinema, it indicates that there is one artist, usually the director, who controls the artistic vision of a cinematic work, which is by definition a collaborative enterprise. In the late 1940s, critics begin using the concept of **auteurism** to distinguish between films made within the studio system, intended for a mass audience and filmed on sound stages and sets controlled by major production companies, and films intended as artistic endeavors filmed "on location" that aim to present a more self-consciously artistic product to an audience of connoisseurs. In this way of thinking about Cinema, the "auteur," or director, is the "author" of the cinematic production. Directors like Francois Truffaut (France), Federico Fellini (Italy), Alfred Hitchcock (United States), Spike Lee (United States), and Steven Spielberg (United States) are typically regarded as exemplars of auteurs in film studies. Today, in an era of **peak television**, we can productively think about the creators or **showrunners** of television series, such as David Lynch (*Twin Peaks*; 1990–1, 2017), Amy Sherman-Palladino (*The Gilmore Girls*; 2000–7, 2016), Matthew Weiner (*Mad Men*; 2007–15), David Simon (*The Wire*; 2002–8), or Sam Esmail (*Mr. Robot*; 2015–19), as auteurs. This theory has also been used in commentary about video games.

Soviet Montage Theory

Whereas auteur theory fundamentally traces the origin of meaning in a work of Cinema back to an author with a singular creative vision, **Soviet montage theory** suggests that meaning in a work of Cinema emerges from the narrative impact of how images and scenes are edited. As a technique, **montage**, which differs from **continuity editing** in production, effect, and intention, is the process of selecting, editing, arranging, and collating different sections of film to form a continuous whole. Although Soviet filmmakers of the 1920s disagreed about how to approach montage, they nevertheless agreed about its centrality to Cinema as a narrative medium. Today, Sergei Eisenstein's ideas about montage in his 1929 foundational essay, "The Dramaturgy of Film Form" (also called "The Dialectical Approach to Film Form"), have the most lasting impact. Eisenstein's work reveals the storytelling power of editing, which involves not only what is being represented on the screen but also how audiences perceive what they watch. For example, in using montage, Soviet filmmaker Lev Kuleshov discovered what we now call **the Kuleshov Effect**, a mental phenomenon wherein viewers discern greater meaning from two sequential shots in a film than from a single shot in isolation.

Just as formalist critics of literature, such as the **Russian Formalists** and **New Critics**, were invested in discovering the ways in which form creates content, so too were proponents of Soviet montage theory, which today remains a lasting contribution of Soviet film theorists to making films and understanding them. Alfred Hitchcock is widely known for his use of montage in films, but many filmmakers after Hitchcock use the technique as well. Films as different as John Hughes's *Ferris Bueller's Day Off* (1986), Christopher Nolan's *Memento* (2000), Sophia Coppola's *Marie Antoinette* (2006), and Disney's *Frozen* (2013) all use montage to engage viewers and heighten the meanings that they attempt to convey. The ability to take different slices of filmed material and to arrange them into a cohesive totality is unique to Cinema.

Theories of Acting

Cinema significantly influences the techniques of performance that actors use. In the context of live theater, actors perform their narratives from beginning to end each night of a show's run, and their performance depends on their ability to remember their lines, to project their voice adequately, and to use their faces and bodies to convey meaning to the furthest seat from the stage. In contrast, actors in cinematic productions often perform their scripts out of narrative sequence, may improvise or offer different performances of the same scene in multiple takes, and use their voices, faces, and bodies to convey very small variations in thought or mood. In this way, Cinema initiates developments in acting, and because Cinema is a collaborative art form, these changes in acting also instigate different types of storytelling both visually and in scripted dialogue.

For this reason, English Studies practitioners benefit from understanding something about acting as a component of cinematic narratives. Cinematic narratives suggest that the physical presence of actors, the **dialects** and **accents** that they choose, and the ways in which they express the language of their scripts can change a story. The most significant transformation in acting that contributes to our understanding of Cinema is **method acting**, or **the Method**, which is an adaptation of a system developed by the Russian theater practitioner Konstantin Stanislavski and was popularized in the United States by Lee Strasberg, Stella Adler, and Sanford Meisner. This range of training and rehearsal techniques emphasizes sincere and emotionally expressive performances, which depend on improvisation, drawing on one's own emotional present or past, and inhabiting the emotional and psychological reality of one's role. This approach depends upon the actor finding motivations and justifications for the actions that a character performs and their feelings about those actions.

Structuralist and Poststructuralist Film Theories

Cinema also encourages English Studies practitioners to find new ways of reading or interpreting stories and to understand audience responses. Subsequent to formalist approaches to Cinema, as exemplified by Soviet montage theory, critics seek interpretive frameworks that they can apply to cinematic texts to understand their philosophical, **ideological**, and literary content. Initially, the approaches that they use originate with **structuralism**, a theory that suggests identifying particular patterns and codes in a text to arrive at its deeper meaning. Structuralist film theory often emphasizes the **temporality** of Cinema as a genre. Nevertheless, it does not assert that the temporal form of Cinema produces all meaning. Structures that can be applied to films in order to interpret them include **feminism, psychoanalysis, Marxism, critical race theory, queer theory**, and more.

Poststructuralist film theory, like **poststructuralism** more broadly, can be seen as both an extension of structuralist approaches to their furthest conclusion and a rejection of those approaches. Poststructuralist theory emphasizes **deconstruction** as a necessary tool in unraveling the infinite meanings that a text can engender. As a method, deconstruction emphasizes a process of ongoing decentering, which, put another way, means that instead of looking for the one true meaning of a cinematic work, we should read the work of Cinema against itself to examine the ways in which doing so will result in a proliferation of possible meanings. For example, in his book *Violence: Six Sideways Reflections* (2007), Slavoj Žižek uses a poststructuralist approach to argue that M. Night Shyamalan's critically reviled *The Village* (2004) in fact is an exceptional commentary on the media's mystifying portrayals of those most responsible for terror, violence, and inequality. Thus, poststructuralist film theory allows critics to "read against the grain" of a cinematic text to discover its broader possibilities for meaning beyond the surface narrative.

Gaze Theory

In **gaze theory**, we can see structuralist and poststructuralist approaches to Cinema exemplified in a political criticism that integrates emergent theories from the disciplines of philosophy, psychoanalysis, sociology, and literary studies. This approach to Cinema particularly emphasizes the ways in which **visual rhetorics** influence our understanding of **class, gender, sexuality**, and **race**. For example, Laura Mulvey's foundational essay "Visual Pleasure and Narrative Cinema" (1975) uses Jacques Lacan's theories about the gaze and **scopophilic desire** to suggest that viewers of Cinema must attend to the ways in which camera angles and shots are used to give some characters in a work of film subjective authority (the power of being the one who actively looks, sees, and judges) and to construct other characters as objects (those who are passively seen, acted upon, and judged). Mulvey's essay examines the ways in which female bodies, and thus female characters, are **objectified** in Cinema, which reinforces **patriarchal** power structures that oppress women in the real world.

These ideas have since been adapted to influence interpretations of films that showcase the representation of other marginalized groups in cinematic works. Thus, by understanding gaze theory, we may gain new insight into the representation not just of women in films but also of people of a range of races, ethnicities, classes, and sexualities.

Five Key Theories and Concepts in Popular Culture Studies

Popular Culture Studies is intimately connected to Cinema, but it focuses more on reception and audience than on production and creativity. Many of the most important theories and concepts in Popular Culture studies relate to understanding Popular Culture as reflective of the larger culture that we inhabit and that is structured through practices of production and consumption.

Mass Culture

When we talk about **mass culture** or **consumer culture**, we are talking about those cultural products that inform our everyday understanding of the world. Rather than thinking about culture as something that happens in museums or libraries, we must think about culture as something that happens all around us in our everyday lives. From this perspective, culture is something that we experience even when we do not seek it out. Culture includes everything: daily news reports, products that we see or hear advertised, spaces of the stores in which we shop, products that we buy, songs on the radio, lifestyle articles in magazines, and more. Popular Culture or consumer culture emerges with enhancements in media and communication technologies that allow more and more people to have a common experience in daily life, and thus it truly comes into being in the twentieth century. As opposed to being siloed in our own communities or regions, we now understand the world in ways that are increasingly similar. Mass culture and consumer culture make the world smaller.

The Culture Industry

Foundational to our understanding of mass culture or consumer culture are the theories of Max Horkheimer and Theodor Adorno. The term **Culture Industry** comes from a chapter in Horkheimer and Adorno's 1944 book *Dialectic of Enlightenment*, "The Culture Industry: Enlightenment as Mass Deception." Horkheimer and Adorno argue that things like radio, films, magazines, and other cultural goods that are marketed to a mass audience produce a passive citizenry who substitute the easy pleasures of Popular Culture for the values of social and economic prosperity. According to Horkheimer and Adorno, following Karl Marx, the consuming public is mystified by the pleasures of Popular Culture into accepting inequality. This term is important because it acknowledges the significant impact that Popular Culture has on individuals' perceptions of their daily lives, and it suggests that mass culture is connected to power relationships in society as a whole. Further, this term has become a stand-in for larger ideas about the relationship between individuals and the products that they consume: in other words, it suggests that Popular Culture products have larger meaning as we seek to understand our identities and our place in the social order of our communities.

Cultural Studies

Emerging from the idea of a Culture Industry, **Cultural Studies** promotes the serious consideration of Popular Culture as an academic subject. Emerging in Britain in the middle of the twentieth century, and spearheaded by scholars such as Stuart Hall and Raymond Williams, Cultural Studies scholarship sought to connect a broader inquiry into mass culture to more traditional ideas about what constituted culture inherited from literary studies, art history, and philosophy. Cultural Studies offers a framework through which to analyze Popular Culture that connects to Marxist, feminist, postcolonial, psychoanalytic, and critical race theories. It expands the definition of culture to include those cultural products that are not typically experienced as "art."

Cultural Hegemony

An important concept that guides Cultural Studies and that also connects to Horkheimer and Adorno's ideas about the Culture Industry is **cultural hegemony**. Cultural hegemony suggests that the beliefs, perceptions, values, ideas, and norms of a culture reflect those of the dominant ruling class of that culture, and that even those people who are oppressed by that value system ultimately espouse and promote them. In other words, oppression is not something that occurs in a systematic or conscious way perpetrated by powerful oppressors onto powerless objects of oppression. Instead, the culture that surrounds all people, and in which they participate, is the product not only of those with power or authority but also of those who are the "losers" in that culture. Basically, the "masses" support cultural ideals, values, perceptions, and beliefs, even they themselves do not benefit from them. This idea is important because it creates a more complicated picture of power imbalance, where even those who are oppressed can be complicit in their oppression because they perceive their oppression as part of something that holds larger cultural value.

Countercultures and Subcultures

Finally, in Popular Culture countercultures and subcultures constitute significant reactions against the idea of hegemony. Countercultures or subcultures oppose the dominant cultural values that hegemony supports and mass culture or consumer culture promotes. Countercultures, such as **Hippie** culture in the 1960s, consciously reject the dominant culture, and they espouse values, ideas, traditions, or practices to which the dominant culture objects. Subcultures are subsets of the dominant culture that adapt those values, ideas, traditions, or practices of the dominant culture, or edit them in significant ways, in order to create a new cultural ideal (**Punk**). Countercultures and subcultures constitute points of resistance against hegemony and against the Culture Industry. Their resistance has the power to create new cultures.

Five Key Theories and Concepts in New Media Studies

The New Media landscape integrates technology with narrative, creating new ways of seeing narrative in its component parts as well as new ways of thinking about how information is stored, cataloged, processed, and disseminated.

Information

In New Media Studies, information constitutes that set of **data** and/or **knowledge** that is communicated in a range of **multimedia** narrative forms. Information can be regarded as something that is processed, not just by readers or viewers but also by machines. In a New Media economy, information is mediated by technology, and may often be characterized as **hypermediated**, or imbedded in a number of different formats, each of which influences a person's understanding of the information at hand. In *Remediation: Understanding New Media* (1999), J. David Bolter and Richard A. Grusin go further and argue that New Media constantly reproduce and replace old media technologies: in other words, New Media texts refashion, or remediate, the texts of mass media. Thus a film based on a book remediates the printed text and can do so without acknowledging the original medium. In such a way, the new medium absorbs the old and, in doing so, gives the user a more vivid experience of reality.

Archives

Because New Media Studies encourages us to view information in this way, it becomes essential to think carefully about how information is stored. One term that can help us to understand this emphasis on the preservation of information is **archives**. Historically, the word "archives" had been used to talk about the place in libraries for storing documents and texts: the archives were a physical place to which a scholar would go to conduct academic study. In contrast, in a New Media environment, archives operates as a conceptual term that connects to the storage of data for backup. For example, you may have heard that once you post something on social media, it is there forever: this idea is informed by the notion of the technological archives that exist for things posted on the internet. Further, the increasing use of **cloud storage** for files basically creates electronic archives of your activities.

The ever-growing body of **digital media** online, however, has given rise to self-designated, nonprofessional archivists who have taken on the task of cultural preservation on the internet. In such a way, they have democratized cultural memory with the creation of online accessible archives of a broad range of information in a wide variety of formats. The temporality of New Media, as Diana Taylor argues in "Save As ... Knowledge and Transmission in the Age of Digital Technologies" (2010), encourages us to "archive"—that is, to save and store—continually and endlessly in order to preserve a sense of self in the unstable environment of digital technologies both now and in the future.

Databases

The concept of archives in digital environments gives us access to more and more types of information as well as more sources of information about given topics. Instead of relying on one authoritative source, like an encyclopedia, if we have a question about something, we are more and more likely to search in a **database**, such as Google or Bing!, in order to find a range of results, which may or may not represent the truth. Thus, it begins to be critical that we understand ourselves as inhabiting a **media ecology** or existing within a network of competing sources of information that shape our understanding of the world and the information that we consume. The idea that media, technology, and communication directly affect human environments was first proposed as a theoretical concept by Marshall McLuhan in *Understanding Media* (1964). Neil Postman named the theory media ecology and formalized it, arguing that technologies, such as the print text or television, are not just instruments to deliver information but environments through which the human condition is expressed.

Interactivity

Perhaps the most important characteristic of a New Media ecology is its **interactivity**. Individuals do not just passively consume media products in a New Media ecology; rather, they actively contribute to New Media discourses, engaging directly with the media products that they encounter and participating in the proliferation of discourses surrounding those discourses. Interactivity relates directly to the concept of **fandom**, which gains traction in **internet subcultures** where people who share a similar interest can connect with **web technologies**, and it connects to the ways in which we now experience events on a global scale.

Simulation

Finally, **simulation** is a critical concept in New Media Studies, and it refers to the virtual representation of reality. Coined in its New Media usage by the theorist Jean Baudrillard, simulation can be understood as the furthest extension of interactivity, wherein an audience can come to experience an event as real, as if it directly happened to them, because of the ways in which they internalize sounds, images, and narratives that they consume. For Baudrillard, simulation leads to the production of **simulacra** or things that we regard as real but that never actually happened. The relationship between simulation and simulacra is integral to New Media Studies as the incorporation of **Virtual Reality**, **Augmented Reality**, and new video technologies in gaming, printed books, and **journalism** increases.

What Are the Conventions of Scholarship for English Studies Practitioners Who Examine Cinema, Popular Culture, and New Media? What Kinds of Research and Interpretation Do Cinema, Popular Culture, and New Media Scholars Do?

In general, English Studies practitioners who examine Cinema, Popular Culture, and New Media are invested in discovering the ways in which Cinema, Popular Culture, and New Media narratives affect their audience. One approach for doing this has much in common with interpretive approaches in literary studies, where scholars perform **close readings** of the texts that they examine and then, based on those close readings and how they integrate those readings with theoretical, historical, social, or cultural context, they offer an interpretation of the texts that they examine. For example, scholars interested in the representation of black womanhood might choose Beyoncé's *Lemonade* (2016) as a text to investigate. They might look at the visual representations in the video through the lens of Cinema studies, also attending to the narrative constructed by the songs and their placement. Such a project might enable them to discover the ways in which Beyoncé deploys stereotypes about blackness and femininity. They might also examine the way that Beyoncé invokes **imagery** reminiscent of the history of slavery and in doing so connects that traumatic history to the personal trauma of infidelity in a marriage. From a Popular Culture perspective, they could then think more broadly about Beyoncé's status as a cultural icon, and how that iconic status influences the representation of black womanhood that she projects in *Lemonade*. Finally, New Media could provide insight into the audiences that *Lemonade* targeted and the ways in which it used a multipronged media plan to supplement the primary text of *Lemonade* and to contextualize its narrative. Ultimately, this type of scholarship privileges the analysis of primary texts, and it suggests that primary texts reveal important truths about culture.

Another approach for scholarship in these areas would be to focus less on the text as artwork and more on the reception of Cinema, Popular Culture, and New Media texts. Scholarship that takes this approach might be less interested in the story that these texts tell than in the technologies through which they are told, the ways in which the audience experiences these texts, and the commentary that these texts produce. Thus, rather than offering an **argument** about how to interpret the text under discussion, these scholars might instead offer an argument about what the audience's reception and interpretations have to say about a text's meaning and cultural impact. To return to the example of Beyoncé's *Lemonade*, scholars who take this sort of approach would be less interested in Beyoncé herself or even in what she has created than they are in the Beyhive, as Beyoncé's fans call themselves, media narratives about the reception of *Lemonade*, social media commentary that appears after the piece's release, and the larger media apparatus that Beyoncé deploys to promote and disseminate her works. Ultimately, this type of scholarship is less invested in the truths that a text can reveal about culture than it is in learning the ways in which the **multimodal** processes of representation and communication work.

What Is Cinema Studies, Popular Culture Studies, and New Media Studies for the Twenty-First Century? How Does It Connect to the Discipline of English Studies, More Broadly Conceived?

An English Studies approach to Cinema, Popular Culture, and New Media in the twenty-first century emphasizes:

1. visual and verbal rhetorics that inform our understanding of the global economy in which we live;
2. the influence of creative writing on the production of Cinema, Popular Culture, and New Media texts;
3. the similarity between critical and theoretical scholarly approaches to literature and those we use for Cinema, Popular Culture, and New Media; and
4. the influence of professional writing and technical communication on the dissemination and promotion of Cinema, Popular Culture, and New Media.

By looking at the ways in which these media formats allow for different types of stories to be told and a wider range of voices to be heard, English Studies practitioners may attend less directly to the technical aspects of cinematic, mass media, or technology-enhanced production and instead may look at those technical aspects of Cinema, Popular Culture, and New Media as tools that individuals and collaborative groups use in the service of creating cultural narratives.

As practitioners of English Studies seek to emphasize **inclusion** as a value of our discipline—defining inclusion broadly in terms of valuing voices from diverse gender, sexual, class, racial, and ethnic backgrounds; valuing diverse intellectual perspectives on the texts that we evaluate; valuing the multiplicity of types of texts that populate our cultural landscape; and valuing the creation of texts using a multiplicity of approaches and techniques—it is important to understand Cinema, Popular Culture and New Media as central to a vision for English Studies in the twenty-first century. Cinema, Popular Culture, and New Media open a forum within which marginalized voices can create and express their unique points of view as well as **critique** the products that they consume. They democratize the production of narrative and critical texts with the aid of new technologies. Further, these texts both reflect and influence developments in linguistics, creative writing, reading practices, theoretical approaches, composition and rhetoric, professional communication, digital humanities in English, and English education.

Further Reading

Bennett, Peter, et al. *Film Studies: The Essential Resource.* London: Routledge, 2007.

Uses popular, academic, theoretical, and journalistic essays to introduce students to key concepts in the study of Cinema.

Bordwell, David. *The Way Hollywood Tells It: Story and Style in Modern Movies*. Berkeley: University of California Press, 2006.
Focuses on the intersection between verbal and visual narratives in movies since 1960.

Charney, Leo, and Vanessa R. Schwartz. *Cinema and the Invention of Modern Life*. Berkeley: University of California Press, 1995.
Links the emergence of Cinema to emerging Popular Culture and media, drawing on the expertise of scholars in film and cultural studies.

Egenfeldt-Nielsen, Simon, et al. *Understanding Video Games: The Essential Introduction*. New York: Routledge, 2008.
Introduces concepts in game studies, issues in the gaming industry, new developments in game design, and scholarly practices in the field.

Gray, Jonathan, et al. *Fandom: Identities and Communities in a Mediated World*. New York: New York University Press, 2007.
Discusses fan communities and the role they play in the reception of cultural products.

MacDougall, David, and Lucien Castaing-Taylor. *Transcultural Cinema*. Princeton: Princeton University Press, 1998.
Explores the narrative conventions of cinematic storytelling with particular emphasis on film as an ethnographic and anthropological genre.

Mahar, Karen Ward. *Women Filmmakers in Early Hollywood*. Baltimore: Johns Hopkins University Press, 2006.
Discusses women in the early film industry.

Neupert, Richard John. *A History of the French New Wave Cinema*. 2nd ed. Madison: University of Wisconsin Press, 2007.
Offers an introduction to Cinema of the French New Wave.

Schreiber, Michele. *American Postfeminist Cinema: Women, Romance and Contemporary Culture*. Edinburgh: Edinburgh University Press, 2014.
Discusses the representation of love and romance in Cinema since 1980.

Smith, Susan. *The Musical: Race, Gender and Performance*. London: Wallflower, 2005.
Explores issues connected to race and gender in classic cinematic musicals.

Tryon, Chuck. *Reinventing Cinema: Movies in the Age of Media Convergence*. New Brunswick: Rutgers University Press, 2009.
Investigates intersections and divergences between Cinema, television, and New Media at the turn of the twenty-first century.

Wardrip-Fruin, Noah, and Pat Harrigan. *Second Person: Role-Playing and Story in Games and Playable Media*. Cambridge: MIT Press, 2010.
Considers the role of narrative in games and other media.

Yearwood, Gladstone Lloyd. *Black Film as a Signifying Practice: Cinema, Narration and the African American Aesthetic Tradition*. Trenton: Africa World Press, 2000.
Discusses the influence of race on Cinema.

In Part 1 of this Case Study, we examine how to approach the adaptation of fiction to Cinema. We then offer engagement activities that you can use to help you better understand how Cinema fits into English Studies.

The Television Series *Game of Thrones*

Case Study, Part 1: From Page to Screen (Cinema)

Who Is George R. R. Martin and What Is *Game of Thrones*?

American author George R. R. Martin rose to fame and wide acclaim with his series of **fantasy** novels *A Song of Ice and Fire*, on which the television series *Game of Thrones* is based. However, Martin had a long career before *A Song of Ice and Fire*. Martin earned a degree in journalism and started his career as a writer by selling short stories to science fiction magazines and anthologies. His interest in science fiction, fantasy, and speculative fiction came as much from a desire to create in those genres as it did from being a fan of those genres. During the 1980s, he worked as a writer and producer for science fiction and fantasy television series including a revival of *The Twilight Zone, Beauty and the Beast*, and the original series *Max Headroom*, but he also regularly attended conventions, conferences, and fan events, and he established himself as a key figure in the science fiction and fantasy community. Martin's background is important because it establishes him not just as a writer of **genre fiction** but also as an actively engaged creator and fan of science fiction, fantasy, and speculative fiction across a range of media.

Martin's first novel in *A Song of Ice and Fire* is titled *A Game of Thrones* (1996), and it introduced readers to Westeros, a roughly medieval world in a crisis of governance, in which the seasons of nature last for years, magic and supernatural creatures are real, and prophecy appears to exert powerful control over people's lives. In this first novel in the series, Martin established a unique approach to narrative in fantasy fiction in which each chapter of his novel, although written in third person, emphasized the viewpoint of a particular character. Readers of his books now refer to this technique as point-of-view narration. The series was originally conceived as containing five books, with the second and third books in the series, *A Clash of Kings* (1999) and *A Storm of Swords* (2000), following the plan that he had originally intended. Martin experienced a block at this point, discovering that his original concept, which dictated that he would skip ahead in time by five years, would not work with his viewpoint-focused narrative style. For this reason, he abandoned the plan of writing just five novels in the series, he abandoned the five-year gap, and he changed his plan to include seven novels that would take place over a continuous span of time.

From this point, the time between the publication of each book in the series lengthened. Book Four, *A Feast for Crows*, was published in 2005, and Book Five, *A Dance with Dragons*, was published in 2011. He missed his deadline in 2015 for the sixth book in the series, *The Winds of Winter*, and though he said in January of 2017 that he expected to finish his manuscript "this year," as the year ended there was no further news about a publication date. Martin has claimed that the seventh novel, *A Dream of Spring*, will be the last in the series, but no timeline has been announced for its writing or completion. In the interim between the publication of *A Dance with Dragons* and the printing of *Introducing English Studies*, Martin has released chapters of *The Winds of Winter* as well as short stories that connect to the world of Westeros that are not part of the *A Song of Ice and Fire* series. He has not published *The Winds of Winter* or *A Dream of Spring*.

The Cinematic Adaptation of *A Song of Ice and Fire*

HBO optioned *A Song of Ice and Fire* for television in 2007. The pilot for the series that would become *Game of Thrones* was produced in 2009, with the nine episodes that would follow in the first season filmed in 2010. At the time that the books were optioned for adaptation, there was concern that Martin's novels might not keep pace with the development of the series and that Martin's health might not allow him to finish the books in time for the television series run. Nonetheless, Martin convinced series showrunners David Benioff and D. B. Weiss and HBO that he would be on track to complete the novels in line with the show's schedule for adaptation.

The first season of the show adhered somewhat closely to the plot and characters of Martin's first novel, *A Game of Thrones*, but from that point the show diverged from the timeline and characters of the show in order to create an episodic plot that would remain compelling to viewers who had not read the books. Notably, the showrunners chose to consolidate certain plotlines, reduce the number of characters, and reorder events of the novels. By the time the show reached its sixth season, it advanced almost entirely beyond the plot of Martin's published novels, drawing primarily on content and outlined material slated to be published in the long-awaited sixth novel, *The Winds of Winter.* The seventh and final season of the series, which concluded in 2019, consisted of entirely original content. The showrunners claimed to develop the conclusion to the television series with Martin's input about his plans for the remaining novels, but since the novels have not been released, it is impossible to know how faithfully the show adhered to Martin's vision.

Thus, what began as a television adaptation of a series of novels evolved into an original fantasy television series inspired by the world that Martin's novels first created. As Cinema, *Game of Thrones* attracted viewers with its high production values, use of technology, nudity, explicit sexual scenes, and violence. *Game of Thrones* established itself as appointment television in an era of peak television, when most viewers rarely watched television shows during their first broadcast airing. The show drew a wide range of viewers who were not necessarily aware of Martin's novels or fans of fantasy narratives or media products generally, and it constitutes an important example of mass culture in a time when mass culture became increasingly stratified and niche-oriented.

Activities for Critical and Creative Engagement

1. *Using* Game of Thrones *or another cinematic text that has been adapted from a poem, short story, play, novel, or memoir, compare and contrast the similarities and differences between the written original and the adaptation for Cinema. How does the story change? What elements of the original are emphasized, what elements are deemphasized, and what new elements are*

introduced? What factors shape narrative decisions for written texts versus cinematic texts? Of the texts that you are analyzing, which do you prefer: the original or the adaptation? Why? (Good texts for this assignment might include Harry Potter, The Hunger Games, Watchmen, The Handmaid's Tale, *or others.)*

2. *Take a text that you have read (a poem, short story, play, novel, or memoir) and outline how you would adapt it for Cinema. What would guide your decisions about casting, setting, plot elements to emphasize, and visual effects? How would your adaptation use the original written text as a foundation, and how would it diverge from the original? Why?*

How Does English Studies Help Us to Think More Deeply about Cinema and Understand Adaptation?

Game of Thrones provides an interesting entryway into thinking about not only the similarities between written works of fiction and their counterparts in Cinema but also the differences between these two formats for creative expression. Evaluating the show's path from page to screen from an English Studies perspective helps readers and viewers to understand how the pressures of the marketplace shape the books and movies that we consume. It also encourages readers and viewers to think about what makes literary narrative distinctive from cinematic narrative and to bring that knowledge to bear on their own interpretations and creations. But the *Game of Thrones* phenomenon does not stop with Cinema. It extends to Popular Culture and New Media, which will be explored in Part 2 of this Case Study.

In Part 2 of this Case Study, we examine the role that Popular Culture and New Media play in our understanding of cultural texts like Game of Thrones. *We then offer engagement activities that you can use to help you evaluate Popular Culture and New Media using the tools of English Studies.*

The Television Series *Game of Thrones*

Case Study, Part 2: Cinema after the Internet (Popular Culture and New Media)

The Role of Popular Culture in Making *Game of Thrones* Popular

The phenomenon of *Game of Thrones* in many ways depended on its ancillary Popular Culture products. Reviews; trailers; cast member appearances at conventions and fan events as well as on broadcast television; published, audio, and video interviews with cast members and showrunners; and episode recaps in respected publications played a large role in making the public aware of the series and in encouraging people to watch it. Rather than waiting for an audience to emerge based on word of mouth, *Game of Thrones* used mass media to create its audience and shape its audience's vocabulary about the show.

Activity for Critical Engagement

1. *Select a cinematic text (a movie or television show) and do research using the internet and library databases to discover ancillary Popular Culture materials that accompany the text of your choosing. You will want to evaluate the marketing materials for the work of Cinema, including such items as trailers, commercials, and movie posters; interviews with producers, directors, and cast members; and reviews and recaps in mass*

media publications. How does the Popular Culture narrative about the work of Cinema shape your response to it or influence your interpretation? How do these different Popular Culture artifacts work together to construct a narrative about the Cinematic text that interests you? What is that Popular Culture narrative?

New Media Appropriations of Game of Thrones

In addition to the conventional promotion of the show, however, New Media appropriations and expansions of series content also played a key role in the cultural significance of *Game of Thrones*. The New Media landscape that governed *Game of Thrones* can be broken into the following categories: **explainers**, **fan theories**, encyclopedias, **spoilers**, **parodies**, real-time commentary, and creative appropriations. Each of these New Media artifacts can be understood as contributing to the fandom of *Game of Thrones*. The **discourse community** of viewers who loved, or loved to hate, the series created these artifacts.

Explainers can be understood as short videos or blog posts that make sense of what is happening during a particular episode of the show, often connecting what happens on the television series to Martin's written source material, commentary on Martin's personal website *Not a Blog* (https://grrm.livejournal.com), or interviews with Martin. On YouTube, fans like Alt Shift X, Rawrist, and Preston Jacobs created videos discussing each episode of *Game of Thrones*. These explainers often gave way to fan theories about where the books, show, or both were heading. These theories often had names, such as "L+R=J," "Southron Ambitions," or "Eldritch Apocalypse," that fans then used as shorthand in their conversations on social media **platforms** like YouTube, Twitter, Facebook, Reddit, and Tumblr. Fans also contributed to online encyclopedias, like *A Wiki of Ice and Fire* (https://awoiaf.westeros.org), detailing every aspect of the show and books.

Beyond this first grouping of New Media interventions in *Game of Thrones* discourse, fans could also go online to find spoilers or advance information about what would happen next on the series based on leaked or hacked material and parodies or parodic commentaries about the show, which often, like Funny Or Die's *Gay of Thrones*, called attention to the ways in which different audience communities responded to what they saw depicted. Real-time commentary about the show also connected fans of similar backgrounds for in-the-moment reactions to the show while it first aired as well as for postshow analysis with the use of common hashtags. For example, the hashtags #thronesyall or #demthrones were often used by Black viewers of the series, and #thronesyall went **viral** when *Game of Thrones* fans protested the showrunners' prospective new series *Confederate*, a fantasy series imagining that the Confederate South won the American Civil War, in August 2017. Finally, viewers could also go online to find creative efforts by fans in which they wrote alternate versions of the plot of Martin's novels (**fan fiction**), participate in **cosplay** connected to the show's characters, or created **fan art** that depicted the characters or landmarks in Westeros as they believed that they should appear.

Each of these New Media interventions created additional context for *Game of Thrones* as well as multiplied the number of texts available for analysis from an English Studies perspective.

Activities for Critical and Creative Engagement

2. *Identify a fan theory connected to Game of Thrones or another popular series and find at least three different New Media texts that examine, discuss, or engage with that theory. What kinds of evidence do commentators use to support their claims? How is this different from the evidence you might use in an academic context? Do different platforms for disseminating this material make a difference to the level of depth through which they explain the theory? Do you find the theory more or less compelling once you look at a range of New Media Sources about it? Why?*

3. *Look at the New Media responses to a different work of Cinema (television or film) from the one that you chose for activity one. Texts you might choose include* Star Trek, Star Wars, Buffy the Vampire Slayer, The Walking Dead, Dr. Who, Twilight, *or* American Horror Story. *Find examples of the various types of New Media texts listed in this section, and immerse yourself in the world that fans of these movies or TV shows have created. What relationship do these New Media texts bear to the sources of their inspiration? How would you characterize the online communities that are invested in discussing these shows? How is fandom different from critical analysis? What role do you believe the internet plays in fostering fan communities? Why?*

How Does English Studies Help Us to Interpret *Game of Thrones*, Its Reception, and Its Cultural Impact and Significance?

By understanding Cinema, Popular Culture, and New Media from an English Studies perspective, it becomes possible for viewers of *Game of Thrones* to interrogate the relationship between these types of texts in creating an interactive environment for audience members. Using the tools of Cinema, Popular Culture, and New Media analysis, we gain insight into formal narrative techniques, visual narrative features, and the impact of technological innovation on storytelling as well as into the vast array of texts that audiences engage as they enter into the television series' discourse. Instead of isolating the book and television series as stand-alone artistic endeavors, we can use the **methodologies** of Cinema, Popular Culture, and New Media Studies in English to look at the broader contexts for these series and to understand their wide-reaching effects in early-twenty-first-century culture.

5

Rhetoric and Composition

Our first exposure to the term **rhetoric** may have occurred after we watched a political **speech** or debate, when news commentators offered their analysis. Typically, commentators deploy the **word** with a negative **connotation**: they describe a politician's words as "empty rhetoric" or "just rhetoric"—all style and no substance—or they use the term "rhetoric" as a **euphemism** for the word "lie." Even if the word rhetoric is deployed more positively, it tends to suggest aggression: "tough" rhetoric or "strong" rhetoric—what we might call "fighting words." While we may be very familiar with these **contexts** for the term rhetoric, we may not have spent time examining rhetoric as a topic of study or thinking about how rhetoric informs the ways in which we communicate. At its most basic level, rhetoric is simply "the **art** of persuasion" regardless of the intent.

In contrast to the term rhetoric, the term **composition** may not seem to have relevance in our daily lives. Although there are "composition notebooks" in the school supplies aisle, or a professor might refer to our college writing course as a "composition course," composition is not a term in common usage, and it can sound old-fashioned or obsolete to modern ears.

This chapter focuses on finding the connections between rhetoric (approaches that speakers or writers use in **language** to reach their **audiences**) and composition (the practical techniques we use to organize our ideas and to express ourselves in written language). Additionally, it delves into the significant role that Rhetoric and Composition as a field plays not only in nineteenth- and twentieth-century attempts to define the **discipline** of English Studies but also in twenty-first-century transformations of English Studies away from a predominant focus on literature.

A careful examination of what we mean by Rhetoric and Composition helps us to understand how Rhetoric and Composition emerges as one of the most dynamic, influential fields in English Studies today. We discover how Rhetoric and Composition articulates both theoretically and practically what we often mean by critical thinking in English Studies, and we learn to distinguish between different analytical approaches to writing that emerge from the various fields in the discipline.

Key Questions

1. How does rhetoric influence the processes of written **communication** and the composition of different types of **texts** for different audiences?
2. What is Rhetoric and Composition and what role has it played in the historical evolution of English Studies? How does Rhetoric and Composition influence and transform English Studies from the middle of the twentieth century onward?
3. To what extent does Rhetoric and Composition as a field codify some of the critical thinking skills that practitioners often associate with English Studies generally?
4. What are the conventions of scholarship in Rhetoric and Composition? What kinds of research and **interpretation** do scholars of Rhetoric and Composition accomplish?
5. What is Rhetoric and Composition in the twenty-first century? How does Rhetoric and Composition connect to English Studies, more broadly conceived?

How Does Rhetoric Influence the Processes of Written Communication and the Composition of Different Types of Texts for Different Audiences?

Before we can investigate Rhetoric and Composition as a distinct field of English Studies, it is important to flesh out important concepts that centrally inform first rhetoric and then composition. We start with rhetoric because rhetoric is the intellectual foundation through which our attempts at communication are organized. Before writers can compose speeches or texts, they must first understand their identities as writers, considering the **purpose** or intention that drives them, the **content** that will best showcase their purpose or intention, and the audience at whom the speech or text is directed. These three elements—writer, content, and audience—are sometimes referred to as the **rhetorical triangle**. The three points on the rhetorical triangle also correspond to **Aristotle's rhetorical appeals: ethos** or the credibility or reputation of the writer; **logos** or the **evidence**, logic, and facts of the information contained in a piece's content; and **pathos** or the emotional impact of the text on the audience. Experienced writers understand that, by using one or more of these appeals to engage with their audience, they have a better chance of communicating effectively and persuasively. Further, a sophisticated **knowledge** of these rhetorical tools helps writers to develop an appropriate **tone** or **mood** for the content being presented and to refine their own **voice** to communicate naturally in a variety of **rhetorical situations**.

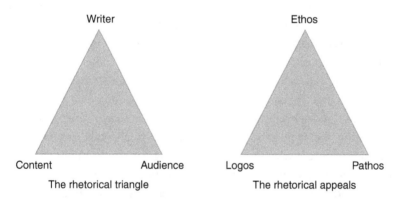

The rhetorical triangle   The rhetorical appeals

For example, students must often submit an **essay** when they apply for admission to a university or when they apply for scholarship funding. First, they must establish their credibility, using ethos: they explain their accomplishments, and they outline the **credentials** that qualify them. Second, they justify their application with facts, using logos: they connect the value of their application to **objective** measures of excellence in a broader context. For instance, they might offer their grade point average or test scores to give evidence of their abilities, or they might describe work they have accomplished in community service or paid positions. Third, they consider the best way to persuade their audience by appealing to their emotions, using pathos: they describe a personal obstacle that they have overcome, or they discuss how their experiences have shaped their passions and ambitions. These rhetorical skills also have practical applications outside of an academic context. For example, when an applicant for a job writes a cover letter to accompany their résumé, they succinctly explain their relevant job experience or educational background (ethos), refer to the requirements listed in the posting for the job (logos), and/or describe their personal reasons for applying for this position (pathos). Applying for acceptance to college, for a scholarship, or for a job are all rhetorical situations in which writers must use rhetorical appeals to reach their audiences.

Once writers understand their given rhetorical situation, which Lloyd Bitzer explains is the event, idea, or topic that compels a writer to communicate and consciously to deploy rhetoric for that communication, they can then move to the work of composition. Simply, composition includes the full range of practices involved in the **writing process** from its initial stages to a finished product. Instead of seeing writing as a static, polished piece of finished communication, experts in composition see writing as a series of coordinated actions. These actions allow us to enter into dynamic **dialogue** with one or more **interlocutors**. Most significantly, experts in composition attempt to **demystify** the writing process and to decouple that process from myths about writers and writing that often compromise effective communication.

Composition specialists fight against these and other myths by investigating the various steps that writers typically take when they sit down to compose a text. Practically speaking, composition specialists are interested in the writing process that transports writers from the blank page to a polished final draft. These include **idea generation** (**brainstorming**, **clustering**, listing, and **freewriting**, to name some common techniques), **drafting, revision, copyediting, proofreading,** and formatting for submission, which includes both **document design** in the appropriate **program** or **platform** (**word processing** or **presentation software** programs or digital platforms like **blogs, wikis,** or **websites**) and, in **academic writing,** conforming to the appropriate **citation style.** Beyond these practical steps in the writing process, composition specialists also focus on breaking down a draft into its component parts, focusing on elements like **argument** (including **thesis statements**), **organization,** evidence, **exposition, transitions, diction** (including the **denotative** and **connotative meaning** of words), and **mechanics.**

What you will notice, by looking at the items of the above lists, is that while composition specialists are interested in how we write and the

Some Myths and Facts about Writers and Writing

Myth	Fact
Good writers are born and not made. If writing does not come easily, then you are doomed to be a bad writer.	With practice, everyone can develop skills that help them to improve their writing and become effective at written communication.
There is one right way to compose a piece of writing, and if you do not do it in that precise way, then it will not be good.	Different writers use different strategies at different times depending on the rhetorical situation, and different strategies can produce equally positive writing outcomes.
Good writers wait for **inspiration** before they sit down to write.	Good writing takes practice and persistence, and good writers know that sitting down to write even when you do not feel inspired or in the mood can nonetheless produce good writing.
Everybody knows the objective standards for what good writing is, and there is no room for debate about what counts as good writing.	We make **subjective** judgments about what good writing includes, and writers make decisions in how they express themselves that others might not enjoy. Nevertheless, although we make subjective judgments about the characteristics of good writing, **discourse communities** typically have general agreement about the qualities that they look for in a piece of effective written communication.

components of written texts, they are less focused on issues of **grammar**, punctuation, or "proper" English. Instead, they emphasize the strategies that writers use to communicate their ideas to a range of audiences in varying contexts and formats. For this reason, composition specialists might show just as much interest in a tweet or a text message as they do in a published essay or full-length book; they might give as much attention to an **emoji** or **abbreviation** as they do to a complex **sentence** or paragraph. From their perspective, all writing counts as rhetorical communication, and the work of specialists in Rhetoric and Composition is to value all types of rhetorical communication and to understand the features that distinguish them. In the end, by understanding the symbiotic relationship between Rhetoric and Composition, students can become more conscious and sophisticated communicators in their writing as well as more savvy and incisive evaluators of the writing that they encounter.

What Is Rhetoric and Composition and What Role Has It Played in the Historical Evolution of English Studies? How Does Rhetoric and Composition Influence and Transform English Studies from the Middle of the Twentieth Century Onward?

Understanding the defining values of *rhetoric* and *composition* individually helps us to see connections between them. It also aids in understanding how Rhetoric and Composition not only becomes a unified field but also finds a home in the larger discipline of English Studies. Clearly, English Studies cares about how people use language to express themselves and reach different audiences (rhetoric) and about the processes for achieving effective written communication (composition). However, the integration of Rhetoric and Composition as a distinct field of English Studies was neither immediate nor obvious in the early days of the discipline. Learning about the history of Rhetoric and Composition can help to reveal the shifting values of English Studies over the past century.

Rhetoric, with its attendant links to the composing process, was historically part of a traditional **classical education**. **Classical rhetoric** emphasized the contributions of Greek and Roman philosophers, paying special attention to the Sophists and to Roman **rhetoricians** like Cicero and Quintilian. Classical rhetoric continues to influence speech and writing studies, and students in both Communication Studies and English Studies today will find references to classical rhetoric in their coursework. However, in English Studies, this was not always the case.

While the fundamentals of rhetoric and writing had long been seen as central to a classical university education, only as access to a university education expands after World War II to include more and more students— for example, women, working-class students, and students of color—does instruction in rhetoric and writing become a cornerstone of **core** or **general education requirements** at most universities. At first, these courses did not generally teach students about the writing process, writing for different audiences, or writing in a wide array of **genres** and formats. Instead, they tended to teach about literary analysis and successful academic essay writing, addressing perceived weak skills in university students as access to higher education expands to formerly underserved populations.

It is also the case that English departments, with the popularization of **New Criticism** in the early part of the twentieth century, became most focused on **close reading** as a technique for literary analysis. For this reason, English departments did not see general writing instruction as a primary goal or responsibility of their curricula. In the middle part of the twentieth century, despite resistance from some faculty trained in the study of literature, that prejudice against general writing instruction began to change.

In the era after World War II, the National Council of Teachers of English (NCTE) perceived a need to assess the role of writing instruction in English courses and to arrive at best practices for writing instruction. For this reason, they inaugurated the Conference on College Composition and Communication (CCCC) in 1949, and this organization, with its attendant publications and conferences, codified the values and standards that we now associate with Rhetoric and Composition as a field of English Studies. Most importantly, CCCC, or "Four Cs" as it is called by English Studies practitioners, attended to administration and compensation issues for those who taught writing at colleges and universities, typically graduate students, part-time **adjunct** faculty, or full-time adjunct faculty without the protections of tenure. It continues to be the case that most required writing courses at universities are taught by **contingent faculty**.

CCCC also established guidelines for appropriate class sizes for writing instruction as well as pedagogical goals for first-year writing courses and university writing more generally. Finally, they looked to English to serve as a departmental home for writing instruction in the postwar American university, and faculty primarily interested in the study of literature agreed, at least in part as a maneuver to assure the political power of English departments on campus in times of uncertain resources, external mandates, and shifts in higher education demographics.

In plain language, when departments of English, which focused primarily on the study of literature, agreed to house university writing programs, they carved out territory for themselves that would:

1. secure smaller class sizes, typically capped at fewer than thirty students, for courses emphasizing writing instruction;

2. allow them to advocate for stronger compensation packages for graduate students and adjuncts as well as to make the case for more tenure-track positions in the English department; and

3. establish English as a department through which every university student would pass during their progress toward an undergraduate degree.

In other words, admitting Rhetoric and Composition into English Studies gave practitioners in the discipline more power on university campuses, but it did not necessarily reflect a commitment to the field itself.

From the 1960s onward, Rhetoric and Composition becomes increasingly critical to defining English Studies for four reasons:

1. its emphasis on writing as a pathway toward self-actualization, self-expression, and self-knowledge;

2. its emphasis on the pedagogical benefits of writing to cognitive processes and learning, not only in the writing classroom but also in courses across the curriculum;

3. its emphasis on practical communication skills that benefit students in a variety of workplace and community settings in their lives after university; and

4. its emphasis on writing as a vehicle for exploring social issues connected to indexes of identity such as **class, race, disability, gender,** and **sexuality** and diverse perspectives that emerge out of those **identity** categories.

These four emphases of Rhetoric and Composition exert profound influence on other fields in the discipline, including long-established fields like literature and linguistics and more emergent fields like creative writing, professional writing and technical communication, and digital humanities in English.

If in their courses students have been asked to keep journals, submit writing assignments in a portfolio format, or visit the campus writing center for peer-to-peer advice about how to improve their writing, they have experienced firsthand the pervasive influence of Rhetoric and Composition on university instruction. These practices reflect the values of social justice movements of the 1960s and 1970s with their emphasis on personal freedom, equality, and the importance of giving individuals a voice to speak their personal truths. Instead of perceiving education through what Paulo Freire calls a **banking concept**, in which instructors possess all power and knowledge and deposit information in students to be stored and then returned to the instructor without question or modification, Rhetoric and Composition emphasizes what Freire calls a **problem-posing method**. The problem-posing method gives students ownership over their learning by encouraging them to identify problems, determine **research questions**, and work independently or collaboratively to discover solutions to the problems that engage them. This pedagogical shift envisions educators as facilitators rather than as authorities with the last word, and it envisions students as independent thinkers who are empowered to challenge authority and to control their own learning. Seeing education this way radically changes the work that we expect education to do, and it changes the English Studies classroom from a place where students passively take notes while a "sage on the stage" pontificates about great works of literature to a collaborative space where student-centered, discussion-based pedagogical approaches are preferred.

To What Extent Does Rhetoric and Composition as a Field Codify Some of the Critical Thinking and Written Communication Skills That Practitioners Often Associate with English Studies Generally?

With this changing cultural landscape, higher education places greater emphasis on honing students' abilities to think critically and communicate effectively. Because rhetoric is closely bound to critical thinking practices, and because composition is closely bound to the practices of written communication, English Studies becomes foundational to the general education of all university students. While all fields in English Studies emphasize critical thinking and written communication skills, Rhetoric and Composition foregrounds those skills in ways that enable practitioners to define them clearly and succinctly as well as to think about the practical value of those skills beyond the classroom. Rhetoric and Composition reveals English Studies as a discipline invested in understanding **literacy** from a variety of perspectives.

Critical Thinking

When we encounter a topic, text, **dataset**, or other object of study, it is natural to react to it. Our reactions might include confusion, identification, frustration, curiosity, or, at a very basic level, liking or disliking what we have encountered. Those reactions alone, however, do not constitute critical thinking. First of all, reactions typically come from "the gut": they are immediate emotional responses that do not reflect deliberative thought. Second, reactions may not reflect an organized cognitive process with clear steps. It is possible to like something without knowing why one likes it. It is possible to feel confusion without ever taking steps to resolve that confusion.

Critical thinking involves those cognitive processes that we use after we have had our initial reactions. At a basic level, it includes deep reflection, which allows us to consider questions of purpose, **methodology**, **value**, context, and **impact**. It may then lead us to engage in further research or theoretical inquiry, through which we can learn additional information or approach our topic from different perspectives. Next, critical thinking demands both direct and comparative analysis: **direct analysis** involves our focused attention to the original object of study; **comparative analysis** involves looking at the original object of study alongside other related objects to trace similarities and differences. Finally, critical thinking leads us to carefully considered conclusions, solutions, and/or further directions for contemplation, creativity, and/or research.

An example can help clarify what we mean by critical thinking. Imagine that a friend recently saw the movie *Black Panther* (Ryan Coogler; 2018), which features one of the few black comic book heroes. In describing the movie, they say, "It was awesome! I loved it!" but this does not explain why they loved it, why others should care about the movie, or what makes the movie interesting. As the friend continues, however, they might offer more analysis, which depends on critical thinking. For example, they might discuss the movie's groundbreaking use of an almost entirely black cast and crew and connect that decision to a broader conversation about racial politics in the United States. Alternatively, they might offer direct analysis of the film's depiction of black bodies in the fight scenes and action sequences or comparative analysis of the similarities and differences between *Black Panther* and other comic book movies, such as *Batman* (Tim Burton; 1989), *Wonder Woman* (Patty Jenkins; 2017), or *Thor* (Kenneth Branagh; 2011). Finally, they might interrogate the cultural impact of the film and investigate the connections between its themes and current events. All of this thinking that extends beyond, "It was awesome! I loved it!" constitutes critical thinking. By engaging in critical thinking, our initial views change, become more complex, or take deeper hold.

Many, if not all, academic disciplines value critical thinking, and English Studies promotes critical thinking across its diverse fields. Rhetoric and Composition does not own critical thinking. It does, however, compel practitioners, with its focus on both the relationship between writer, content, and audience and its use of rhetorical appeals in written communication, to approach critical thinking systematically as the prerequisite not only of **rhetorical analysis** but also of the production of written texts. Rhetoric and Composition avoids emotional and **aesthetic** interpretive responses common in the study of literature, cinema, popular culture, new media, and creative writing, and it also is less inclined toward scientific and data-driven approaches common in linguistics, professional and technical communication, and digital humanities. Thus, Rhetoric and Composition is well positioned to help students in English Studies to understand in a concrete way what critical thinking includes so that they might then apply that knowledge to their work in other fields of English Studies, in courses beyond the discipline, in the workplace, or in the community.

Written Communication

Rhetoric and Composition also codifies what English Studies practitioners value in written communication by demystifying the writing process and breaking it down into the systematic steps that writers take to produce texts for different audiences. The term "written communication" emphasizes the **dialogic** relationship between **authors** and their audiences, and it also emphasizes the connection that becomes possible between authors and audiences through writing. Written communication values not just the expression of authors but also the impact that authors' words have on diverse audiences. Indeed, through texts, authors have productive relationships with audiences, and the rhetorical triangle of author, text, and audience allows us to see that texts do not exist in a vacuum but circulate through social, environmental, cultural, and economic networks.

While other fields in English Studies may implicitly understand written communication in this way, Rhetoric and Composition makes this view of written communication explicit, and it allows practitioners of English Studies to talk concretely about the work that they do when they produce texts as writers or interpret them as readers. These skills as producers and interpreters of texts connect directly to desirable attributes that employers look for, and a foundation in Rhetoric and Composition can help those with backgrounds in English Studies to communicate with employers about their abilities in this area.

What Are the Conventions of Scholarship in Rhetoric and Composition? What Kinds of Research and Interpretation Do Scholars of Rhetoric and Composition Accomplish?

Scholars in Rhetoric and Composition use a range of methods and approaches to make discoveries about relationships between authors, the content that authors communicate, and the audiences that authors attempt to reach. While some practitioners rely on theoretically based analyses of how rhetoric works in texts, others conduct **applied research** connected to the writing process, best practices for writing instruction and assessment, and business and/or community impacts of writing projects. Scholars interested in theoretical approaches in Rhetoric and Composition may focus more on the rhetorical analysis of written texts, theorizing about the writing process, or understanding those situations that give rise to the use of rhetoric. In contrast, scholars interested in applied approaches may focus more on amassing **data** (samples of written communication) and evaluating that data in order to trace patterns in the use of rhetoric or better understand the steps in the writing process. Additionally, some scholars may combine these theoretical and applied approaches. Given the range of approaches to scholarship in Rhetoric and Composition, it makes sense to identify five major areas of Rhetoric and Composition research and to discuss how researchers within these fields approach their topics.

Theoretical Research in Rhetoric

Scholars of rhetoric, much like their peers in literary studies and other fields in English Studies, use critical theory to evaluate the rhetorical impact of texts. By applying theory to texts as diverse as articles, essays, promotional materials, images, physical spaces, and many more, these researchers examine how texts work and make interpretations that connect to authors' purposes and the impacts that different rhetorical situations and choices make on audiences. Particularly indebted to thinkers such as Kenneth Burke, who believed that written communication can be understood as **symbolic action**, or expression that conveys beliefs and desires so strong that they count as a kind of action in themselves, theoretical rhetoricians pay particular attention to the **dialectical** relationship between authors and audiences. For example, a theoretically oriented scholar might evaluate the rhetoric of **Pride** celebrations that promote **LGBTQ** rights. Using a **Marxist** approach, they might examine the corporate sponsorship of these events as an attempt to attract affluent LGBTQ people to certain kinds of products and services. Alternatively, they might use **discourse theory** to interrogate the slogan "y'all means all," evaluating how regional **dialect** has been deployed for a message of **inclusion**. They also might take a **psychoanalytic** approach to look at the **visual rhetoric** of the rainbow flag to consider the messages that it sends to people outside of the LGBTQ community.

Digital Rhetoric

Scholars of **digital rhetoric** focus their attention on the ways in which **digital media** are used to inform, persuade, and motivate action. They attend to writing in digital platforms, including Twitter, YouTube, Instagram, wikis, blogs, and more, in order to:

1. understand the uses of these platforms;
2. explore the processes of creation, composition, and distribution that take place through them; and
3. examine the differing impacts on audiences when they encounter digital texts versus encountering other sorts of texts.

These researchers seek to invigorate research in rhetoric by considering how rhetoric changes through technological advancement. Perhaps most significantly, attention to digital rhetoric allows scholars to make bold connections between rhetorical analysis and scholarship in cinema, popular culture, and new media.

Scholarship in digital rhetoric—such as Douglas Eyman's *Digital Rhetoric: Theory, Method, Practice* (2015), which seeks to establish an analytical methodology informed by and appropriate to digital texts—demonstrates the ways in which English Studies approaches to communication can assist in understanding the ways in which technology influences and transforms our communication practices in the twenty-first century. For Eyman, **digital technologies** initiate new approaches not just to written communication but also to thinking, analyzing, and interpreting. Therefore, digital rhetorics provide a methodological framework not for creating or teaching students to create texts across multiple platforms (for that, see **multimodal** composition below) but for reading, researching, and understanding digital texts and theorizing their relationship to classical rhetorical forms.

Medical Humanities and the Rhetorics of Science, Technology, Engineering, and Math (STEM)

Rhetoric and Composition scholars may also emphasize issues that pertain to written and oral communication in fields that may at first appear to diverge from the typical interests of English Studies in order to investigate how different communication styles effect patient experiences, the research questions and interpretive lenses that shape scientific data, cultural differences in written communication, and much more. For example, the scholarly, peer-reviewed journal *Rhetoric of Health and Medicine* integrates scholarship from humanities and social scientific perspectives with a goal of focusing attention on how communication impacts health outcomes, medical intervention, wellness, illness, and healing. Often, this type of research focuses on cultural difference. Using applied methodologies, such as interviews and collection of writing samples, as well as theoretical methodologies, researchers in this emerging area of Rhetoric and Composition attempt to demonstrate the impact of rhetoric on scientific knowledge and the ways in which we communicate in scientific, medical, and technical fields.

The Rhetoric of Social Justice

Rhetoric and Composition scholars have also done substantial work to understand not only the impact of rhetoric on social and cultural inequality but also to situate Rhetoric and Composition as tools in movements for social justice connected to groups marginalized on the basis of class, gender, race, sexuality, and disability. In this regard, scholars invested in the rhetoric of social justice deploy methodologies similar to their colleagues who focus on STEM rhetorics, conducting studies that are applied or theoretical, depending on their specific research questions. Perhaps one of the most famous theoretical foundations for this work is Freire's *Pedagogy of the Oppressed* (1968), which argues for a problem-posing method of education rooted in dialogic exchange in order to give students ownership over what they learn and to promote liberation through self-expression. Scholars who address topics connected to social justice see Rhetoric and Composition as a field of English Studies with activist potential to assist in a broader project of advancing values of inclusion and equality.

Multimodal Composition

Just as scholars of digital rhetoric are interested in analyzing texts that are produced in a range of formats, scholars of multimodal composition are interested in studying those processes of composing texts in different "modes" including but not limited to written language—such as audio, video, photographs, or drawings, to give just some examples. Most notably, scholars like Cheryl E. Ball have worked to establish how composition across media and platforms can assist student learning. These scholars also assert the value of **webtexts**, collaborative digital learning spaces such as wikis or blogs, and other digital environments for expression. Scholars of multimodal composition believe that the work of Rhetoric and Composition centers not just on verbal or linguistic literacy but also on literacy across a range of communication "modes," which may include digital modes but need not do so. Any text that engages multiple modes of communication—even a medieval manuscript with illuminations—can be considered multimodal. Additionally, multimodal composition does not necessarily mean **multimedia** composition, since it is possible to compose across modes of communication without including different media forms. Most significantly, scholarship on multimodal composition has influenced the way that written communication is taught in both K-12 and university settings, making a case for broadening the scope of the writing classroom to include compositions that go beyond the traditional academic essay.

In this regard, Rhetoric and Composition specialists who do research on multimodal composition influence scholarship in the field of English education.

First-Year Writing, Writing Instruction, and Writing Program Administration

Finally, like scholars of multimodal composition, scholars whose research emphasizes questions connected to students' writing experiences in their first year of university, best practices in writing instruction and assessment, and writing program administration have strong connections to the field of English education. Unlike scholars of multimodal composition, however, these scholars are not as invested in research questions about the writing process. Instead, scholars of first-year writing, writing instruction, and writing program administration focus their scholarship on the institutionalization of composition instruction in community colleges and universities, and their work emphasizes inquiry into the institutional structures that shape **pedagogy** and student learning in writing classrooms. While most undergraduates are unlikely to conduct their own research in this area, those interested in pursuing graduate study in Rhetoric and Composition should be aware that many academic jobs in this field of specialization expect expertise in first-year writing, writing instruction, and writing program administration regardless of other research interests.

Experts in this type of research are particularly invested in understanding how we teach students about Rhetoric and Composition and how that education prepares them to succeed in a range of rhetorical situations both inside and outside of academic settings. Further, these scholars take care to think about how we assess our classroom practices and how we judge our effectiveness in helping students to become better writers and thinkers. Since at least the late 1980s, as Richard H. Bullock argues in his foundational article, "When Administration Becomes Scholarship: The Future of Writing Program Administration" (1987), the issues that preoccupy writing program administrators—including curriculum development, course scheduling and staffing, and program assessment—should be regarded as a primary area of scholarly inquiry in Rhetoric and Composition.

What Is Rhetoric and Composition in the Twenty-First Century? How Does Rhetoric and Composition Connect to English Studies, More Broadly Conceived?

Rhetoric and Composition holds an important place in both the past of English Studies and its future. Because the field emphasizes literacy—reading (interpretation of how texts work) and writing (the composition of texts)—it shares common ground with all of the discipline's other fields, and it helps practitioners across those fields to explain the work of English Studies to nonspecialists. Additionally, it has become increasingly common for university students only to encounter English Studies through required first-year writing courses that emphasize rhetorical analysis and the writing process unless they choose to major or minor in English. This makes Rhetoric and Composition a critical pathway into English Studies for the next generation of scholars, and it increases the influence that this field has on how students experience their English Studies education. Consequently, engaging with Rhetoric and Composition is essential to a well-rounded, twenty-first-century engagement with the broader discipline of English Studies.

Further Reading

Adler-Kassner, Linda, and Elizabeth Wardle, eds. *Naming What We Know: Threshold Concepts in Writing Studies, Classroom Edition.* Boulder: University Press of Colorado, 2016.
Collects essays from leading scholars in Rhetoric and Composition about fundamental concepts of the field, important debates, and emerging areas of scholarly inquiry.

Biesecker, Barbara A. "Rethinking the Rhetorical Situation from within the Thematic of *Différance*." *Philosophy and Rhetoric*, vol. 22, no. 2, 1989, pp. 110–30.
Reevaluates Lloyd Bitzer's theory of the rhetorical situation from a feminist theoretical approach.

Bitzer, Lloyd F. "The Rhetorical Situation." *Philosophy and Rhetoric*, vol. 1, no. 1, 1968, pp. 1–14.
Theorizes the characteristics that give rise to the use of rhetoric.

Booth, Wayne C. *The Rhetoric of Rhetoric: The Quest for Effective Communication*. Williston: Blackwell, 2004.
Argues that the quality of our everyday lives is improved by studying rhetoric and understanding its influence.

Brereton, John C., ed. *The Origins of Composition Studies in the American College, 1875–1925: A Documentary History*. Pittsburgh: University of Pittsburgh Press, 1995.
Collects historical commentary about the role of Rhetoric and Composition in college and university classrooms.

Douglas, Eyman. *Digital Rhetoric: Theory, Method, Practice*. Ann Arbor: University of Michigan Press, 2015.
Defines digital rhetoric, explaining the historical context for its emergence and discussing the unique manifestations of rhetoric in digital environments.

Elbow, Peter. *Writing without Teachers*. Oxford: Oxford University Press, 1973.
Advocates for process-oriented writing that eliminates restrictive rules for composition and instead emphasizes free writing, multiple drafts, journaling, and reflection.

Rice, Jeff. *The Rhetoric of Cool: Composition Studies and New Media*. Carbondale: Southern Illinois University Press, 2007.
Explores the connections between the development of new technologies and media practices as they parallel the evolution and emergence of composition studies as a distinct field of English Studies.

Tinnell, John. *Actionable Media: Digital Communication beyond the Desktop*. Oxford: Oxford University Press, 2017.
Explores rhetoric in the context of digital culture.

Vitanza, Victor J. *Negation, Subjectivity, and the History of Rhetoric*. Albany: State University of New York Press, 1996.
Revisits classical rhetoric and explores how it is regarded and used in different historical contexts.

*In this Case Study, we examine how a common rallying point on **social media** platforms like Twitter, the hashtag, operates rhetorically, particularly in a social justice context, and how the hashtag participates in a long history of rhetorical slogans and rallying cries. The hashtag can thus help us understand some of the central concerns of Rhetoric and Composition today. We then offer engagement activities that you can use to help you better understand why hashtags matter and what the rhetorical impact of hashtags can be.*

Hashtag Activism: Social Movements in the Internet Age

What Is the Rhetoric of a Hashtag? Do Hashtags Count as Writing?

When the *Oxford English Dictionary* added the word "hashtag" in 2014, media outlets buzzed. Historically, the **dictionary** has taken its time adding new words, and people were somewhat surprised to see a term that had existed for just seven years had earned a spot in the most comprehensive dictionary in the English language. Nevertheless, no one could doubt the ubiquity of the term or the swiftness with which hashtags had become one of the most succinct ways to define an audience, make an argument, organize information, and communicate in writing. Indeed, the hashtag today is an essential part of our rhetorical landscape.

Activities for Creative and Critical Engagement

1. *Create a hashtag of your own and explain your thought process as you put it together. Things to consider include the following: do you use capital letters to preserve differences between words? Would other people immediately recognize the meaning of your hashtag, or does it require explanation? How would you like people to respond to your hashtag? What about the hashtag might inspire that response? As you complete this exercise, it may be useful to think about how other popular hashtags work: for example, #yolo, #blessed, or #lifegoals.*

2. *Identify a hashtag that is currently trending on social media (Twitter, Instagram, or Facebook). Evaluate that hashtag. What does it mean? Is it an effective rhetorical gesture? Why or why not? Do you think this hashtag will be important in the future? Why or why not? Who is the audience for this hashtag? What is the rhetorical situation that gives rise to this hashtag? How does this hashtag connect with other types of communication to create a broader discourse about a topic?*

Slogans, Pamphlets, Polemics, and Zines: Composing Activism before the Hashtag

At first, hashtags might seem like a thoroughly contemporary, twenty-first-century mode of communication that has little in common with the kinds of communication that people used in the past. Social media and its forms can seem quite distinct from longer-form, analog modes of communication. However, before there were hashtags like #blacklivesmatter or #metoo, activists still depended on attention-grabbing rhetorical strategies. Instead of hashtags, activists used slogans, which they would chant at protests, post on signs, invoke in underground publications like pamphlets and **zines**, and then finally disseminate through traditional media outlets. Like people who use hashtags today, activists would attempt to distill their message down to something short and memorable in order to connect with audiences that shared their views, work for social change, and fight against those who agreed with the status quo. For example, the women's liberation movement popularized the phrases "The personal is political" and "My body, my choice." Civil Rights activists propagated "Freedom now!" and "I'm black, and I'm proud." The pro-life movement promoted "A child, not a choice." By looking back at activism throughout the twentieth century and earlier, we can understand that hashtags participate in a rhetorical tradition that connects to the rhetorics of earlier social justice movements.

Activity for Critical Engagement

3. *Identify an activist movement of the past that interests you. Once you have identified a movement, identify key slogans that have been associated with it in history. Do some research in one or more library databases (Academic Search Complete, Project MUSE, or JSTOR might be good starting points) in order to find out about that social movement and to discover how the movement's agenda connected to the slogans that it deployed. Were this group's slogans effective? Why or why not? Who was the group trying to reach with its slogans? How did audiences react to the words and phrases that the group used to communicate its agenda?*

Going Viral: Discourse Communities after the Internet

With the advent of digital **computing technology**, affordable personal devices that can connect to the internet, and digital platforms designed to share information quickly and efficiently, people have access to more information faster than ever before. Historically, people might have only been exposed to the communications of groups of which they themselves were members or with whose beliefs they themselves were sympathetic. Today, in contrast, the internet offers access to many discourse communities beyond our real-world environment and our local frame of reference. The biggest change that this makes is the speed with which activists can organize and get information out to the public.

When we talk about something "going **viral**," we are talking about the efficient, high-speed dissemination of information. Most of the time, those things that go viral do not have larger significance to our political worlds, our rights, or our identities. Instead, they are silly things that entertain us: videos of cats playing piano or a wedding proposal flash mob, for example. However, when a hashtag or **meme** connected to activism goes viral, it has the power to raise millions of dollars (#icebucketchallenge or #noshavenovember), to rally people to protest (#blacklivesmatter or #womensmarch), or to start a revolution (hashtags associated with the Arab Spring uprisings in 2010 and 2011 in Tunisia, Libya, Yemen, Syria, Bahrain, and Egypt as well as vigorous protests in other countries throughout the Middle East and North Africa). Whereas historically discourse communities would be made up of people in close proximity to each other, who either had direct knowledge of each other or were acquainted by association with another person whom they had in common, the internet expands our discourse communities and allows us to connect with many more people much more quickly, which profoundly influences the ways in which people can organize around causes that they care about.

Activity for Critical Engagement

4. *Choose a hashtag that connects to an activist movement today. Go to Twitter, and do a search for that hashtag. You may even need to use Twitter's Advanced Search tool (https://twitter.com/search-advanced?lang=en). Once you have come up with your results, spend some time reading through the tweets that use this hashtag. What kind of people use this hashtag and why? What do you learn from reading the various tweets that invoke this hashtag? What are the social change or social justice objectives of the people who deploy this hashtag on social media?*

How Does English Studies Help Us to Think about the Power of Hashtags?

Like any other piece of written communication, hashtags allow their users to engage rhetorically with an audience. Hashtags help to organize information and to give people access to it. They also communicate information, try to elicit emotional responses, and speak to the credibility of those who use them. As practitioners of English Studies with knowledge of rhetoric, we can delve into the deeper power of hashtags in today's culture.

6

Creative Writing

Telling **stories**; representing situations visually and with **dialogue** for the page, stage, or **screen**; writing **poems**; or putting one's own personal experience into **words** are familiar activities to most people, regardless of whether they choose to immerse themselves in English Studies as a **discipline**. No special **credential** is required to do these things, and many people with a variety of educational backgrounds write creatively to process their feelings, to express ideas that are important to them, to relax, to entertain others, or to satisfy a desire to make **art**. Sometimes people seek to get their writing published or to publish it themselves, and sometimes they are content to regard their writing as a private hobby. Sometimes people appear to possess a natural aptitude for the rhythms of **language**, how to pace a story, or how to make an **audience** see or feel something with the words that they use. Sometimes people's creative efforts in writing appear to be a labor of love, something that they work very hard at and enjoy but that is not, in the end, very good. Significantly, people have used language as a creative outlet long before a field called Creative Writing existed in English departments at universities, and people outside of English Studies still write creatively.

Nevertheless, students of English Studies today usually understand Creative Writing as a term that practitioners use to designate a specialized field in our discipline. They may have taken courses in Creative Writing, or they may look forward to learning about Creative Writing in advanced coursework. What skills does coursework in Creative Writing teach? What values does the field of Creative Writing espouse? How do those values connect to and distinguish it from the broader concerns of the larger discipline? The aim of this chapter is to unpack what we mean by Creative Writing, both as an **aesthetic** practice and as an academic enterprise, to explain this field's dramatic growth over the past fifty years.

Key Questions

1. What is Creative Writing? What distinguishes Creative Writing from other fields in the discipline?
2. What is the relationship between reading creative **texts** and the creation of one's own original works?
3. What are the **genres** of Creative Writing, and what media do creative writers use to disseminate their creations to the public?
4. What methods and approaches are promoted in Creative Writing as a field of English Studies in an academic **context**? How do research, analysis, workshopping, and reflection shape Creative Writing **praxis**?
5. What is Creative Writing in the twenty-first century? How does Creative Writing connect to English Studies, more broadly conceived?

What Is Creative Writing? What Distinguishes Creative Writing from Other Fields in the Discipline?

Creative Writing is the field of English Studies that seeks to train students to write in **creative genres**, primarily including the **short story**, the **novel**, poetry, or **creative nonfiction**. Creative Writing instructs students about how to approach the **creative process**, provides students with feedback on their own creative efforts, and mentors students in important skills like **networking**, sharing their work with public audiences, and navigating the publication process. It may seem obvious today that a field with these interests would find a home in English Studies: Creative Writing anatomizes and promotes the essential skills and work habits required for imaginative writing and for bringing imaginative writing to publication. In so doing, Creative Writing emphasizes the creation and dissemination of those works that other fields of English Studies spend their time analyzing. However, Creative Writing did not always do this work.

When English departments entered the modern university in the nineteenth century, they could primarily be understood as devoted to the study and **criticism** of literary works and, to a lesser degree, dedicated to written **communication**. Creative Writing became part of the English Studies classroom in the twentieth century not as an independent field of study but rather as a method through which to promote deeper analysis of literature. By requiring students to practice writing in the literary forms that they encountered, instructors believed that they could promote student understanding of the formal structures of literature, help students to connect with the **content** of literature that might feel culturally or historically distant from them, and foster student appreciation of canonical authors and texts. Even today's students might have been introduced to Creative Writing in this way. For example, when studying Shakespeare's sonnets, they might have been asked to write sonnets of their own, or when reading Henry David Thoreau's *Walden* (1854), they might have been asked to write their own personal **narrative** about a place that is meaningful to them. Taken from this perspective, Creative Writing existed as a supplementary support to the study of Literature, and it was not afforded a central place in the curriculum of "traditional" English departments.

Today, however, Creative Writing has emerged as a central, independent field in English Studies. Creative Writing no longer subordinates itself to the study of Literature. Instead, it establishes concerns and values connected to imagination, creativity, and the making of art as in their own right possessing great significance to English Studies. For this reason, the focus of Creative Writing is not **evidence**, analysis, or criticism, as it typically is in many other fields of the discipline, including history of the English language, linguistics, literature, cinema, or rhetoric and composition. This focus on the imaginative work of English Studies has enhanced the popularity of Creative Writing. The number of students who want to study Creative Writing has increased exponentially over the past fifty or so years. In fact, the number of colleges and universities with active memberships in the Association of Writers and Writing Programs (AWP), the primary academic organization for creative writers in the United States, grew from just twelve in 1967 to over five hundred in 2018.

As Creative Writing evolved throughout the second half of the twentieth century, it came to focus on three main areas that are foundational to the creation, **revision**, and dissemination of creative written works:

1. An emphasis on technical skills, known as **craft**, that go into creating written works of poetry, fiction, or nonfiction as well as theatrical, cinematic, or digital **scripts**.

2. Participation in a feedback process known as **the workshop method**, popularized by the famous Iowa Writer's Workshop, intended to engender careful revision and formal polishing of manuscripts prior to releasing them to a wider audience.
3. A focus on direct mentorship of students not only in how to approach the creative and writing processes but also in how to find an audience for one's writing.

With these three areas of importance, Creative Writing can sometimes seem to have more in common with other **studio arts** fields like music, theater, and visual arts, where students receive practical training from mentors who themselves are artists and creative practitioners, or with applied fields like editing and production for **television**, **movies**, or **digital media**. Unlike many other fields in English Studies, which typically use texts composed by others as the focus of their analysis and which typically approach those texts using traditional scholarly methods involving academic research, **data** collection, and dissemination of findings in **peer-reviewed journals** or books, Creative Writing emphasizes the writing of one's own original texts. Creative writers draw on creative **inspiration**, influence, and background information to produce works that enrich, entertain, and emotionally resonate with their audiences.

What Is the Relationship between Reading Creative Texts and the Creation of One's Own Original Works?

The different fields of English Studies practice different approaches to reading creative works, and they emphasize reading for different reasons. In history of the English language or linguistics, we read creative works to determine patterns of language that help us better understand the structures of written English in a particular moment, how words are formed, or how the meanings of words change over time. When we study literature, our reading focuses on critical **interpretation**, which seeks to discover the aesthetic qualities that justify a text's place in the canon, to reveal the political or **ideological** premises that govern a text's creation or reception, or, on a very basic level, to understand the deeper significance of what the text is trying to communicate. When we approach creative works from the perspective of rhetoric and composition, we read to understand the relationship between the writer, the text, and the audience and to make sense of the methods of persuasion that are used to engage the audience. In Creative Writing, practitioners read to learn and understand those techniques that produce effective or excellent imaginative works so that they can use them as a model in their own creations. This is what we mean by craft.

In general, each of us experiences written texts when we read them as, on some level, models for our own writing. Reading helps us to expand our vocabulary; recognize more complex structures for **sentences**, paragraphs, and longer pieces; and learn how to organize ideas. Most of reading's positive influence on our writing happens subconsciously, however, and we do not necessarily approach texts that we read with an intentional purpose of learning how to become better writers or storytellers. As a field in English Studies, Creative Writing seeks to take these subconscious ways in which we use those creative works that we read and to make those processes conscious. By creating methods by which writers can both analyze craft techniques in others' writing and practice craft techniques in their own writing after having completed that analysis, Creative Writing makes visible the link between reading creative works and creating one's own.

What Are the Genres of Creative Writing, and How Do Creative Writers Bring Those Genres to Audiences?

Genre can sometimes be confusing for students of English Studies because different fields in the discipline use the term in different ways. In general, genre means the "kind" or "type" of writing under consideration. For literature-focused practitioners of English Studies, genre is the kind or type of literature that one chooses to study or read, but for Creative-Writing-focused practitioners of English Studies, genre is the kind or type of writing that one hopes to do. Thus, while there is some overlap between how the fields use the term genre, there are also some differences because one field focuses on interpretation (literature) and the other field focuses on practice (Creative Writing).

Undergraduate Creative Writing programs, whether they stand alone as distinct majors or operate as "tracks" of more broad-based English majors, typically offer students exposure to three primary genres: poetry, fiction (which includes the short story and the novel), and creative nonfiction. While students may prefer one genre to the others, undergraduate Creative Writing programs tend to emphasize a comprehensive approach to teaching students to read and write across the creative genres. Graduate Creative Writing programs, like their undergraduate counterparts, also focus on these three primary genres, but usually these programs, which include the more common terminal Master of Fine Arts (MFA) degree and now a growing number of Doctor of Philosophy (PhD) programs in Creative Writing, expect students to specialize in one genre over the others. Thus, if you have interest in pursuing the academic study of Creative Writing, it is important to understand how the field defines these genres.

Poetry

Poetry includes **verse** compositions that emphasize image, **sound**, and rhythm as primary factors in creative representation. Poetry may or may not be narrative in nature, and it can include consistent **rhyme** and **meter**, or it can be composed as **free verse**, which eschews formal consistency in rhyme and meter. What unites texts across the genre of poetry is their commitment to engaging poetic **figures of speech** as tools for the concrete representation of emotions or experiences.

In the context of the academic field Creative Writing, poets are encouraged to attend carefully to the ways in which they craft each line of each poem that they write, putting poems through multiple rounds of revision based on feedback from peers and mentors. Some **poetic forms**, including but not limited to **avant-garde** free verse, **lyric poetry, language poetry, prose poetry,** or strict **metrical** verse compositions like the **sonnet, villanelle,** or **pantoum,** lend themselves to this approach. A poet with whom you might be familiar who emerges out of this form of training is African American poet Rita Dove, who won the Pulitzer Prize in 1987 for her book *Thomas and Beulah* (1986) and who served as the United States Poet Laureate from 1993 to 1995. Dove's poetry is recognized for the precision with which it articulates complex emotions, the artfulness of her poetic **diction,** and the sweeping scope of the topics and narratives that she uses poetry to explore.

By contrast, other poetic forms are marginalized by this methodological emphasis, for example, **spoken word**. Spoken word is a poetic form that is rooted in public performance, may be accompanied by music, and traces to an oral tradition. Like rap music, it makes heavy use of rhyme, repetition, and improvisation to engage its audience, and it does not emphasize revision in the same way that more academically revered poetic forms do. In fact, poetry that emerges out of an academic context may not utilize these techniques common to spoken word at all. Further, while poets may perform spoken word texts as part of their political commitment to social justice issues or as an activity that connects to their cultural heritage, it is less likely that poets will submit these works for scrutiny in a workshop or publication environment. For this reason, perhaps the best way to experience spoken word is either in person at events like **poetry slams** or by seeking recorded performances of such events online. Notable spoken word poets include Kevin Coval, a Jewish-American poet and activist from Chicago, and Shaggy Flores, a **Nuyorican** poet, writer, and scholar of the African diaspora.

Nevertheless, one of the primary outlets through which poets disseminate their work is public performance, even if they are not doing spoken word. **Open mic nights**, where poets read their creations to a public audience, typically include a host who keeps the event running smoothly and poets who volunteer to read either one work or multiple works within an agreed-upon time frame. These events might be sponsored by literary magazines or the venues, such as coffee houses or bars, in which they take place, and usually the audience is made up of other writers who will also read their work and friends of the writers in attendance. By contrast, **invited readings** solicit one or more notable poets to perform a longer reading, often ranging from thirty to forty minutes. Invited readings recognize established poets who have already developed a professional network through publication, and these appearances are often organized in connection with the promotion of a new publication and include opportunities to have the poet autograph copies of their books.

Publication is the most prestigious means through which poets writing today share their work with audiences, although it is also the case that fewer people today read contemporary poetry and buy books of poetry than have done so historically. The possible outlets for publishing poetry include the following:

1. Online and print **anthologies**, literary journals, or **literary magazines**, some of which focus on Creative Writing across genres and some of which focus on poetry alone.

2. **Chapbooks**, which are small collections of poetry typically by a single author, published in pamphlet format and focused on a particular theme.
3. Books, which are larger collections of poetry typically by a single author, and which have higher production values than chapbooks.

Poets typically begin by submitting individual poems for consideration to anthologies, journals, and magazines, and once they have established their reputation, they may publish chapbooks or books. Poets typically receive no or little payment for the publication of individual poems, nor do most poets earn much, if any, money from the publication of chapbooks or books. For this reason, most active poets today have "day jobs," which often include teaching Creative Writing at a university.

Fiction

Fiction can be defined as **prose narratives** that originate in the imagination. Unlike poetry (a performance-oriented genre that typically privileges sound, rhythm, and **imagery**), fiction (a genre geared toward silent reading by individuals) emphasizes elements of **storytelling** such as **plot**, **description**, **exposition**, and **characterization**. The form that fiction takes often connects to its length, though writers have a great deal of freedom even within established forms. Further, fiction is often divided into content-oriented types such as **literary fiction**, **science fiction**, **young adult fiction**, **fantasy**, **romance**, **horror**, and more. Learning about some of the dominant characteristics of the two primary fictional forms—the short story and the novel—can help us to discover how writers approach composing fictional narratives and how the academic field of Creative Writing influences the fictional narratives that we read.

Short stories are fictional works that, as their name indicates, are shorter in length and more focused in scope than their longer counterparts, the novel. While short stories still demand a fully developed plot, characters, and theme, they may not include structures as complex or passages of description or exposition that are as intricate as those in novels, due to the length constraints of this type of fiction. The short story rises to prominence in an academic context because it is well suited to the workshop model of instruction, in which writers read their works aloud and then receive feedback from their peers. For this reason, students may be more likely to study short stories in the context of Creative Writing, reading authors such as

Alice Munro, who won the Nobel Prize in Literature in 2013 in recognition of her body of work as a short story writer, or Raymond Carver, who is very influential on contemporary approaches to the short story genre. Further, the publication of short stories is accorded value in an academic context that aligns with the value assigned to scholarly article publications in the promotion and review processes for professors in English departments.

Today, there is a sharp divide between practitioners of Creative Writing about the genre of the short story. Writers, literary agents, and editors associated with **mainstream commercial publishing** believe that the short story has declined in relevance to a general reading public because those readers do not tend to buy books that collect short stories and because mainstream magazines and newspapers are less likely to publish short stories on a regular basis. In contrast, creative writers associated with higher education, academic publishing, and boutique or experimental literary journals and publishing houses continue to hold short fiction in high esteem, and academic practitioners see the short story as an essential form that creative writers must master.

Ultimately, this divide pertains to who gets to assign value in the field of Creative Writing: professionals in the commercial marketplace of major publishing cities like New York or London or professors in the intellectual marketplace of higher education. In 2013, this debate entered the mainstream first with the fall 2010 publication of Chad Harbach's **essay** "MFA vs. NYC" in the online magazine *n+1* and later with the 2014 publication of the collection inspired by that initial essay, *MFA vs. NYC: The Two Cultures of American Fiction*. The essay, and then later, the book, exposed the biases, values, and practical realities that shape the works that writers produce as well as the ways in which changes in the publishing industry have made it more difficult to make a living from one's writing. Continuing the conversation, Junot Diaz wrote an essay for *The New Yorker*, "MFA vs. POC," in which he articulated the unique challenges that writers of color face in writing and publishing literary fiction. Mainstream media including *The New York Times*, *National Public Radio*, *The New Republic*, and *Slate* picked up the story. This collection of articles, essays, and reports painted a picture of the contemporary publishing landscape in which advance payment for work on manuscripts was rare, in which all but established best-selling authors must foot the bill for the promotion of their books, and in which securing an agent to represent one's writing was the only pathway to publishing fiction. Further, it revealed the ways in which gargantuan student debt, the workshop culture of universities, and the professionalization of Creative Writing in the academy influenced the kinds of writing that authors of fiction could produce.

In spite of the divisions that such debates reveal, the type of fiction about which there is more agreement is the novel. Novels are long-form works of fiction that offer complex portrayals of characters and situations in book-length form, typically with some degree of **realism** in their representations. Important novelists today include Jonathan Franzen (*The Corrections, Freedom*), Kazuo Ishiguro (*The Remains of the Day, Never Let Me Go*), Zadie Smith (*White Teeth, On Beauty*), and Chimamanda Ngozi Adichie (*Half a Yellow Sun, Americanah*). Novels may be divided into chapters that are either numbered or titled, they may be divided into larger parts, or they may not include any of these reader-friendly divisions. Ultimately, what distinguishes the novel from other forms of fiction, such as the short story or the **novella**, which we can define as a very long short story or a very short novel, is the breadth of its scope and the complexity with which it delves into its characters' psychologies.

Because fiction, unlike poetry, does not have a long tradition of oral performance and because fiction becomes a more central genre of Creative Writing with growing **literacy** rates among women and the working classes in the nineteenth century, publication is by far the most significant means by which fiction writers disseminate their work. Fiction is widely read among academic audiences and the general reading public, and fiction is widely available for purchase in online outlets, at bookstores, and even in places where you buy groceries, clothing, household items, or office supplies. The possible outlets for publishing fiction include the following:

1. Online and print literary journals and magazines, some of which focus on Creative Writing across genres and some of which focus on fiction alone.
2. Books of collected short stories, which may be by a single author or may be anthologies with multiple authors contributing.
3. Books, which are the primary form of publication for novels.

Unlike poets, writers of fiction depend much more heavily on securing the representation of a **literary agent** in order to get publishers to look at their manuscripts for book-length projects. Like poets, however, writers of fiction may present their creations and promote their publications at open-mic nights or at invited readings, though when they do so, they are likely to read only very short pieces or excerpts of longer works. For writers of fiction, such readings are often connected to the promotion of their published works, and they may conceive of these appearances as "tours" at which they will inscribe their publications and autograph them for fans. Most writers of fiction must self-fund such promotion of their books, and they receive little support from their publishers for this kind of promotion.

Creative Nonfiction

Creative nonfiction is a relatively new genre in the field of Creative Writing, although people have been writing prose works that tell true stories using the techniques associated with imaginative writing for hundreds of years. The newness of creative nonfiction to Creative Writing says less about the genre than it does about the ways in which the academic field historically valued the genres, seeing less worth in writing that it regarded as **journalism** in comparison with writing that it regarded as art. In the twenty-first century—especially with the explosion of communication and media technologies that accompany the widespread use of the internet—creative nonfiction becomes one of the fastest-growing, best-selling genres of Creative Writing. Creative nonfiction encompasses personal narrative forms such as **autobiography**, **life writing**, and **memoir** as well as narrative forms more public in nature, including **occasional writing**, long-form **feature** or **investigative reporting**, **biography**, and **commentary**. Each of these forms can appear across ranges of length, from short-form essay to book-length work. Creative nonfiction writers also sometimes practice **mixed-genre writing**, in which they merge elements of the above creative nonfiction forms into a piece that does not fit neatly into just one of the forms. Truman Capote, David Foster Wallace, Elizabeth Gilbert, Helen Macdonald, Ta-Nehisi Coates, and Karl Ove Knausgard are well known for their writing in the creative nonfiction genre.

The focus of creative nonfiction on producing aesthetically pleasing narrative using the techniques more commonly associated with literary genres of poetry and fiction is what distinguishes it from journalism, a writing form that focuses less on aesthetics and more on providing the public with important information needed for daily living. While writers of creative nonfiction root their creations in true stories, their emphasis, like writers of fiction, is more on telling a good story than on timeliness or relevance, the criteria that typically guide journalists who report the news. Instead, by creatively packaging the truth in narrative form, writers of creative nonfiction seek to represent greater human truths, just as writers of fiction or poetry do.

One challenge for readers and writers of creative nonfiction connects to its status as an emergent creative genre. Given the emphasis of using creative techniques to tell true stories, sometimes there is uncertainty about the line between fictional and factual creative representation. Perhaps the most famous controversy connected to this issue occurred with Oprah Winfrey's selection of James Frey's *A Million Little Pieces* (2003) for Oprah's Book Club in 2003. The book, which was marketed as a memoir, was later revealed to include significant passages that were untrue or significant modifications of the truth. Ultimately, Winfrey, embarrassed by the revelations about the fictionalized accounts in the book, rescinded the book's status as part of her book club. This example offers just one illustration of some of the issues that writers of creative nonfiction must negotiate and that shape the ways in which readers receive their works.

Like writers of fiction and poetry, writers of creative nonfiction present their work in public venues at open-mic nights or at invited readings as well as publish their works in the following venues:

1. Online and print literary journals and magazines, some of which focus on Creative Writing across genres and some of which focus on creative nonfiction alone.
2. Books of Collected Essays or Shorter Nonfiction Pieces, which may be written by a single author or may be anthologies with multiple authors contributing.
3. Books, which are the primary form of publication for longer creative nonfiction works.

As is the case for authors of fiction, authors of creative nonfiction depend on securing an agent to represent their book-length manuscripts to publishers, and all but established authors take a large portion of the responsibility for initiating and funding the promotion of their publications.

Additional Genres

While the three preceding genres are the ones on which academic practitioners of Creative Writing currently focus most of their attention, other genres that might attract creative writers include **playwriting** (writing scripts for theatrical, live production), screenwriting (writing **screenplays** for digital, television, and feature-length cinematic productions), and **game narrative** (writing scripts for **analog game** and **digital game** environments).

These genres, however, tend to be marginalized within the academic study of Creative Writing for the following reasons:

1. Programs dedicated solely to the study of each of these genres are often located in academic units (departments, schools, or colleges) that house theater (playwriting), film (screenwriting), or media and digital studies (game narrative).
2. Dissemination of these types of writing depends on collaborative productions, and they do not find an outlet in conventional venues such as public readings, publication in digital or print magazines or literary journals, or publication in electronic or print book form.
3. These types of writing are marginalized in the critical fields of English Studies, and it is rare to see scholars study the language or writing of these texts in isolation from their broader production context.

As Creative Writing evolves in the twenty-first century, however, authors are inspired by these narrative forms, and they are more likely to explore creating in those forms and to teach students how to do so as well.

What Methods and Approaches Are Promoted in Creative Writing as a Field of English Studies in an Academic Context? How Do Research, Analysis, Workshopping, and Reflection Shape Creative Writing Praxis?

Instructors of Creative Writing, much like those in other studio arts fields such as music, theater, and painting, are themselves creators and artistic practitioners. While they often have degrees to qualify them to teach in university classrooms, their primary qualification to teach Creative Writing is their own achievement as writers themselves. Unlike specialists in other fields of the discipline, the work of creative writers is not to produce scholarly studies of other people's writing: it is to create writing themselves.

This foundation guides the way that students experience Creative Writing in an academic context as well.

Methodologically, practitioners in criticism-based, scholarly fields of English Studies orient their research around **close reading** and deep analysis of primary texts that they then situate by placing those analyses into context with **secondary source** research. These scholars then organize their claims around citations to primary sources and secondary source material to put themselves into critical conversation with other scholars. In contrast, those in practice-based, creative fields of English studies orient their writing of creative works around their own inspiration, which derives context from the writer's life experiences, emotions, or ideas; the influence of other writers, past or present, on the form of the creative work (craft); current events understood as historical, cultural, anthropological, or sociological; or other research that informs the story that the writer hopes to tell or the image that the writer hopes to represent. They generally do not cite sources in their creative efforts, and they do not organize their creative works to foreground their relationship to other people's ideas. Instead, they foreground the creative work as a world in its own right, even as they sometimes imbed allusions to other writers or descriptions of external events or ideas in what they have created. Thus, creative writers do not compose their pieces in a vacuum, but they also do not foreground the context for their pieces in their completed creative works.

Because creative writers do not foreground the sources that inform their final products, research and analytical **methodology** in Creative Writing does not follow the same rules as those methodologies used in other English Studies fields. Research or the reading of other creative works may lead to the execution of writing exercises, journaling, outlining, or other activities connected to the creation of an original piece of writing. Once a piece is drafted, unlike counterparts in other fields in English Studies, creative writers in an academic context put their pieces through many rounds of **critique,** presenting them in writing workshops where they receive oral and written feedback on what they have shared with the group. In a classroom context, they will often submit a final draft of their piece accompanied by an **artist's statement,** which explains how the final composition was informed by research, the influence of other writers, personal experience, emotions, or ideas, and the feedback of the workshop. Only then, in an academic context, is a writer likely to read a piece publicly or to submit it to be considered for publication.

It is important here to acknowledge that not all authors subscribe to the above methodologies, and that many authors, outside of an academic context, approach the creative process with their own idiosyncratic practices. Indeed, for as many writers that emerge out of academic Creative Writing programs, such as Jeffrey Eugenides, Curtis Sittenfeld, and Sandra Cisneros, there are those who become acclaimed authors without an academic pedigree in Creative Writing, such as J. K. Rowling, Toni Morrison, and Neil Gaiman. The fact that becoming an author does not require specific academic training distinguishes Creative Writing from most other fields of English Studies, which originate and are almost exclusively practiced in educational institutions.

What Is Creative Writing in the Twenty-First century? How Does Creative Writing Connect to English Studies, More Broadly Conceived?

The main challenge facing Creative Writing today is the management of its growth in a way that confronts the harsh reality that all students who pursue training in Creative Writing in an academic context may not find a pathway toward paid employment as authors or writing instructors. Accompanying this challenge is the ongoing tension between Creative Writing as an academic field and Creative Writing as a commercial product to be bought and sold in the literary marketplace. Nevertheless, in the twenty-first century, Creative Writing is one of the fastest-growing academic fields of English Studies.

More and more institutions are adding or expanding undergraduate and graduate programs in Creative Writing, and by doing so, they demonstrate the increasing value accorded to the accomplishments of creative writers, not just in higher education generally but in English departments specifically. Creative Writing has proven highly attractive to students, drawing greater numbers into English departments when numbers of students interested in pursuing some of the other fields have declined. It has also expanded the possibilities of English Studies as a discipline that returning students pursue for personal enrichment disconnected from their chosen career paths.

Furthermore, Creative Writing, like other studio arts disciplines, fosters connections between universities and the broader communities of which they are a part through:

1. outreach to K-12 education in the form of contests, workshops for school students and teachers, and events aimed at a K-12 audience;
2. performances of creative works in both campus and community venues that welcome general audiences; and
3. publication of works that everyday people can enjoy.

While some other fields of English Studies, such as linguistics or literary studies, face harsh criticism for their use of **jargon**, their engagement with esoteric topics that might not seem critical to twenty-first-century life, and their seeming alienation from the creative process through which texts come into being, Creative Writing marshals the common human investment in expressing feelings, telling stories, and making art, and it does so in a way that is, at least some of the time, accessible to people outside of the **ivory tower**.

These features make Creative Writing one of the most important fields of an English Studies for the twenty-first century. Creative Writing, like rhetoric and composition, demonstrates in easy-to-understand terms why English Studies matters. It provides people with the tools to create written works and to understand the creative process that many of their favorite writers follow.

Further Reading

Bishop, Wendy, and David Starkey. *Keywords in Creative Writing*. Logan: Utah State University Press, 2006.
    Provides basic definitions for key concepts in Creative Writing and a framework for novices to understand Creative Writing today.

Gardner, John. *The Art of Fiction: Notes on Craft for Young Writers*. New York: Random House, 1983.
    Discusses the craft of writing fiction, focusing on basic skills, common errors, exercises for writers, and everything in between.

Gioia, Dana. *Can Poetry Matter? Essays on Poetry and American Culture*. St. Paul: Graywolf Press, 1992.
    Ponders the role of poetry in the broader culture in a collection of essays considering the business, aesthetics, and relevance of poetry as a genre.

Harbach, Chad, ed. *MFA vs. NYC: The Two Cultures of American Fiction*.
New York: Farrar, Straus, and Giroux, 2014.
Collects essays that detail the experiences of authors writing today with
graduate programs in Creative Writing, getting published, and succeeding
at a writing career.

Karr, Mary. *The Art of Memoir*. New York: HarperCollins, 2015.
Draws on personal experience, excerpts from other memoirs, and anecdotes
from other writers to investigate the process of memoir writing and the
cathartic power of telling our own stories.

Longenbach, James. *The Art of the Poetic Line*. St. Paul: Graywolf Press, 2008.
Uses examples from canonical poets from Shakespeare up to the present
day to describe the function of the line across types of poetry.

Sampson, Fiona. *Creative Writing in Health and Social Care*. London: Jessica
Kingsley, 2004.
Investigates the uses of Creative Writing for connecting patients, clinicians,
and other health care professionals.

Sharples, Mike. *How We Write: Writing as Creative Design*. London:
Routledge, 1999.
Offers a guide to the writing process that pays particular attention to
intersections between creativity and technological advancements in
document design and medium.

Singer, Margot, and Nicole Walker, eds. *Bending Genre: Essays on Creative
Nonfiction*. London: Bloomsbury, 2013.
Asks leading writers of creative nonfiction to consider what it means to
push the boundaries of literary genre and to demonstrate in the essays that
they contribute the key forms that creative nonfiction can take.

Stein, Lorin, and Sadie Stein, eds. *Object Lessons:* The Paris Review *Presents the
Art of the Short Story*. New York: Picador, 2012.
Investigates what makes a great short story by asking short story writers to
share their ideas and to select exemplary short stories from the pages of one
of the most important literary journals for short stories, *The Paris Review*,
to illustrate their answers.

In this Case Study, we examine how to go about analyzing the craft techniques that a creative work deploys in order to use them in our own writing. We then offer engagement activities that you can use to help you better understand craft in Creative Writing and how it connects to the establishment of Creative Writing as an academic field in English Studies.

Reading for Craft, Writing with Craft: Writing like a Successful Author

While telling stories or writing poems might feel like a natural activity to many of us, what training in Creative Writing does is help to denaturalize the creative process and writing process to help authors to elevate their natural talent to something that we recognize as art. This case study provides a format for thinking about craft in Creative Writing. When writers self-consciously approach Creative Writing through craft, they gain the skills to emulate techniques that they appreciate in others' writing in the writing that they themselves produce.

Identify Something to Read

When writers discuss their "influences," they basically are talking about the authors and texts that they themselves have read and in which they have found inspiration. Whether they enjoyed these authors and texts or felt anger, frustration, or irritation in response to them, they count these authors and texts as influences because in them they could identify something to emulate. The first step in becoming a skilled creative writer is thus to become a thoughtful, sensitive reader. When you read as a creative writer, you attend specifically to those formal elements of creative representation that you might use in your own writing. Your agenda is neither to read for entertainment nor to read with an eye toward critical analysis but rather to use the chosen reading as a model for your own creative endeavors.

Activity for Critical Engagement

1. *Reflect on what makes a piece of writing a good model to use for thinking about your own creative endeavors. What criteria guide your reading choices and why? Write a "craft philosophy" that describes how you believe readings should be selected for those interested in using them as material to guide their own development as creative writers.*

Choose a Craft Technique or Element on Which to Focus in Your Reading

Once you have chosen a text to read, you will want to choose a formal element, narrative technique, or poetic device on which to focus so that you can analyze how the writer uses it and how you might apply it similarly in your own writing. You may have chosen this text because it is listed on a course syllabus, in which case your instructor might have told you that a particular story is notable for its use of characterization, that a particular poem is notable for its use of imagery, or they might have given you some other insight into some aspect of craft on which to focus. You may have chosen something that you have read before, in which a technique or element stood out to you, inspiring you to want to analyze it more deeply. You also may have selected a text that you have never read before and know very little about, and if that is the case, you should read the text once to identify the element on which you will focus for your craft exercise.

Learn More about the Technique You Chose

Before you begin a craft exercise, it can be helpful to gain a deeper **knowledge** of the technique or element that interests you.

Activities for Critical Engagement

2. *Do an internet search for the type of craft that interests you. How do people discuss this writing technique or element? Is this similar to how you previously understood it, or is it different?*
3. *Using a dictionary of figures of speech and literary devices, find the definition for the technique or element that you would like to explore. Think about how this definition can help you to "read for craft" in order to enhance your own Creative Writing. What do you think your writing will gain from deeper engagement with this term, device, or element?*
4. *Research what scholars have had to say about this writing element in either this literary work or in others. How does the scholarly conversation help you to think about your own motivations for using this technique?*

Trace the Use of the Element or Technique throughout the Work

You will want to make note of not only the appearance of the element or technique but also of how you notice the author incorporating it. Does it appear in different ways at different times? Does there appear to be a rationale driving the author's decisions? What do you think of how the author is using the element or technique? Why? How might you draw on what this author does in your own writing?

Activities for Critical Engagement

5. *On a photocopy of your chosen text, use a highlighter on one copy to mark each instance where the author uses this particular technique. How frequently does the author use this technique? Does the author use this technique in conjunction with others that you did not choose to explore for this exercise, and, if so, is this significant? What are the similarities between how this technique is used throughout the entirety of the piece? What are the differences? How might you use similar strategies in your own writing?*

6. *Using a photocopy of your chosen text, cut out each example of the technique, separating all of your examples into one pile and discarding those parts of the work that do not help you to see this technique. Once you have done this, read through each instance of the technique in order. How does this direct comparison of the uses of this technique change your perception of how the technique works? What is the effect of the author's use of this technique when you isolate examples of it? How does it make you feel? What does it achieve either poetically or narratively?*

7. *Using a photocopy of your chosen text, make marginal notes about your responses to this technique as you read. What emotions does this technique evoke? What does it make you think about? How does your perception of this technique at work influence your ideas about what it can do in your own writing?*

Practice the Craft

Now that you have analyzed the use of a particular strategy, technique, or element in the text of your choosing, try to write something in which you incorporate that strategy, technique, or element into your own writing. The goal in practicing the craft is to learn by doing—not just by reading or thinking. You may decide to model your "practice" exactly after the text that you evaluated for craft, or you may decide to write something very different from the text that you evaluated. The idea is that the text that you evaluated will serve as a source, influence, or inspiration for your own creative work.

Activities for Creative and Critical Engagement

8. *Compose a poem, story, essay, or scene in which you practice the craft that you studied through your reading. Take care to model what you do after your source text as precisely as possible, and think about how your own writing changes when you use this model. What differences do you notice in your own creative process by emulating this source text? In what ways does your writing benefit or suffer as a result of this craft exercise? Why?*

9. *After you have practiced your craft by writing your own poem, story, essay, or scene, reflect on what you have written in comparison with the source text. In what ways is the "influence" of the source text visible? In what ways does your own creative vision and voice still come through in the piece? Is this a craft that you will deploy again in your Creative Writing? Why or why not?*

How Does English Studies Influence Creative Writing?

As we can see from the systematic approaches that this case study offers both for analysis and creation, when Creative Writing enters the discipline of English Studies, it becomes more "academic." Instead of regarding the creative process as ineffable, mysterious, or guided by inspiration, Creative Writing as a disciplined field breaks down the creative process into its formal elements, offers strategies for approaching different creative situations and problems, and imagines authors as artisans who train in the use of specific tools and who hone specialized skills to make their art.

7

Professional Writing and Technical Communication

Lots of people have struggled with assembling a newly purchased piece of furniture with complicated instructions and inadequate tools for the job. One company that is known for instructions that can sometimes be challenging is the Swedish store IKEA. The instructions for its furniture explain the assembling process using images rather than the written word.

IKEA, as a global corporation with stores worldwide, provides its customers with an easy-to-use visual aid that is not language-specific, and in doing so, it keeps company costs down by eliminating the need to translate directions into a multitude of languages. The customer who purchases a Billy Bookcase in Japan uses the exact same set of instructions as the customer in the United States. The print document successfully communicates the information using a cartoon-like visual design that is comprehensible to most users. But, occasionally, the visual is not enough.

You may wonder what such instructions have to do with English Studies. Quite a bit, actually. The creation, written and visual, of such professional documents as IKEA's paper instructions for assembling the Billy Bookcase draws on the expertise of practitioners of Professional Writing and Technical Communication.

At least since the 1980s, English departments have featured limited course offerings in business and technical writing, which have served students in programs across campus as well as in the English major. Such courses directly addressed demands of local employers for skill in workplace writing genres and conventions. Most recently, many English departments have devoted greater attention to these types of courses, adding such courses to their programs for the first time, making existing courses more robust, and expanding the number of courses students may take addressing different types of workplace writing toward completing degree requirements.

The concern about preparing writers for the workplace, however, is not a new one. In fact, Professional Writing and Technical Communication began initially as a response to workplace needs in late-nineteenth-century America. But that response has evolved into a rich and vibrant field over the years, reflecting many of the same concerns about understanding the processes we use in written communication and about establishing writing as equally central to English Studies as interpretation. At the same time, Professional Writing and Technical Communication is different from other fields in the discipline in that it has a history of responding quickly to needs outside of academia. This chapter will focus on how current writers in this field organize and present information in multiple formats as well as the importance they place on concise written content, engaging **visual rhetoric**, **usability**, and effective **document design**, particularly for emerging technologies.

Key Questions

1. What counts as Professional Writing and Technical Communication? Why is this field often housed in English departments?
2. What sorts of texts are produced and studied in Professional Writing and Communication? How are they analyzed? Who is their audience?
3. How does Professional Writing and Technical Communication differ from the other writing fields? What kinds of writing can students expect to see and do when they take a Professional Writing or Technical Communication course?
4. What are the conventions of Professional Writing and Technical Communication scholarship? What kinds of research and interpretation are Professional Writing scholars interested in?
5. What is Professional Writing and Technical Communication in the twenty-first century? How does it connect to English Studies, more broadly conceived?

What Counts as Professional Writing and Technical Communication? Why Is This Field Often Housed in English Departments?

Professional Writing goes by many names, including business writing, business communication, technical writing, and even technical communication, although technical communication has become a growth area in its own right. Whatever name you use, however, Professional Writing is, essentially, writing appropriate to workplace settings. People in many different lines of work do this type of writing. Students might expect people in professions such as public relations, journalism, technical writing, and advertising to do this type of writing, and they do. Students might be surprised, however, that people in many other professions, including teaching, law, medicine, sales, accounting, research, and government, also benefit from training in Professional Writing and Technical Communication. Any person whose work requires them to write a report, give a PowerPoint presentation about an ongoing project, apply for funding, or write an annual review uses the central skills of Professional Writing and Technical Communication. Practitioners can, in fact, be anyone in any profession in which writing and document preparation are expectations of the job. Much like rhetoric and composition, Professional Writing requires the careful consideration of **purpose**, **audience**, **genre**, and **rhetorical situation**. Practitioners in the field use their expertise to connect businesses and organizations in both for-profit and nonprofit sectors with their target audiences. Professional writers do not simply write: they design, analyze, and edit in order to communicate ideas that are verbally and visually powerful.

As a field of study, Professional Writing originated between 1890 and 1910, when American colleges began creating profession-centered courses in areas such as engineering and agricultural studies. At first, writing instruction was largely ignored in most of these new courses, but poor writing was soon in evidence among college students and graduates. As a result, a "cry for more English" was soon voiced both inside and outside the university. Freshman English, a relatively new course, could not supply emerging professionals with the writing ability they needed. Harvard University became the first institution to develop upper-division classes to address this concern. The early instructors of these courses worked toward preparing professionals for writing in journalistic, literary, and other careers. Harvard's books and techniques, such as the in-class practice of writing skills, were adopted by a number of other schools. However, these efforts were not enough.

As the specialization and segmentation of the professions and the university increased, so did the demand for specialized writing instruction. The first specialized courses were developed in English departments and provided those departments with their own marketable "real-world" courses. Professional Writing began to be viewed as a set of skills to be mastered in college and applied in specific careers. The debate arose as to who should teach these writing courses: instructors trained in literature and linguistics or instructors with expertise in target careers such as journalism and engineering. At many institutions, journalistic writing departed entirely from the English department. Other genres of Professional Writing more typically stayed within English, but they were largely marginalized from literature and creative writing. Professional Writing ultimately developed as a field in American colleges in the twentieth century because of the belief that modern universities could teach everything and prepare students for almost any type of profession. The explosion of scientific knowledge and business enterprise during this period demanded the creation of agricultural, business, and technical writing courses. Curricular decisions, textbooks, and the feedback instructors gave to students were guided by practical, professional concerns.

Although Technical Communication was once an alternate name for Professional Writing, it has rapidly evolved into its own area within Professional Writing with the increased use of technology in the workplace and in our daily lives. Today, it is viewed by many professionals as parallel to Professional Writing to the extent that it is often taught in place of more general business writing courses in many writing programs at universities across the United States. Consequently, the field once known as Professional or Business Writing has become Professional Writing and Technical Communication. These practitioners are not all that different from those in Professional Writing; they just communicate more about technology-related topics and do so in increasingly complex digital environments using increasingly complex digital tools. Students who focus their education on Professional Writing and Technical Communication may choose to seek a career path outside of academia, although all English majors use the writing skills of this field.

The first major textbook on technical writing was published in 1908, and as with Professional Writing more generally, there was a significant division between instructors of the technologies and instructors of writing, most of whom were literature professors. In the mid-twentieth century, Technical Communication split from Professional Writing when a group of writing teachers identified themselves more narrowly as instructors of technical writing. The technical advancements of World War II inspired returning soldiers to seek training in technical writing. In the 1950s, the Society of Technical Writers was established, giving the field a professional status. The Space Race and emerging technologies continued to increase interest in what would become Technical Communication. However, recognition as a field of English Studies was considerably more challenging. The Modern Language Association (MLA) is the principal professional organization in the United States for scholars of literature and languages. Founded in 1883, the MLA resisted including the fields of writing studies. It took over fifty years for the MLA to recognize technical writing as a legitimate field, offering the first panel on technical writing at its convention in 1976. By 2000, membership in the Society for Technical Communication exceeded twenty thousand. Undergraduate and graduate programs in Professional Writing and Technical Communication continue to proliferate, making the field one of the fastest growing in English Studies.

Professional Writing and Technical Communication originated in English departments. Today, it may be housed in either the English department or in the business program. The field is **interdisciplinary**, drawing on disciplines such as Business and Communication in addition to English. Professional Writing and Technical Communication scholars often teach business majors in addition to English students. Their research draws as much on the scholarship of business practices as it does on the scholarship of writing studies. Today, instructors in Professional Writing and Technical Communication are unlikely to be literature and language professors, as they were when the field first emerged. Instructors with both scholarly and practical expertise in the field teach the courses, and there is much greater recognition and acceptance of the field within English Studies than there was in its early days. Professional Writing and Technical Communication has much in common with the other writing studies fields, especially rhetoric and composition. In particular, both emphasize the verbal and visual rhetoric of writing. Becoming a Professional Writing and

Technical Communication practitioner does not mean that you will become a scholar or pursue research in the field, although you might; and becoming a Professional Writing and Technical Communication professional does not mean that you will work in the field outside of academia, although you might.

What Sorts of Texts Are Produced and Studied in Professional Writing and Technical Communication? How Are They Analyzed? Who Is Their Audience?

Professional Writing teaches the composition and design of both simple documents (**memos**, business letters, **résumés**, and email) and complex genres (**proposals**, multimedia presentations, **white papers**, and **formal reports**). Those simple documents are important and allow an English major working in the field to demonstrate their abilities to write quickly and succinctly. Getting the message across clearly and without any "fluff" is essential in the workplace, since the audience is broad and often intimidated by lengthy text. Writers also have to be able to "ramp up" their writing to meet the goals of longer, more complicated documents and to do so with writing that is equally clear and concise. And not all writing in the workplace involves creating documents. Copyediting and revising the writing of others are just as important. Most often, texts will be created and finalized collaboratively, so writers in this field have to be able to find a common "voice" with others, and not necessarily other writers, in the workplace. The basic principles of Professional Writing and Technical Communication include the following:

- Writing for your audience: the document should reflect your audience, their needs, and your purpose.
- Writing ethically: keep in mind your duty to yourself, your profession, your employer, your colleagues, and the public.
- Achieving a readable style: your writing should be concise and effective in terms of words, sentences, and paragraphs.

- Designing effective documents: your document should visually engage the reader and be easy to read and understand.

Written and visual rhetoric are equally important. Unlike writing in many of the other fields of English Studies, such as literature and critical theory, the inclusion of charts, graphs, diagrams, illustrations, photographs, and other images is common in the documents produced for the workplace. It is essential that writers in the field understand the impact that the visual design of a document can have on its audience.

The importance of document design and layout cannot be overemphasized. An understanding of purpose and function is key to creating effective and readable documents. Understanding what information must be presented, how the document will be used, and if the document must be provided in printed or online form is essential to good design. People expect English majors to recognize the purpose of a written document, but they may be surprised to learn that specialists in Professional Writing and Technical Communication are also expected to understand how to determine or create the best visual layout for pieces of written communication. For academic essays, we employ MLA and other styles, but other documentation formats may be more challenging. And even if we think we know the standard layout for nonacademic texts, we may not be familiar with the variations that are possible.

Document layout, in its most basic sense, is the art of arranging "blocks" of content (text and images) on a visual plane (the page). It includes making judgments about balance, dominance, order, flow, alignment, and space. Well-designed documents make content easier to read and thereby enhance comprehension. As important as text is to a document, white space can be used effectively to improve readability, to provide visual balance, and to guide the flow of information.

Many businesses have their own style guide for document design. However, an excellent general resource is published by the American Printing House (APH) for the Blind, Inc. Their "Guidelines for Print Document Design" (https://www.aph.org/aph-guidelines-for-print-document-design/) for people with **low vision** provide excellent recommendations for designing professional documents that are readable by all users.

Design Choice	Justification
Use a readable typeface or font.	It is easier for individuals of all ages to read a **sans serif font**, one that is made up of straight lines without the little "tail" at the end of the main strokes of the letter.
Use white space.	White space makes print more readable because it provides contrast and luminance around the text.
Use headings and subheadings.	They serve as navigation aids for readers and organize information logically.
Avoid excessive use of uppercase letters or bold.	Large sections of text in uppercase letters or bold font imply shouting.
Avoid italics.	Because individual letters lean into the next one, italics can be difficult to read.
Use lists.	Information is easier to read when it is grouped and broken down into lists.
Use bullets.	Bullets for lists of three items or more make information easier to read and retain.
Use hanging indents but do so sparingly.	Only the enumerating symbol of the bulleted list or paragraph should hang to the left.
Use an unjustified or "ragged" right margin.	Depending on the typeface, unjustified right margins may make the text more readable by eliminating excessive spacing between words.
Use footnotes or reference section at end of document.	This strategy minimizes cluttering in the body of the text.
Use no more than sixty-two characters per line.	A line of text is easiest to read if there are no more than sixty-two characters.
Use plain backgrounds for text.	A busy graphic as a background prevents the text from being easily read.
Maintain same standards for images in terms of readability and usability.	Consider color and font to ensure that images are readable and usable.
Bind for usability.	Consider how a document will be used before binding it, and select an appropriate binding if it is needed.
Print on light-colored paper.	To ensure sufficient contrast with text, use nonglare white, ivory, cream, pale yellow, or pale pink paper.
Use fills with even dots or diagonals for graphics.	Even dots and diagonals are the most readable fills for graphics.

First impressions are very important with document design. A document that helps the reader locate important information quickly and easily will be more persuasive.

The primary audience for Professional Writing and Technical Communication often extends beyond academic experts, such as professors in English Studies or scholars in Professional Writing and Technical Communication. It can include employers, employees, clients, consumers, and even the general public.

How Does Professional Writing and Technical Communication Differ from the Other Writing Fields? What Kinds of Writing Can Students Expect to See and Do When They Take a Professional Writing or Technical Communication Course?

Although practitioners of Professional Writing and Technical Communication do write résumés, letters, memos, and technical instructions among other documents both in their courses and in the workplace, their skills go beyond just composing and formatting workplace documents. Professional writers often play the role of codifying company policy, documenting organizational changes and the rationales for those changes, and recording the history of a business or institution. One of the challenges for a company is finding a way to store the business knowledge that its employees have. Such knowledge is called **tacit knowledge**: the skills, ideas, and experiences that a person has that cannot be easily transferred to others because they have not been recorded in a format that allows for such transfer. Tacit knowledge does not necessarily require language, so it is not necessarily written down. For example, an apprentice may learn a craft by watching, imitating, and practicing. However, unless the employee passes that knowledge along to others, the information could be lost if the employee is fired or takes a job at another company.

Accordingly, it is essential that a business convert the tacit knowledge of its employees to **explicit knowledge**. The most common forms of explicit knowledge are documents, manuals, and recorded procedures. Writing in the workplace often involves documenting a process in writing so that other employees can perform the same task. Explicit knowledge can be accessed easily because it is well articulated, codified, and verbalized. Like an iceberg, explicit knowledge is what can be viewed from the surface of the water; tacit knowledge is the expanse of the iceberg underneath the water. With their skills in document design, understanding of audience, and ability to write clearly and succinctly, practitioners of Professional Writing and Technical Communication can successfully transfer the elusive tacit knowledge to the readily available explicit knowledge. The example of the printed instructions for assembling IKEA's Billy Bookcase that opened this chapter demonstrated just how easily tacit knowledge can be made explicit.

Professional Writing and Technical Communication as a practice has a very specific primary objective: writing professional documents for the financial health of the business or organization. Therefore, it may seem that the field differs significantly from creative writing, in which the creative writer is primarily motivated by a desire to create art, evoke emotion, and delight the reader. However, that is not the case. Creative writers whose work is purchased do not earn an income just for themselves but also for their **literary agent** and publishing house. Professional Writing and Technical Communication also has much in common with rhetoric and composition with its focus on effective writing, visual rhetoric, and document design. They are just more likely to be practitioners, rather than scholars, of their field. Nevertheless, Professional Writing and Technical Communication does differ from the other fields of English Studies in more subtle ways:

- Audience need: writing helps organizations to run efficiently with the goal of minimizing legal and safety concerns; audience is less concerned with the aesthetic appeal of the writing and its ability to entertain.
- Writing style: value is placed more on brevity, clarity, and simplicity than on complexity and sophistication.
- Recognized authorship: writers usually remain anonymous because writing impact, not writing credit, is the goal.
- Content and design: both are valued equally rather than content over form.

As a result, Professional Writing and Technical Communication students can expect their courses to encourage them to write in very different ways and with very different goals in mind than they do in their other English courses.

What Are the Conventions of Professional Writing and Technical Communication Scholarship? What Kinds of Research and Interpretation are Professional Writing Scholars Interested in?

While both areas of the field engage with scholarship on the teaching of workplace writing, Professional Writing researchers often explore topics such as rhetoric, practice, and theory that also interest rhetoric and composition scholars. Professional Writing is much more than simply applying writing skills learned in the classroom to the workplace. It is a **social action** that goes beyond the organization. Scholars are interested in the complexity of the rhetorical act that requires the writer to theorize within a variety of rhetorical situations. Particular attention has been paid to Professional Writing as **organizationally situated authorship**, making business writers more than just packagers and distributors of knowledge; they are knowledge creators and collaboration managers.

Scholarship in Technical Communication has grown significantly in recent years, helped by an increase in scholarly journals and an interest by publishers in book-length studies. Academics are particularly interested in the history of the field and its place in English Studies as opposed to a professional department. Likewise, it should be no surprise that Technical Communication scholars study genre, including the variety of document forms, the move from print to digital, and writing about new and old technologies. They are interested in visual theories and practice, usability, research methods, and philosophic approaches. Both Professional Writing and Technical Communication explore gender and diversity in the workplace and their effect on writing. As such, the field's breadth of scholarly interests touches on and, at times, embraces those of the other fields of English Studies.

Because most people qualified in the field are practitioners rather than academics, research can be less common than in the other fields of English Studies. **Peer-reviewed articles** and essays are more typical than books and follow American Psychological Association (APA) style, much like linguistics does. Since Professional Writing and Technical Communication is so entrenched in the workplace, **field research** (the collection of data outside a library or laboratory), with the appropriate university permissions to work with human subjects, is often required. For example, scholars may want to explore writing practices in entrepreneurial business or nonprofit organizations. To do so, they need to collect data from the appropriate workplaces in order to analyze how writing is being conducted and valued. Scholarly articles are typically written by two or more authors, unlike the **single-author research** approach found in other fields of English Studies like literature and critical theory. Significantly, Professional Writing and Technical Communication research does not just explain how writing is being practiced in the workplace; it directly informs those practices and influences how such writing is conducted, interpreted, and valued outside of academia.

What Is Professional Writing and Technical Communication in the Twenty-First Century? How Does It Connect to English Studies, More Broadly Conceived?

Although Professional Writing courses developed initially in response to a need for effective writers in the workplace, the field has evolved far beyond that goal. In particular, it has had to address the cultural shift from print to digital environments for both writing and document design. While many of us may still read print books for pleasure, reading in the workplace is increasingly done in digital environments. Redesigning and rewriting documents, such as human resources materials, for the Web and the digital screens of computers, tablets, and smartphones has changed not just how Professional Writing practitioners write but also the technology with which they do that writing. They have to know more than just Microsoft Office Suite and the tools that each product offers for designing documents; they also have to be able to evaluate those tools and select the best ones for the purpose of audience of their writing. For example, a writer needs to know when a table created in MS Word really should be transferred and revisioned in an Excel spreadsheet or when the conclusions of a word-processed report would be better represented in PowerPoint slides. And the writer may also have to make decisions as to whether more powerful design software, such as Dreamweaver or InDesign, are warranted. The workplace is becoming much more of a digital environment, with employees often working virtually with each other and seldom face to face. Consequently, Professional Writing practitioners today are often the ones who ensure that the purpose and tone of written communication does not get lost.

With the rapid development of technology, there is an increasing interest in and need for Technical Communication rather than Professional Writing. As technology becomes more and more specialized, technical writers are having to rely on experts in the industry to write the primary documentation; as a result, the technical writer's role may become more that of an editor and document designer. In addition, **Virtual Reality, Augmented Reality, Artificial Intelligence, social robotics,** and the **Internet of Things** are changing the way we work and live our lives. Technical Communication practitioners are having to write for virtual environments that are far more immersive than just reading a printed page or computer screen. As businesses try to keep control over their products, consumers demand greater access and involvement through **transmedia experiences** and a greater participatory process.

Games, books, movies, and other media are largely experienced online now, forcing corporations to create digital worlds for our entertainment, work, and social lives. We are no longer just a consumer culture but a **participatory culture**—one in which we act as **prosumers** (contributors or producers) rather than simply as consumers. For example, rather than posting a job advertisement on their website and inviting prospective applicants to submit their materials online, a company may have human resources browse résumés available on **LinkedIn** and contact suitable job candidates directly. The documentation will be created by the prosumer, not by the technical writer. Technical communicators will have to figure out what sort of documentation should be sought by an employer surfing the virtual world of LinkedIn rather than design the webpage and write the text for the job advertisement to be posted online.

Similarly, consider changes in a visit to the doctor. Doctors now use mobile technology to interact with patient records instantly. They have to pull together a patient's medical history, X-rays, blood tests, and insurance information and then generate various digital and print documents that are personalized and secure. In the ever-increasing participatory culture, patients now expect immediate access to those documents and the ability to update their own medical information. The technical communicator no longer creates the simple documents to be filled out but now helps to design a suitable database interface in addition to templates for a variety of digital devices that structure and format the content components.

Consequently, Professional Writing and Technical Communication is experiencing the same pressure that other fields of English Studies are from new technology and more immersive digital environments. And the field is discovering that technology does not just change the way we read but also the way we write.

Further Reading

Allen, Jo. "The Case against Defining Technical Writing." In *Teaching Technical Communication: Critical Issues for the Classroom*, ed. James M. Dubinsky, pp. 67–76. Boston: Bedford/St. Martin's, 2004.
Argues for a broader understanding of technical writing as a field.

Bernhardt, Stephen A. "The Shape of Text to Come: The Texture of Print on Screens." *College Composition and Communication*, vol. 44, no. 2, 1993, pp. 151–75.
Discusses the move from print to digital text changes document design and user interaction.

Connors, Robert J. "The Rise of Technical Writing Instruction on America." *Journal of Technical Writing and Communication*, vol. 12, no. 4, 1982, pp. 329–52.
Presents a history of the development of technical writing at colleges in the United States.

Katz, Steven B. "The Ethic of Expediency: Classical Rhetoric, Technology, and the Holocaust." *College English*, vol. 54, no. 3, 1992, pp. 255–75.
Studies the role of ethics in professional writing using the example of the Holocaust.

Kynell, Teresa C., and Elizabeth Tebeaux. "The Association of Teachers of Technical Writing: The Emergence of Professional Identity." *Technical Communication Quarterly*, vol. 18, no. 2, pp. 107–41.

Examines how Professional Writing and Technical Communication became an academic field.

Miller, Carolyn R. "A Humanistic Rationale for Technical Writing." *College English*, vol. 40, 1979, pp. 610–17.
Argues for the inclusion of technical writing in the humanities.

Rude, Carolyn D. "Mapping the Research Questions in Technical Communication." *Journal of Business and Technical Communication*, vol. 23, 2009, pp. 174–215.
Explores how research in Professional Writing and Technical Communication should be conducted.

Selfe, Cynthia L., and Gail E. Hawisher. "A Historical Look at Electronic Literacy." *Journal of Business and Technical Communication*, vol. 16, no. 3, 2002, pp. 231–76.
Examines how digital environments affect written communication.

Stolley, Karl. "Integrating Social Media into Existing Work Environments: The Case of Delicious." *Journal of Business and Technical Communication*, vol. 17, 2009, pp. 350–71.
Discusses the influence of social media on workplace writing.

Wood, Julia T. *Gendered Lives: Communication, Gender, and Culture.* Boston: Wadsworth, 2011.
Explores issues of gender in workplace writing and communication.

In this Case Study, we examine the importance of visual design and meaningful content for professional documents, specifically the résumé. This document is one that all of us will likely write and rewrite during our careers, but it often challenges us in terms of the best form and content for our needs. We offer engagement activities that you can use to help you better understand how to design a successful résumé, particularly as an English major.

Document Design and Content

Thinking "Outside the Box" with Document Design

As English majors, we are typically taught formatting requirements, usually according to the MLA guidelines rather than true document design. The conformity to these "rules" is essential so that the reader is not distracted from the page's content by its visuals. However, professional documents require conscious and conscientious document design in order to fully engage their audience, make their written text accessible, and allow the reader to interpret the information quickly and efficiently. **White space** and visual images require just as much consideration as **typeface** and **font style** in order to highlight the document's message.

Activities for Creative and Critical Engagement

1. *Write your name out in full by hand on a blank piece of paper. If you wrote it in cursive, print it in upper and lowercase letters and then in all uppercase letters. Now try writing it in different colors. What is the impact of these variations on the eye? Using a word-processing program, type your full name on the screen in three different fonts that you believe reflect your personality. What font styles did you choose and why? How does word processing your name differ from handwriting it? What are the effects of changing the color and/or weight of the letters? Now, have someone else look at the different versions of your name. How do other people react to the styles you have chosen? Do they find a particular font style conveys your*

personality more effectively than others? Why or why not? Based on your experimentation, how does typeface convey visual meaning?

2. *Take an academic assignment that you wrote for another course. An annotated bibliography would be a good choice since it has a variety of layout requirements. Completely change the layout of the pages by using columns for the text rather than paragraphs. Give each column a title. How does comprehension of the text change with this new format? Are the columns of text easier to read if you convert complete sentences to a bulleted list?*

3. *Now take an academic essay in MLA style that you wrote for another course. Select a nonstandard font (something other than Times New Roman, Garamond, Georgia, or Bookman), and reformat the text. Divide the text into sections with block paragraphs (no tab indentation), and add subtitles. Make the typeface of the subtitles larger, a different style, and/ or a different color. Add some additional white space and a few images and/or graphics that relate to the content of the text. How does this new layout change the reading of your essay? Which format elements improve your essay in terms of comprehension? Which ones do not? Why? Why do you think MLA style is used for academic essays on literary texts in English Studies?*

Creating Content for a Document

No matter how well-designed visually, a professional document will have little to no impact if it does not contain meaningful content. Creating that content in the workplace is usually a team, rather than an individual, effort. One particular genre of professional document that everyone produces on their own at some point in their careers is the résumé. Although a résumé consists largely of factual information, such as education and employment history, it also lists the individual's skills. Describing those skills clearly and succinctly can make the difference between a successful and unsuccessful document when applying for a prospective job.

Activities for Critical Engagement

4. *Locate copies of the syllabi for all the English courses you have taken so far in your undergraduate program. If necessary, find a copy in your university's syllabus bank (if there is one) or ask the instructor of the course to send you one. Identify other courses you have taken, such as Communication, Marketing, etc., that you believe have enhanced your professional abilities for the job market. Using the course description and learning objectives found on each course syllabus, write a bulleted list of all the skills you learned that are suitable for the job market. If you need help finding the right verb to describe your skill, search for "résumé verbs" online or go to the textbook website for a list of action verbs suitable for résumés.*

5. *For each job (full-time or part-time) you have held, identify three or four broad skills that you have learned in the position. Typical skills relate to communication, leadership, research, and time/project management, but you may come up with additional and/or more specific skills depending on your employment history.*

6. *Using general headings, such as Communication, Leadership, Research, and Time/Project Management, combine the skills from both lists in the appropriate categories. Add categories as needed and rank the skills under each one in order of importance and/or expertise.*

Designing a Document with Meaningful Content

A **skills-based résumé** is a document that lists a person's job qualifications in skill categories rather than in reverse chronological work experience categories. Although the **reverse-chronology résumé** is the standard format, a job applicant may choose the skills-based résumé for a number of reasons, including insufficient work experience, employment changes or gaps, and a background that may seem atypical for the advertised position. For English majors, this type of résumé can be particularly powerful because, if done well, it effectively showcases your writing talents in terms of creativity, wordsmithing, and **Standard American English (SAE)** to prospective employers in addition to listing your education, skills, and employment history.

The layout of your résumé is just as important as its content. The Purdue OWL provides excellent guidelines for résumé design (https://owl.english. purdue.edu/owl/resource/631/01/):

- Divide your résumé into quadrants and be sure that the text and white space are balanced with the information you wish the prospective employer to see first in the upper left quadrant.
- Consider using columns (no more than three) to present text.
- Select the font style with care, and be sure that it is easily readable.
- Be consistent with emphasis, and do not overuse bold, italics, underlining, and uppercase.
- Try the "20-second test" on your résumé to determine the immediate takeaways of a prospective employer.

Basic format for a skills-based résumé:

STUDENT NAME

Street Address—Town, State Zip Code—Telephone Number—Email
    LinkedIn—Online Portfolio URL—Twitter

EDUCATION

> University
> Major
> Minor
> Relevant Coursework
> Anticipated Graduation Date
> Accomplishments

SKILLS & EXPERIENCE

Communication

> Skill 1
> Skill 2
> Skill 3

Leadership

> Skill 1
> Skill 2
> Skill 3

Organization/Coordination

> Skill 1
> Skill 2
> Skill 3

EMPLOYMENT HISTORY

Position	Employer	Dates of Employment

VOLUNTEER EXPERIENCE

Position	Organization	Dates of Involvement

Activity for Critical Engagement

7. *Using the résumé model above and the list of skills that you compiled from your university courses and job experiences, prepare a suitable skills-based résumé for yourself. What font(s) will you use? How readable is your choice of typeface? How effective is the overall layout?*

8. *Review the design guidelines for résumés provided by the Purdue OWL (https://owl.english.purdue.edu/owl/resource/631/ 01/). How well does your résumé conform to those guidelines? What are the results of the "20-second test"? What final changes do you need to make in order to have a well-designed résumé with the most meaningful content?*

How Does English Studies Influence Professional Writing and Technical Communication?

All writing in English Studies depends on organization, visual design, consistent formatting, readability, accuracy of information, and error-free writing. What you write and how you write can reveal who you are as a writer. Writing in the workplace, be it a résumé or any other professional document, offers an impression of you to an employer; therefore, you need to control the message it conveys.

8

Critical Theory

Think back to the first time that you realized you loved a book, **play**, or **poem**. What attracted you to it? Did you connect with the characters? Were you fascinated with the world that it depicted? Were you enchanted by how the **words** sounded? Alternatively, think about the things that you enjoy about writing. How do you make decisions when you are writing an **essay**, **story**, or poem? Do you think about how others will respond to what you write, or are you focused on your own need to express yourself? You may not have given these questions much thought before, and you may wonder what they have to do with something called Critical Theory. Critical Theory is the field of English Studies that helps us to answer the above questions, making it possible to build upon those answers to think in more sophisticated ways about those **texts** that we care about.

As a field of the **discipline**, Critical Theory provides practitioners of English Studies with analytical tools that denaturalize the practices of reading and writing: it provides us with clearly articulated intellectual frameworks and practical **methodologies** for approaching the **interpretation** and creation of texts. Through the approaches that Critical Theory makes available, which draw on the perspectives of many different disciplines, readers and writers can better understand the structures and assumptions that undergird their interpretations and creative and rhetorical choices. At first, students new to Critical Theory can find its procedures and vocabulary intimidating, but once they learn a bit about it, they discover that they have nothing to fear. In this chapter, students will discover how Critical Theory informs the work of English Studies practitioners, about the debates and controversies that arise out of the "turn to theory" in English Studies and about the influence of Critical Theory on the public perception of English Studies as a discipline.

Key Questions

1. How is theoretical reading different from simply reading to understand or to analyze? What are the rewards and risks of theoretical reading?
2. What are the origins of Critical Theory? Why are ideas from other disciplines important to English Studies?
3. Why has Critical Theory been influential in English Studies? Why have some practitioners objected to Critical Theory's influence?
4. What are the conventions of theoretically oriented work in English Studies? How do practitioners of English Studies engage with Critical Theory to inform the work that they do?
5. What is Critical Theory in the twenty-first century? Is Critical Theory dead? How does it connect to English Studies, more broadly conceived?

How Is Theoretical Reading Different from Simply Reading to Understand or to Analyze? What Are the Rewards and Risks of Theoretical Reading?

Reading, at a basic level, involves two components: **fluency,** or the ability consistently and efficiently to process the words that we see upon the page as **language**, and comprehension, or the ability to understand the message of what we are reading. Fluent readers with strong comprehension skills can answer fact-based questions about the texts that they read, such as the following:

- What are the definitions of important vocabulary in the text?
- Who are the characters in the text and/or who is speaking?
- What are the main events or topics of the text?
- When and where do the events of the text take place?
- What are the conclusions of the text?

They can understand what they have read and summarize it.

As you know from English courses you have taken in the past, however, our discipline asks students to build on those basic skills, encouraging both interpretation and analysis. Interpretation and analysis begin with questions that generate **subjective** or opinion-based answers, such as the following:

- Does important vocabulary in the text carry with it **connotations** that deepen or change its meaning? Why?
- How does this text make me feel? Why?
- What motivates the main characters or the speaker of the text?
- How does this text connect to other written or cultural texts or to events in the real world? Do those connections change how we feel about the text? Why?
- What is most important about this text, and what is the text's larger message?

The answers to these questions produce **arguments** or assertions that differ from reader to reader.

When we read theoretically, or take a theoretical approach, we apply a standard framework to shape our analysis. Many times, this kind of framework guides the topics that instructors assign to students, even if the instructor never mentions Critical Theory. For example, an essay topic that asks students to analyze the depiction of **race** and slavery in Toni Morrison's *Beloved* provides students with a framework that implicitly connects to **critical race theory**. Alternatively, a topic that asks students to analyze the **impact** of chants and slogans in public protests provides students with a framework that implicitly connects to **rhetorical theory**. By paying explicit attention to theory, however, and systematically engaging with its methods, our interpretations can grow in richness, depth, and complexity.

For example, let's say that a student has read J. K. Rowling's *Harry Potter* series (1997–2000) and finds Hermione to be an appealing character. An initial interpretation might be that Hermione is the real hero of the series because she is central to solving all of the problems in the books and because she, as a witch without magical parents, symbolizes the egalitarian society that the books promote. That interpretation may be rooted in the student's **gender** identity, personal reactions while reading, or any number of other subjective factors. If the student decides to attempt a theoretical interpretation, however, they would need to subscribe to a set of rules that would guide their analysis. Since the student is interested in a female character, they may want to approach the series using a **feminist** theoretical lens, which would allow them to focus on the representation of women in the text. The student's appreciation of Hermione as their favorite character would constitute the **inspiration** for the project, but Critical Theory would give them tools to move beyond that initial inspiration to consider the deeper consequences of gender in the series. For example, a feminist theoretical approach could encourage the student to investigate the characteristics of the feminine gender role and evaluate how Hermione fits into conventional ideas about femininity. It could also allow for a deeper consideration of **patriarchy**, the organizing principle that puts men in positions of power in social institutions, and the ways in which patriarchy limits what Hermione can accomplish. Not only would the student marshal examples from the **novels** for support but also the student would draw on theoretical **knowledge** to explain the broader consequences of Hermione's **characterization**.

This example demonstrates some of the rewards of theoretical reading. Theoretical reading gives readers new terms to contextualize their ideas, and it gives them clear steps to organize their interpretive process. It also lets readers move beyond immediate, individual reactions to arguments supported by **evidence** and logical **argumentation**, which can make their claims more persuasive to others.

Of course, taking a theoretical approach also involves risks. For example, limiting our interpretation to one theoretical approach may discourage us from attending to features of the text that do not relate to it. Returning to the case of *Harry Potter*, taking a feminist approach may encourage us to neglect other equally important features of the **narrative**, such as its **commentary** on social **class** or its adherence to the formal characteristics of the **bildungsroman**, a **genre** of literature that details a protagonist's development from childhood to adulthood. Additionally, as we introduce theoretical terms to contextualize our claims, we might alienate readers who are not familiar with or who might object to the theory that we have chosen. Finally, we risk using the text to advance a theoretical agenda that is incompatible with it, rather than using the theory to illuminate the text that we read. As long as readers are aware of these risks and take care to avoid them, reading theoretically can expand the possibilities of their analysis and lead to a deeper, more sophisticated understanding of the texts that they encounter.

What Are the Origins of Critical Theory in English Studies? Why Are Ideas from Other Disciplines Important to English Studies?

People mean different things when they use the term Critical Theory, depending both on their fields of expertise within English Studies and on their own beliefs about the appropriateness of using Critical Theory in English Studies. According to the broadest understanding of the term, Critical Theory is as old as language itself. Stretching back to the philosopher Aristotle's criteria for tragedy, comedy, poetics, and rhetorical communication, **audiences** for written works have tried to categorize them, to assess their merit, and to use established methods or invent new methods for understanding their formal composition and emotional or intellectual impact. From this perspective, even if you have never heard of a formal field called Critical Theory, you still "do" theory every time you analyze something: Critical Theory is just **jargon** for deep inquiry and systematic evaluation.

Such a broad definition, however, might feel so wide-ranging that it does not actually help those new to this field to understand what Critical Theory is, who uses it, or what kinds of frameworks it promotes in its various guises. For this reason, students benefit from learning about Critical Theory as a historically situated, multidisciplinary apparatus, which allows people to ask deeper questions of the cultural texts that they encounter. Indeed, a basic understanding of Critical Theory remains important to disciplinary literacy in English Studies, even for those who choose not to rely on Critical Theory in their own creative or scholarly endeavors.

Structuralism as a New Beginning for Critical Theory

To say that Critical Theory is historically situated is to acknowledge that its meaning both changes over time and depends on social, cultural, and **ideological contexts**. Early scholars in English Studies fields traced the origin of Critical Theory back to Ancient Greek philosophy, and they saw

criticism as a process designed to reveal the formal qualities of texts and the **aesthetic** responses that those formal qualities produced. Furthermore, they used criticism to establish the superiority of some works over others, and they often did so by tracing the accomplishments of a work back to the genius of its **author**, using the author's **biography** as evidence for their assertions.

In the early part of the twentieth century, linguists, **rhetoricians**, and literary critics attempted to establish "new" foundations for criticism. Instead of referring their analysis to Ancient Greek philosophy or to the life or intentions of the author, they looked to the text itself, through the practice of **close reading**, to provide the framework for its own analysis. For the purposes of this introduction to Critical Theory, we can understand how this works through three different approaches: **Structural Linguistics**, **Russian Formalism**, and **New Criticism**. These three approaches have much in common with each other.

Approach	• **Key figures** • **Important Concepts** • **English Studies Fields of Greatest Impact**
Structural Linguistics	• Ferdinand de Saussure; Roman Jakobson • 1. The nature of language is arbitrary. • 2. Words only have meaning in relation to other words. • 3. Words create the world in which we live—they do not merely describe it. • Linguistics; Rhetoric and Composition; Literature; Cinema
Russian Formalism	• Vladimir Propp; Viktor Shklovsky • 1. Literature is autonomous, and literature and those activities that make it different from other human enterprises should be the focus of literary theory. • 2. Literature should be studied using a "scientific" method, and psychological and cultural-historical approaches should be avoided. • 3. Literary "facts" must be prioritized over the interests of the critic. • Rhetoric and Composition; Literature

New Criticism
- I. A. Richards; Cleanth Brooks; T. S. Eliot
  - 1. "Close reading," or the deep analysis of literature in isolation from cultural-historical context, is the method critics should use to understand the meaning in a literary work.
  - 2. Literary works are fundamentally impersonal, and their merits do not trace back to the life experiences or intentions of the author.
  - 3. The structure of a text connects intimately to its meaning, and the two cannot be analyzed separately.
  - Literature

Structural Linguistics, Russian Formalism, and New Criticism constituted the dominant critical modes in English Studies for the first half of the twentieth century, and they each anticipate **structuralism**, a theoretical approach that encourages critics to analyze larger structures to determine the meaning within. In general, structuralist approaches have the following beliefs in common:

1. There is such a thing as **objective** meaning, and the critic or scholar holds the responsibility of discovering it.
2. Analysis and understanding of the structure that contains the object of study is essential to revealing its one, true meaning.
3. The process of analyzing structures requires an objective, scientific methodology that follows carefully established procedures.

Structuralist approaches to finding meaning do not only become popular in English Studies: they also exert considerable influence in philosophy, sociology, economics, political science, anthropology, psychoanalysis, and many other disciplines. Furthermore, as critics in English Studies use theory to organize their analysis and interpretation, they begin to draw on the structuralist contributions of other disciplines to expand their own perspectives beyond close reading and formal linguistic or rhetorical analysis.

How Do Other Disciplines Influence Structuralism in English Studies?

The structuralist moment in Critical Theory formalizes **interdisciplinary** approaches to texts in English Studies. Below, you can get an overview of three foundational structures to Critical Theory, which connect to other

disciplines and prove highly influential in English Studies: **Marxism,
psychoanalysis,** and **feminism.** These are not the only structures through
which practitioners of English Studies evaluate texts, but they remain most
influential on the discipline today, particularly because they allow English
Studies practitioners to connect their work to important social issues as
well as to a more scientific understanding of representation and human
nature.

Structure	**• Disciplines outside English Studies** **• Foundational Figures** **• Uses in English Studies** **• Example**
Marxism	• Philosophy; economics; political science; history: sociology, among others. • Karl Marx; Friedrich Engels; Antonio Gramsci; Theodor Adorno; Max Horkheimer. • In English Studies, practitioners use Marxist theory to evaluate power relationships rooted in socioeconomic class status in written texts. • A Marxist reading in Cinema might evaluate the film *Fight Club* (David Fincher; 1999). Using ideas about use value versus exchange value, a critic could evaluate the film's protagonist's transformation from a passive consumer at the film's opening to one who controls the means of production (and, thus, destruction) at the film's end.
Psychoanalysis	• Psychology; anthropology; philosophy, among others. • Sigmund Freud; Carl Jung; Melanie Klein. • In English Studies, practitioners use psychoanalytic theory to investigate the subconscious meanings in a text. Their approach might involve evaluating the psychologies of characters, exploring the psychological underpinnings of relationships between characters, or connecting the author's psychological state to the text that they have produced. • A psychoanalytic reading in Literature might use Freud's concept of the Oedipus Complex to evaluate the relationship between Hamlet and his mother, Gertrude, in William Shakespeare's famous play, *Hamlet* (~1599–1602). A psychoanalytic approach could assist the critic in making sense of Hamlet's jealousy when his mother marries his uncle after his father's death, and the critic could argue that Hamlet's indecision connects to his subconscious and taboo desire for his mother.

Feminism	• Philosophy; psychology; history; sociology; anthropology, among others. • Virginia Woolf; Simone de Beauvoir; Kate Millett. • In English Studies, practitioners use feminist theory to investigate the influence of gender on both the meanings in a text and on our practices for assigning meaning as readers. • A feminist approach in Rhetoric and Composition might evaluate slogans on protest signs, hashtags in **social media** campaigns, and other protest **discourses** that have emerged around the #MeToo and Women's March movements in the wake of the 2016 United States presidential election. By evaluating these various discourses, a rhetorician could look at how protestors have appropriated cultural stereotypes about femininity to battle against what they perceive as widespread misogyny in the United States.

Fundamentally, structuralist theoretical approaches extend the scope of what English Studies practitioners can examine in their scholarship, which dramatically changes the discipline:

1. The scope of inquiry in English Studies begins to extend beyond discussions of formal elements, intuitive emotional responses, or the link between an author's life and their writing.
2. Concrete, objective methodologies for analysis in English Studies begin to dominate the discipline.
3. English Studies scholars begin commonly to draw on the work of other academic disciplines to situate their analyses of written texts.

In these ways, structuralism will lay the foundation for how practitioners "do" English Studies up to the present day.

Poststructuralism and the "Turn to Theory" in English Studies

At the middle of the twentieth century, Critical Theory changes yet again, taking a leap from structuralist approaches, which believe that the "true meaning" of a text is to be discovered through structural analysis, toward poststructuralist approaches, which question the very notion of meaning. **Poststructuralism** argues that structural analysis, by its logical extension, creates additional structures that must be endlessly unraveled.

As a result, poststructuralism questions the value of structures—such as language, power, history, and discourse—as pathways toward meaning, and it instigates new theoretical approaches, such as **reader response theory, cultural studies, postmodernism, new historicism, queer theory,** critical race theory, **postcolonial theory, ecocriticism,** and more.

The rapid growth of theoretical approaches, which privilege the reader as the producer of an infinite array of possible textual meanings and which diminish the emphasis on the formal attributes of literary works or on authors as creative geniuses, is often described as the turn to theory in English Studies. This turn, and the poststructuralist theories that enable it, changes the ways that people read and transforms the discipline of English Studies. Students new to Critical Theory should remember three important ideas about poststructuralism and the turn to theory:

1. Poststructuralism understands knowledge as contingent, political, and subjective and challenges structuralist beliefs in truth, meaning, and objective reality.
2. Poststructuralism invests itself in the proliferation of possible meanings; it does not seek one answer to a scholarly question but rather exhaustively to catalog the many potential answers that a scholarly question might elicit.
3. Poststructuralism both extends the concerns of structuralism, searching for objective methodologies to drive critical **praxis**, and rejects them, drawing attention to the ways in which structures themselves are subjective constructions of the critic.

As poststructuralism comes to influence and shape the branches of Critical Theory that fit under its larger umbrella, these three ideas determine the directions that they take.

Critical Theory's Influence in Different Fields of English Studies after Poststructuralism

While Critical Theory exerts notable influence across English Studies, it has the longest history and most powerful impact in the following fields: linguistics; literature; cinema, popular culture, and new media; rhetoric and composition; and digital humanities in English. Within each of these fields, individualized methodologies develop for how to engage with Critical Theory and how to use Critical Theory to promote that field's values. Examples from Literature and Rhetoric and Composition can demonstrate how this works and give a sense of the different appraisals of Critical Theory that emerge from specialized fields within English Studies.

Scholars of literature sometimes think of Critical Theory interchangeably with **literary criticism**, which we can define as a body of texts committed to examining, advocating for, and interpreting works of literature. This general definition for literary criticism encourages the inclusion of three types of texts as broadly connected to the work of theorizing literature:

1. **Nonfiction** literary works by prominent canonical authors that explain their own artistic vision. For instance, Philip Sidney's "An Apology for Poetry" (1595), Mary Wollstonecraft's "A Vindication of the Rights of Women: With Strictures on Political and Moral Subjects" (1792), T. S. Eliot's "Tradition and the Individual Talent"(1919), and Zadie Smith's "Two Paths for the Novel" (2008) might fit into a literature scholar's idea of what counts as Critical Theory.

2. Works of literary scholarship, which might include **peer-reviewed scholarly journal articles** and books that offer interpretations of literature. A book like Sandra Gilbert and Susan Gubar's *The Madwoman in the Attic: The Woman Writer and the Nineteenth-Century Literary Imagination* (1979), for example, is a work of academic scholarship, but it possesses deep connections to theoretical conversations about sex, gender, representation, and equality.

3. Nonfiction works from philosophy and other disciplines. To list just a few examples, scholars of literature will often contextualize their interpretations with theoretical concepts from outside of English Studies that connect to issues of social class (Pierre Bourdieu, sociology), gender (Judith Butler, comparative literature and philosophy), language (Jacques Derrida, philosophy), **sexuality** (Michel Foucault, history), or race (Frantz Fanon, philosophy and psychiatry). The examples that fall under this category directly fall under the category Critical Theory, and scholars of literature would share an interest in these works with scholars not only in other English Studies fields but also in other academic disciplines beyond English Studies.

When a scholar of literature discusses Critical Theory, they do so with a precise definition that assumes knowledge of these three types of critical discourse.

In contrast, specialists in rhetoric and composition often associate Critical Theory with rhetorical theory, which emphasizes how authors communicate with audiences for purposes of persuading, informing, and entertaining. Because of these interests, rhetoricians include different types of texts in their definition of theoretical discourse:

1. Works of ancient philosophy, which form the foundation of the study of rhetoric. For example, they might turn to Aristotle's *Poetics* (~335 BCE) or Plato's *Phaedrus* (~370 BCE).
2. Contemporary treatises on rhetoric, which connect the work of speaking and writing to the practices of everyday life. These treatises may be more theoretical in nature, or they may adhere more closely to our ideas about traditional, peer-reviewed academic scholarship. For instance, works of rhetorical scholarship like Kenneth Burke's *Language as Symbolic Action: Essays on Life, Literature, and Method* (1966) and Geneva Smitherman's *Black Talk: Words and Phrases from the Hood to the Amen Corner* (1994) assist specialists in rhetoric and composition with tying their understanding of how discourse works with broader theoretical concepts.
3. Nonfiction works from philosophy and other disciplines. As with their counterparts in literary studies, rhetoricians engage with theorists from outside of English Studies to provide a broader context for their claims. The lists of ideas and theorists that interest rhetoricians may differ from that of their counterparts in literary studies, but they also might use the same ideas and theorists to talk about their own area of interest.

As these categories make evident, scholars of rhetoric and composition have a slightly different understanding of Critical Theory than scholars of literature do. Both groups of scholars—as well as scholars across the many other fields of English Studies—would characterize themselves as engaging with Critical Theory, but their theoretical approaches include different types of readings and different ways of using theory to enhance their understanding.

Ultimately, specialists in different fields of English Studies engage with Critical Theory for different reasons, use it according to different methodologies, and encounter it from different perspectives. The most important thing for students new to Critical Theory to recognize as they immerse themselves more deeply in English Studies is that their coursework and reading will teach the theoretical vocabulary that they need to assist their intellectual endeavors.

Why Has Critical Theory Been Influential in English Studies? Why Have Some Practitioners Objected to Critical Theory's Influence?

Critical Theory has been influential in English Studies because it offers new ways to see texts, formalizes disciplinary procedures for thinking about texts, and provides new ways to articulate the larger significance of textual creation and analysis. Critical Theory "disciplines" the approaches that we take to reading and writing, and in so doing, it justifies the specialized training and conventions of analysis and expression that characterize English Studies as an academic discipline. As when a mathematician solves a problem and "shows their work" so that others can see how they arrived at the solution, practitioners of English Studies can point to their theoretical approach and its methodologies to "show their work" or explain how they arrive at an interpretation or mode of expression. Instead of interpretation or expression being a matter of opinion—"Everyone sees something different in a story" or "Different people have their own ways of expressing themselves"—interpretation and expression become regulated by the patterns of thought, methods, and outcomes that Critical Theory makes possible.

It is no accident that the rise of Critical Theory corresponds to the rise of the contemporary university. The interventions of state and federal governments, funding bodies, and accrediting agencies to regulate institutions of higher learning instigate new requirements for disciplines, including English Studies, to describe their work in terms that reflect common language for assessment and reporting. Critical Theory provides English Studies with that language, rendering "objective" those subjective processes of interpretation and expression that our discipline fundamentally values. Critical Theory creates a technical jargon through which to explain the analysis and creation of texts, and it institutes methods of analysis and creation for practitioners to follow. Further, after the radical political movements of the 1960s and 1970s, Critical Theory provides justification for disciplinary transformation and renewal, which includes revision of the **literary canon** to be more inclusive of writers of different genders, races, ethnicities, class statuses, and sexualities, as well as attention to issues of activism, social justice, and discrimination across the fields of the discipline.

Perhaps most importantly, Critical Theory has influenced English Studies because it inspires English Studies practitioners to ask different kinds of questions in their scholarship and offers new pathways toward expanding and deepening the possibilities for English Studies scholarship. Critical Theory makes it possible to advance interpretations that differ from the author's stated intentions, to evaluate the political impacts of texts on readers outside of a text's own historical context, and to understand texts not as works of genius but as cultural products. Further, it allows writers to codify their decisions as well as to situate themselves within larger social, cultural, and political conversations. Critical Theory frees scholars from some of the oldest conventions of English Studies, and it initiates new ways of seeing language, literature, rhetoric, and cinema.

Despite the powerful influence that Critical Theory has exerted over the evolution of English Studies into the twenty-first century, some teachers, scholars, and public intellectuals rejected the turn to theory or came to criticize it after watching what they believed to be its negative impact on the discipline. Critics of Critical Theory's influence on English Studies have tended to orient their objections in the following ways:

1. Critical Theory distracts practitioners of English Studies from their true purposes: understanding how language works; evaluating the conditions of rhetorical communication and reception; understanding the language, genres, and forms of literature; and celebrating literature as a unique human accomplishment.
2. Critical Theory introduces jargon into English Studies that alienates the public and makes it more difficult for us to communicate the value of English Studies to public audiences.
3. Critical Theory instigates interpretations that violate the legitimate purpose of scholarship in English Studies; training in English Studies does not prepare its practitioners responsibly to execute political, historical, sociological, anthropological, and philosophical projects, and scholarship that takes these pathways is not a genuine or authoritative contribution to new knowledge in the discipline.

At their heart, these reactions against Critical Theory reveal the anxieties that many English Studies practitioners feel about preserving what they see as the legitimacy of our discipline, our discipline's ability to connect to public audiences and to convince them that our work has value, and our discipline's deeply held beliefs about the proper boundaries and methods for analysis, scholarship, and creativity. Furthermore, some scholars today object to teaching undergraduates about Critical Theory. They believe that its moment has passed, and so students shouldn't learn about it, or they believe that Critical Theory is so thoroughly integrated into the discipline's methods that it does not require discussion independent from the other fields of English Studies. These shifting attitudes toward Critical Theory anatomize the ways in which our analytical, scholarly, and creative practices shift over time, and they show the ways that our personal values, convictions, and professional stature shape the work that English Studies practitioners do.

What Are the Conventions of Theoretically Oriented Work in English Studies? How Do Practitioners of English Studies Engage with Critical Theory to Inform the Work That They Do?

Theoretically oriented work in English Studies takes many different forms depending on the field in which one works. Specialists in the history of the English language, creative writing, professional and technical communication, English education, or digital humanities in English might be aware of theoretical perspectives that connect to Marxism, feminism, critical race theory, or **discourse theory**, among others, and that knowledge might influence the ways in which they write or teach, but it is not necessarily central to their goals. Theoretical approaches might inform their choices, but their objectives do not necessarily reflect what we might regard as a theoretical agenda or perspective. In contrast, Critical Theory holds larger sway over interpretation-focused fields of English Studies: literature; cinema, popular culture, and new media; and rhetoric and composition. Even still, these interpretation-focused fields of English Studies use Critical Theory in different ways, they find value in different theoretical approaches, and not all scholarship in these fields depends on Critical Theory.

Theoretically Oriented Scholarship in Literature

In literary studies, Critical Theory allows scholars to contextualize claims about works of literature beyond the author's intention and beyond the interpretations that the work itself elicits. The theoretical approaches that they take sometimes bleed into each other, but for the purposes of introduction, it is useful to view them as separate enterprises. In general, scholars of literature focus their engagement with Critical Theory through three predominant methodologies:

1. **new formalism;**
2. new historicism; and
3. theories of **identity**.

Learning a bit about each of these broad areas of theoretically oriented literary criticism assists students in understanding the scholarly conversation about the works of literature that they study.

Scholars invested in new formalism begin with the work of literature that they wish to examine. Much like the New Critics, they evaluate the formal structures of a text and the language that is used. From that point of entry, they evaluate the linguistic properties of the text that they analyze, the **performativity** of its language, and the ways in which the text's **lexicon** corresponds to philosophical ideas about **epistemology** and **ontology** as well as the temporal and geographic indexes through which we can understand the language of the text. This methodology for evaluating a literary work emphasizes its formal accomplishments, but unlike traditional formalism, it understands that forms are constructed categories and not universal truths.

Scholars invested in new historicism begin with the premise that any literary work is a product of the culture in which it was produced. They believe that by understanding the culture of the time—which includes nonliterary written works, **art**, technological innovations, political changes, and historical events, among others—we can then understand the work of literature. New historicists root their analyses in a broader cultural analysis that extends beyond the literary work, and they believe that approaching texts from this broader perspective allows new interpretations both of the work's significance in its own time and in ours.

Scholars invested in theories of identity focus either on the context of the work of literature that is their focus or on the author of that work. Their starting point is an identity category—social class, ethnicity, race, gender, or sexuality—that they believe the text or the author exemplifies. Evaluating the text through that identity category, their interpretation rests on whether the text exposes structural inequality, advances the cause of a marginalized other, or reveals a new model for understanding humanity.

In each of these cases, the critic strives to use the theory in order to come to a deeper understanding of the literary text under review. Whether that understanding is formal, historical, or in relation to identity, the desire is to create a broader critical context for understanding the work of literature. It is also the case that many critics deploy approaches that cross the divisions of these categories. Critics might ask theoretical questions that breach the divides between new formalism and theories of identity, between new historicism and formalism, and so on. In the end, theoretically oriented literary criticism encourages scholars to rely less on authors' stated intentions or their personal reactions as readers and more on objective, rational rubrics to ground their analysis.

Theoretically Oriented Scholarship in Cinema, Popular Culture, and New Media

In the study of cinema, popular culture, and new media, Critical Theory allows scholars to situate their claims about texts both in terms of their production and consumption as well as in terms of the ideas that they promote. Scholars in these fields focus on:

1. the distribution and technical decisions of studios, publishers, showrunners, producers, and directors that determine audience reception;
2. the performance decisions of actors and creative and rhetorical decisions of writers; and
3. audience reaction and broader cultural impact.

While the theories that dominate literary analysis also hold sway here, we should also pay attention to psychoanalytic theory and **fandom** theory as important components of this field.

Psychoanalytic theory drives theories of cinema, popular culture, and new media because it provides a structure for understanding visual representations of relationships between characters. Using psychoanalytic theory, critics discuss the power of the gaze or the power that some characters—or the film's director or audience—exert to **objectify** others or strip them of agency by perceiving them as passive things that exist only for the viewer's pleasure. Further, psychoanalytic theory provides a framework for understanding what audiences desire to see in cinema, popular culture, or new media, and how studios, publishers, showrunners, and directors attempt to meet the demands of that desire.

Fandom theory focuses more on the audience reception of cinema, popular culture, and new media texts, discussing the ways in which such texts create communities, discourses, and identities. By engaging with this theory, English Studies practitioners learn about how fans directly connect with texts by creating costumes for themselves that embody characters in them (**Cosplay**), writing new narratives that correspond to and extend to what happened in the published works for those characters (**fan fiction**), or that envision new possible futures for those characters, which are typically new sexual possibilities (**slash fiction**). Furthermore, they think about how fan cultures promote some texts over others and the influence that audiences exert over the production of certain types of texts.

Theoretically Oriented Scholarship in Rhetoric and Composition

Theoretically oriented scholarship in rhetoric and composition also borrows from the concerns of other fields, but it is not identical to them. Rhetoric and composition invests itself in addressing both the objective situations that produce rhetorical communication, as in Lloyd Bitzer's foundational "The **Rhetorical Situation**" (1968), and the subjective situations that shape speakers' rhetoric, such as Richard E. Vatz's "The Myth of the Rhetorical Situation" (1973). Rhetoric and composition finds a pathway through Critical Theory that not only addresses abstract ideas about identity and politics but also attends to the forms of written expression, both in regard to how we analyze it and how we create it.

What Is Critical Theory in the Twenty-First Century? Is Critical Theory Dead? How Does It Connect to English Studies, More Broadly Conceived?

Critical Theory remains central to English Studies today, even as practitioners of English Studies question its motives, utility, and outcomes. We cannot erase from our collective psyches the discipline that we have learned from Critical Theory, nor can we run from the changes in our discipline that the turn to theory initiated. The canon of literature is undoubtedly changed— and many would argue for the better—because of the interventions that Critical Theory has made, and the approaches of other fields in the discipline are also irrevocably changed, to acknowledge new ways of thinking about how language works, how identity impacts expression, and how written texts connect to broader social concerns.

In this regard, Critical Theory is not dead, nor is it dying anytime soon. That said, in the twenty-first century, many scholars have turned their backs on unilaterally theoretical readings, which ignore the author's intentions, disregard the emotional or personal responses of readers, and object to purely historical analyses. Theory is not dead, but we also are not consigned to its constraining orthodoxies as practitioners a generation ago might have been.

Further Reading

Barry, Peter. *Beginning Theory: An Introduction to Literary and Cultural Theory*. 3rd ed. Manchester: Manchester University Press, 2009.
  Introduces students to foundational Critical Theory approaches and helps students to use them.

Braudy, Leo, and Marshall Cohen. *Film Theory and Criticism: Introductory Readings*. 6th ed. Oxford: Oxford University Press, 2004.
  Anthologizes foundational readings in Critical Theory connected to cinema that span the twentieth century.

Macey, David. *Dictionary of Critical Theory*. London: Penguin, 2002.
Offers definitions and explanations of important terms and ideas that
students encounter in a Critical Theory Context.

Eagleton, Terry. *Literary Theory: An Introduction*. 1983. Anniversary Edition.
Oxford: Blackwell, 2008.
Explains the turn to theory in English Studies and discusses the
philosophical modes of thought that contribute to the rise of high theory at
the end of the twentieth century.

Foss, Sonja K. *Rhetorical Criticism: Exploration and Practice*. 4th ed. Long
Grove: Waveland Press, 2009.
Explores the processes of rhetorical criticism and the methodologies that
guide the use of Critical Theory in Rhetoric and Composition.

Lane, Richard J. *Global Literary Theory: An Anthology*. 1st ed. London:
Routledge, 2013.
Anthologizes significant essays and excerpts of Critical Theory looking
toward new developments in the twenty-first century; places special
emphasis on non-Western identities and theoretical approaches after 1990.

Lynn, Stephen J. *Texts and Contexts: Writing about Literature with Critical
Theory*. 7th ed. Boston: Pearson, 2016.
Introduces students to foundational Critical Theory approaches specifically
geared toward literary criticism and analysis.

Moi, Toril. *Sexual/Textual Politics: Feminist Literary Theory*. 2nd ed.
London: Routledge, 1985, 2002.
Offers an overview of Anglo-American and French Feminist approaches to
literary criticism.

Parker, Robert Dale. *Critical Theory: A Reader for Literary and Cultural Studies*.
Oxford: Oxford University Press, 2012.
Anthologizes key readings in Critical Theory from New Criticism through
Postcolonial Theory.

Porrovecchio, Mark J., and Celeste Michelle Condit. *Contemporary Rhetorical
Theory: A Reader*. 2nd ed. New York: Guilford Press, 2016.
Collects significant examples of Critical Theory in rhetoric spanning from
the middle of the twentieth century onward.

In this Case Study, we demonstrate techniques for integrating primary, critical, and theoretical sources to give your interpretations depth and breadth. We then offer engagement activities that you can use to help you better understand how to approach Critical Theory.

Everybody's a Critic—or Can Be: Reading Critical Theory and Becoming Part of the Critical Conversation

When we encounter a text—watch a movie, read a poem, sit in a public space, or view a performance—we often develop an opinion about what we have encountered. We react, and we make judgments about what we liked or did not like, what was good about it and what was bad, or what was most or least interesting or innovative. These opinions might be critical, but they do not really count as "criticism" by the academic definition that we use in English Studies. Criticism involves opinions, reactions, and responses, but it also involves entering an ongoing conversation in the discipline to complicate it, to add to it, or to change its direction completely. Part of that critical conversation involves an engagement with Critical Theory, which provides an apparatus for contextualizing our critical endeavors in English Studies within a larger intellectual framework that emerges out of many different disciplines. Your objective as a practitioner of English Studies is not primarily to write your own Critical Theory. Rather, it is to enter the existing critical conversation by engaging directly with the Critical Theory that informs it. This case study offers steps first for how to evaluate primary and **secondary sources** and then for how to integrate Critical Theory to enhance evaluations of primary and secondary material.

Reading to Interpret: The Primary source

Simply, a primary source is the primary object of analysis for a scholar in English Studies. Practitioners in different fields of the discipline focus their scholarship through different types of primary sources: linguists might use a word or example of a linguistic phenomenon; literary scholars might use a story, novel, play, or poem; scholars of cinema might use films, **television** shows, or videos; and rhetoricians might use political **speeches**, **blog** posts, or other examples of rhetorical communication. In general, across the fields of English Studies, criticism begins with primary source analysis, and that analysis attends to issues of **content**, form, and reception.

Activities for Critical Engagement

1. *Identify a primary source that you would like to analyze. What type of primary source have you chosen? Which field in the discipline focuses on this type of primary source? Refer to the chapter in this textbook that covers this field and perform a primary source analysis of the text of your choosing according to the conventions of the relevant field. Your analysis should recount your reactions, but it should not stop there. It should also deeply analyze both the content and the form of the source that you have chosen.*

2. *After you have analyzed the primary source of your choosing, evaluate what you have discovered. What about your analysis is unique? What questions arise from your judgments about content or form? What are the important takeaways of your analysis? Once you have answered these questions, propose a thesis statement in which you (a) make an observation about the primary source and (b) explain what that observation reveals or why it is significant to understanding the text as a whole.*

Assessing the Critical Conversation: What Can Secondary Sources Tell Us?

A secondary source provides background information, commentary, or interpretation that supplements or provides a context for your primary source analysis. The format of secondary sources varies. Most commonly, secondary sources that you and other scholars use will be published, written works. Other times, however, secondary sources may be interviews, voice recordings (podcasts or radio broadcasts), or video recordings, among other things. Some secondary sources have more authority than others. Scholarly, peer-reviewed sources:

a. are authored by a person or people with advanced training in the area of inquiry (a PhD);

b. include citations for quoted and paraphrased material as well as a list of works cited;

c. pass a rigorous review process wherein other experts on the topic confirm that the research is of publishable quality and contributes to new knowledge in the discipline; and

d. address an audience of experts.

In contrast, nonscholarly, non-peer-reviewed sources do not pass a rigorous review process, typically do not include citations and a bibliography of works cited, may not be authored by a person with advanced, specialized training, and often address a general audience. Both types of secondary sources may be valuable to understanding the larger conversation about a topic, but scholarly, peer-reviewed secondary sources hold more weight in an academic context.

When we want to establish our ideas in English Studies, it is important that we put those ideas into the broader context of what other scholars have already said. Sometimes, scholars will have directly commented on the primary source that is the focus of our own interpretation. Other times, scholars will have commented on issues that are tangentially related to our area of focus, or they will have commented on texts that are adjacent to the one that we are discussing. It is our responsibility as critics ourselves to attend to the existing critical conversation and to situate ourselves within it.

Activities for Critical Engagement

3. *Using a scholarly database available through your university's library, such as the* Modern Language Association International Bibliography, *find a scholarly, peer-reviewed book, journal article, or article in a book of collected essays that connects to your primary source analysis. What you choose may be directly about the primary source, or it may connect to your ideas about it. Then, conduct an evaluation of that source:*

   a. *Who is the author of the source and what are their credentials?*

   b. *What is the overall argument of the source? How does that argument agree with, contradict, contextualize, or complicate your ideas?*

      c. *Does this source use Critical Theory to provide a context for its analysis? If so, what are its theoretical engagements and/or biases?*

      d. *If you were writing a fully developed research paper on this topic, would you use this source? Why or why not?*

4. *Scholars often prepare for their scholarly endeavors by compiling an annotated bibliography. An annotated bibliography is a list of secondary sources, formatted according to a conventional citation format (APA, MLA, Chicago Manual of Style, etc.). Taking the secondary source evaluation that you conducted in the preceding activity, create an annotated bibliography entry:*

      a. *Cite the source according to the appropriate citation format for the field of English Studies that connects to your topic.*

      b. *Create a brief annotation (no more than three to five sentences) that summarizes the source's argument, explains its critical and theoretical context, and discusses its connection to the topic of your inquiry.*

5. *Having completed a full annotated bibliography, scholars may also prepare a literature review, a narrative piece that synthesizes their findings in their annotated bibliography. A literature review provides an overview of the critical conversation about a topic, grouping together sources with common points of view, drawing attention to conflicts or debates that shape the discussion about the topic, and noting the gaps in the critical conversation where new scholarship might be able to intervene. Most scholarly, peer-reviewed journal articles in English Studies provide some type of literature review, either integrated throughout the entire article or in one discrete section. Look back at the journal article that you have selected. Does it have a literature review? What does it highlight about the critical conversation that informs its own claims? What debates shape the field? How does the article intervene in the critical conversation?*

Confronting Critical Theory: How to Read Theoretical Sources and How to Use Them to Become Part of the Existing Critical Conversation or to Start a New One

While you may have had prior experience with analyzing primary sources and with conducting secondary source research, you likely are new to Critical Theory. Reading theory can feel at first like learning a foreign language. Its narrative structures are different from what you might be used to seeing (particularly in theoretical pieces by French authors, the argument of a theoretical piece will often come at the end and not the beginning), the vocabulary is unfamiliar, and the concepts are often abstract or feel disconnected from your areas of interest. However, as with studying a foreign language, the more practice that you get, the easier it is to understand and to use.

Activities for Critical Engagement

6. *Identify a theoretical piece to read. Your instructor may assign you something, or you may need to find something on your own. If you have received no other guidance, Roland Barthes's "The Death of the Author" is one option you might consider. Once you have identified what you will read:*
   a. *Read the piece for the first time, listing any words with which you are unfamiliar and that you do not understand in context.*
   b. *When you have completed this first pass through the text, take one to two minutes to jot down your initial reactions. What do you think the argument of the piece is? What did you find confusing about the piece? What, if anything, did you object to? Explain your answers.*
   c. *Look up the words that you listed on your first reading and define them. You might find the Johns Hopkins Guide to Literary Theory and Criticism, to which your library may have a subscription, helpful. Additionally, you might consider consulting a dictionary of Critical Theory.*
   d. *Once you have defined the words that you did not know, read the piece again, this time aloud. While you read, note any ideas that you think are particularly interesting or that*

> you find particularly applicable to a primary source or texts that you have encountered.
> e. Spend five minutes composing a paragraph in which you summarize the piece, explaining its main argument and supporting points, react to the piece, discussing your points of agreement and disagreement as well as how the piece might be useful in an English Studies context, and connect the piece to one primary source, describing how you could use the theory to understand the primary source more deeply.

How Does English Studies Help Us to See How Scholars Can Use Critical Theory to Find Their Own Voices?

Scholarship in English Studies often requires us to make interpretive claims that are, at least superficially, entirely subjective. By actively engaging with the larger critical conversation in secondary sources, as well as by understanding the theoretical underpinnings of that conversation, we can better understand our own critical allegiances, and we can do a better job of articulating where our interpretations come from.

9

English Education

When does a student first decide to major in English? Is it after they start their undergraduate program or before? Although English majors often declare their major after they begin their studies at university, they were usually inspired to read and to write by a high school English teacher. High school English classes provide a student with their first opportunity to read challenging literary works, such as a Shakespeare play, or to experiment with their own writing creatively and present it to their classmates. And if they were lucky enough to have had a teacher who encouraged them and pushed them to strive to be a better reader and writer, they may have come to college wanting to be an English teacher too. That positive experience in a high school English class can be a strong motivator to pursue a career as an English high school teacher. As an **English secondary education major** or English major with **Education Licensure or Certification**, students may have a much more focused career path at university than other English majors. To prepare students for a career in public high school teaching, English Education emphasizes coursework both in English Studies content—the study of literature and writing, for example—and in pedagogical approaches to classroom instruction, assessment, and student learning.

This chapter explores the typical secondary education program in English in the United States with careful consideration of the standards-based curriculum that oversees how English Education programs are structured at universities. We will explore some of those federal and state standards in order to understand how English Education is taught and regulated. Particular attention will be paid to the English courses that English secondary education majors must take to be fully prepared to teach English at the high school level and the controversies and concerns in English Education that inform how to teach high school students in the classroom.

Key Questions

1. What is English Education? How are English Education programs typically structured?
2. Why does the individual state have so much say over what prospective high school English teachers study?
3. What sorts of texts are studied in English Education? How are they analyzed? What are the similarities and differences between how English Education approaches texts and how English Studies more generally approaches them?
4. What are the conventions of English Education scholarship? What kinds of research and interpretation do English Education scholars do?
5. What is English Education in the twenty-first century? How does it connect to English Studies, more broadly conceived?

What Is English Education? How Are English Education Programs Typically Structured?

English Education, which we also call **English Language Arts (ELA)**, is the field that focuses on how to teach English in high school. It includes learning about language, reading, writing, and interpreting texts. According to the Center for Excellence in Education, ELA education is committed to justice, equality, and diversity. For this reason, its teaching and learning must be broadly and inclusively defined, and its practitioners—high school English teachers—must be both prepared to teach in the classroom and supported professionally. ELA teaching does not just require a passion for reading and writing but rather demands a passion for content, curriculum, instruction, and students. Issues of justice, equality, and diversity are central to the teaching and learning of ELA, shaping approaches to curriculum creation and assessment, **literacy** and language practices, the professional lives and identities of ELA teachers, and research about ELA teaching and learning.

At some universities, the English Education program is a single major that is taught by English and Education specialists. However, it is becoming more common for English secondary education majors to complete their program as a double major in both English and Education. Both approaches are highly structured, leaving little room for students to take many elective courses. Furthermore, English education majors do not typically complete minors in disciplines outside of English or Education. Secondary Education requirements for the English major usually include survey courses in British and/or American literature and a course in Shakespeare as well as courses that address non-English literature in translation and language study. As a result, English secondary education majors often require courses like **global literature**, history of the English language, or linguistics. Additionally, English secondary education majors usually take a **subject-matter methods course** in the teaching of ELA. Such a course focuses on the expectations of ELA at the secondary level, lesson planning, assessment, and classroom management. Prospective English teachers must understand the subject matter—that is, English Studies—in terms of content and in terms of how that content is taught most effectively to high school students. English secondary education majors will also gain field experience through classroom observation, practice teaching, and more formal student teaching near the end of their program, often called **clinical experience**.

English Education programs place considerable emphasis on pedagogical practice, classroom assessment, and the application of national and state standards to the teaching of ELA in addition to learning ELA content. As a result, the English Education major does not just learn how to adapt their own studies in an English program to the high school classroom but also gains practical experience in the teaching of those materials in order to be licensed as an English secondary education teacher.

Why Does the Individual State Have so Much Say over What Prospective High School English Teachers Study?

By state law, education is compulsory in the United States until sometime between the ages of 16 and 18, depending on the state. States are the primary regulators of K-12 education. High school English teachers play a critical role in the lives of adolescents and young adults because they provide the last opportunity required by law to ensure that American children are literate and able to succeed in a twenty-first-century world. In order to ensure that these teachers are able to fulfill this duty, English Education programs must conform to both federal and state requirements that are designed to guarantee literacy for all Americans. For example, the **Common Core State Standards (CCSS) Initiative** is an educational initiative from 2010 that details what K-12 students throughout the United States should know in ELA and mathematics at the conclusion of each school grade. The initiative sought to establish consistent educational standards across high schools; it also sought to ensure that students graduating from high school are prepared to enter credit-bearing courses at two- or four-year college programs or to enter the workforce.

There are five key components to the standards for ELA in the CCSS: Reading, Writing, Speaking and Listening, Language, and Media and Technology. Students and schools participating in the CCSS must show **adequate yearly progress**, meaning that some improvement each year is required. Periodic **standardized tests** are given to students to determine this progress. During high school, usually in Grade 11, students take one or more standardized tests, including for ELA, depending on their postsecondary education preferences and their local graduation requirements.

The CCSS has been controversial. In general, teachers and parents have viewed the standards as too many and too general. In terms of ELA, concerns have been raised that high school students are no longer required to emulate the writing of great authors nor to learn about those authors' lives. As a result, critics argue that students read literature with insufficient historical context and do not get the opportunity to practice good writing based on the texts they read. However, the CCSS has also encouraged curricular change that could have a positive impact on teaching ELA. It promotes an interdisciplinary approach to literacy that motivates students to develop expertise not only across reading, writing, speaking, and listening but also in general knowledge and the various disciplines. There is a new focus on **argumentation**, leading students to create effective argument or a position, defend it, write and speak about their ideas, listen to others, and ask questions. Students need to be able to read a text and evaluate the argument in it, both for reasoning and the evidence provided. Students are also expected to be prepared to read and write more complex texts by graduation. The notion of complexity applies both to the texts students read independently and to the increased complexity of the texts they learn to write. **Close reading** remains central to teaching ELA and often involves rereading with a goal toward understanding the author's message and making sense of the actual text. The use of technology and digital media is embedded throughout the Reading, Writing, and Speaking and Listening Standards in order to prepare students for the twenty-first-century workplace.

Thanks to these new initiatives and standards, new areas of emphasis in ELA have developed that English education programs must address. English education programs have had to adapt their courses to better prepare English education majors to meet the K-12 content standards. The changes help teachers align their instruction with the standards when they get to their own classroom. For example, English teachers are now required to teach technology and multiple literacies in the English classroom. For this reason, technology is now integrated into English education courses rather than taught separately to help English education majors learn how to incorporate it into their own classrooms. In previous decades, reading and writing skills were taught mostly at the early childhood and elementary levels. However, English high school teachers are increasingly responsible for reading and writing instruction as more and more struggling readers and writers enter the high school classroom. English education programs are including more instruction on teaching diverse learners as well as **English as a Second Language (ESL)** students.

For the English Education student who came to the field because they found their own high school experience in the English classroom so inspiring, all these standards and regulations can come as a surprise and may seem unappealing. Often students find the English Education program very different from what they imagined it would be. Rather than just talking about their love of books, English secondary education majors must spend a significant portion of their program learning how to create lesson plans that meet the requirements of the **College and Career Ready (CCR)** academic standards of their state. Their education courses can seem very disconnected from the love for reading and writing that first drew them to English Education. However, the global approach of standards, such as the CCSS, guarantees that ELA learning experience is of the same quality and consistency across high schools in the state. These standards also provide the tools English Education students need to identify and handle such problems as literacy issues or an inability to comprehend complex texts in any high school classroom.

What Sorts of Texts Are Studied in English Education? How Are They Analyzed? What Are the Similarities and Differences between How English Education Approaches Texts and How English Studies More Generally Approaches Them?

Like other English majors, English secondary education majors complete the standard requirements of the English program, but they also complete many courses focused on Education, which include instruction in pedagogical methods and the processes of learning. In their English courses, English Education students study the same literary works as other English majors, and they take many of the same courses as other majors. The CCSS states explicitly that high school students must read across **genres** including **prose**, **poetry**, and **drama** as well as **nonfiction essays** in Grades 9 and 10. It also states explicitly that high school students must read a play by Shakespeare and at least one by an American dramatist as well as engage with the foundational works of eighteenth-, nineteenth-, and early-twentieth-century American literature in Grades 11 and 12. Thus, to prepare to teach this content, English education majors must study literature. In addition, the CCSS provides a reading list of text exemplars for each grade.

What these reading lists make very clear is that, in order to learn the content needed to teach high school English, English secondary education majors must read broadly across American, British, and World literature. They will need to study literary works across genres and historical periods.

In addition to learning content, English secondary education majors must learn how to teach that content to high school students. Part of that instruction may come from modelling how literary works were taught to them in a university English course, but it will be the **English methods course** required for the English Education program that will provide most of the instruction in how to teach literary texts to high school students. This course teaches them about the national and state English standards and how these standards are applied to the teaching of ELA. Students

CCSS Grades 9–10 Text Exemplars

Stories	Drama	Poetry
Homer. *The Odyssey*	Sophocles. *Oedipus Rex*	Shakespeare, William. "Sonnet 73"
Ovid. *Metamorphoses*	Shakespeare, William. *The Tragedy of Macbeth*	Donne, John. "Song"
Gogol, Nikolai. "The Nose"	Ibsen, Henrik. *A Doll's House*	Shelley, Percy Bysshe. "Ozymandias"
De Voltaire, F. A. M. *Candide, Or The Optimist*	Williams, Tennessee. *The Glass Menagerie*	Poe, Edgar Allan. "The Raven"
Turgenev, Ivan. *Fathers and Sons*	Ionesco, Eugene. *Rhinoceros*	Dickinson, Emily. "We Grow Accustomed to
Henry, O. "The Gift of the Magi"	Fugard, Athol. *"Master Harold" … and the*	the Dark"
Kafka, Franz. *The Metamorphosis*	*Boys*	Houseman, A. E. "Loveliest of Trees"
Steinbeck, John. *The Grapes of Wrath*		Johnson, James Weldon. "Lift Every Voice
Bradbury, Ray. *Fahrenheit 451*		and Sing"
Olsen, Tillie. "I Stand Here Ironing"		Cullen, Countee. "Yet Do I Marvel"
Achebe, Chinua. *Things Fall Apart*		Auden, Wystan Hugh. "Musée des
Lee, Harper. *To Kill a Mockingbird*		Beaux Arts"
Shaara, Michael. *The Killer Angels*		Walker, Alice. "Women"
Tan, Amy. *The Joy Luck Club*		Baca, Jimmy Santiago. "I Am to You"
Álvarez, Julia. *In the Time of the Butterflies*		
Zusak, Marcus. *The Book Thief*		

CCSS Grades 11–12 Text Exemplars

Stories	Drama	Poetry
Chaucer, Geoffrey. *The Canterbury Tales*	Shakespeare, William. *The Tragedy of Hamlet*	Li Po. "A Poem of Changgan"
de Cervantes, Miguel. *Don Quixote*	Molière, Jean-Baptiste Poquelin. *Tartuffe*	Donne, John. "A Valediction Forbidding
Austen, Jane. *Pride and Prejudice*	Wilde, Oscar. *The Importance of Being*	Mourning"
Poe, Edgar Allan. "The Cask of Amontillado."	*Earnest*	Wheatley, Phyllis. "On Being Brought from
Brontë, Charlotte. *Jane Eyre*	Wilder, Thornton. *Our Town: A Play in*	Africa to America"
Hawthorne, Nathaniel. *The Scarlet Letter*	*Three Acts*	Keats, John. "Ode on a Grecian Urn"
Dostoevsky, Fyodor. *Crime and Punishment*	Miller, Arthur. *Death of a Salesman*	Whitman, Walt. "Song of Myself"
Jewett, Sarah Orne. "A White Heron"	Hansberry, Lorraine. *A Raisin in the Sun*	Dickinson, Emily. "Because I Could Not Stop
Melville, Herman. *Billy Budd, Sailor*	Soyinka, Wole. *Death and the King's*	for Death"
Chekhov, Anton. "Home"	*Horseman: A Play*	Tagore, Rabindranath. "Song VII"
Fitzgerald, F. Scott. *The Great Gatsby*		Eliot, T. S. "The Love Song of J. Alfred
Faulkner, William. *As I Lay Dying*		Prufrock"
Hemingway, Ernest. *A Farewell to Arms*		Pound, Ezra. "The River Merchant's Wife: A
Hurston, Zora Neale. *Their Eyes Were*		Letter"
Watching God		Frost, Robert. "Mending Wall"
Borges, Jorge Luis. "The Garden of		Neruda, Pablo. "Ode to My Suit"
Forking Paths"		Bishop, Elizabeth. "Sestina"
Bellow, Saul. *The Adventures of Augie March*		Ortiz Cofer, Judith. "The Latin Deli: An Ars
Morrison, Toni. *The Bluest Eye*		Poetica"
Garcia, Cristina. *Dreaming in Cuban*		Dove, Rita. "Demeter's Prayer to Hades"
Lahiri, Jhumpa. *The Namesake*		Collins, Billy. "Man Listening to Disc"

learn the current language arts methodologies and strategies for teaching various genres, literary perspectives, visual and digital literacies, and language approaches as well as their application in the classroom. They develop lesson plans in which objectives are aligned to state and national standards and assessments are aligned to the objectives. These plans also include a variety of teaching strategies, with an emphasis on meeting the diverse needs of students. The course helps them to understand how to access resources to improve instruction, advance the knowledge and practice of the field, and develop professionalism. English secondary education majors often explore in the methods course the developmental factors of adolescents and young adults that affect the teaching of ELA skills to this population. In doing so, they learn how to respond to the affective and cognitive needs of diverse populations and cross-cultural literacies through ELA curriculum.

Literature can enrich the lives of its readers by challenging them to think more deeply and perceptively about the lives of others. High school students often find challenging literary works rewarding, but these texts can be problematic for high school teachers. As prospective teachers of adolescents and young adults, English Education students must learn how to work constructively with the parents of their students. Often, teachers encounter conflict with parents who are unhappy with ELA curriculum and how it is being taught. Parents may even challenge the inclusion of particular texts in the high school classroom. However, the books typically targeted are usually ones that offer more diverse perspectives to young readers. Elie Wiesel's book *Night*, published in English in 1960, is one such text. It details Wiesel's experiences as a teenager with his father in two concentration camps during the Holocaust near the end of World War II. As a literary work, the text raises questions about genre. Is it a **novel**, **memoir**, or a **deposition** (as Wiesel has described it)? How much of it is true? Is it **creative nonfiction?** Along with other Holocaust literature such as Anne Frank's memoir *The Diary of a Young Girl* (publishes in English in 1952) and Marcus Zuzak's novel *The Book Thief* (2005), *Night* presents themes that are complex: the grief and sadness associated with war and violent death, the trauma and horror of genocide, the sexual abuse of children at the hands of adults, and the questioning of the existence of God. For these reasons, parents may view *Night* and similar books as inappropriate for study in a high school English class.

Nevertheless, such literary works provide meaningful insight into humanity—into both human strengths and flaws throughout history and around the world. In describing his experience during the Holocaust, Wiesel gives students the opportunity to better understand the horrors endured by Jews in the past and explore challenging concepts, including the role that **race** and discrimination play in violence, the different forms that resistance—spiritual, physical, or nonviolent—can take, and the attempts people make to maintain their dignity in the most dehumanizing situations. Students will, hopefully, empathize with Weisel's experience and recognize similar social injustices in the lives of people today. As a result, *Night* can initiate broader discussions about genocide, leading to a greater appreciation of the trauma experienced by enslaved Africans during the Middle Passage in the eighteenth and nineteenth centuries as well as the horror of the mass slaughter of Tutsis by the Hutus in Rwanda in 1994 and of Syrians by Syrian armed forces, Syrian opposition fighters, and members of the militant group Islamic State of Iraq and the Levant since 2011, the beginning of the Syrian Civil War. It can raise questions about human trafficking and sexual exploitation at home and globally. By allowing high school students to navigate worlds so different from their own, there is the likelihood that they will apply the lessons they learn from these texts to their own lives.

In addition to teaching literature, English secondary education majors introduce their students to language and literacy, creative writing, rhetoric and composition, and possibly even professional writing. The CCSS encourages teachers to move beyond literature to include nonfiction in their courses and to have their students write across a variety of genres, including **nonliterary expository essays**, poetry, **short stories**, and **digital storytelling** (text and visuals created on a digital platform). High school students today are more than interpreters of literary works. They are also active in the creative process, an experience that helps them to understand more fully the form and meaning of literature.

What Are the Conventions of English Education Scholarship? What Kinds of Research and Interpretation Do English Education Scholars Do?

Scholarship in English Education generally explores teaching methodologies and the student learning experience, requiring the collection of data in the field. With the advent of new technologies for collecting data more widely and deeply, research can now be conducted that uses **big data** rather than data collected from a limited number of classrooms with the result that the findings have broader implications than ever before. Additionally, interest in comparing U.S. education to that of other countries has become easier and, therefore, more common. English Education scholarship typically follows American Psychological Association (APA) style for publications in education journals but Modern Language Association (MLA) style for English Studies journals, reflecting the different emphases and values of research in Education versus those of research in English Studies. Because scholars in this field examine English Education in the high school classroom, **field research** (the collection of data outside a library or laboratory), with the appropriate university permissions to work with human subjects under 18 years of age, is required. Scholarly publications can be written by a single author or by multiple authors depending on the scope of the research project. English Education scholars explore all aspects of the field, but, not surprisingly, considerable attention focuses on **pedagogy**: the teaching of English secondary education majors at university and the teaching of English in the high school classroom.

One significant approach in English Education scholarship is to examine controversies that arise in the high school English classroom. In 1996, the Oakland Unified School District school board of Oakland, California, passed a controversial resolution recognizing the legitimacy of **Ebonics** or **African American English (AAE)** as an African language. The resolution set off a firestorm of media criticism and ignited a national debate. In the case of the Oakland Unified School District, African Americans were not a minority. Rather, they comprised 53 percent of the school district population. Students K-12 were all adversely affected by Oakland's lack of a language education policy around the issue of Ebonics. The resolution sought to address the problem by providing education in Ebonics, using the students' primary/home language as a bridge to teaching them **Standard American English (SAE)**. English Education scholars have examined the controversy over the intervening years in order to determine the lessons learned by educators from the debate and the furor that followed. Even today, this is the situation for twenty-first-century African American students in urban districts nationwide. Despite the national uproar and negative, distorted media treatment around Oakland's Ebonics Resolution, the District was on the right track—that is, using the students' home/mother tongue to teach them language and literacy skills.

As this example makes clear, concerns about diversity in English Education extend to literacy. In 2016, the Conference on College Composition and Communication (CCCC) issued a revised statement on Ebonics and **students' right to their own language**, advocating for new research and teaching that will build on existing knowledge about Ebonics to help students value their linguistic-cultural heritage, maintain Black **identity**, enhance their command of the **Language of Wider Communication**, and master essential reading, writing, and speaking skills. Ebonics is crucial to Black identity and, like Black lives, it matters. Consequently, teachers need training to provide their students with adequate knowledge about Ebonics and help them overcome the prevailing stereotypes about the language and learning potential of African American students (and others) who speak Ebonics.

In addition to recognizing language variation among students of color, English Education is moving toward **decolonizing the English curriculum** and classroom in the twenty-first century. High school English courses have long been dominated by white authors, largely European, thereby marginalizing minority authors in the process. Even though the curriculum for ELA has increased diversity and multiculturalism, whiteness remains the focus with no radical revisioning of language and literary study. Many of the English texts studied and the approaches to analyzing those texts privilege middle-class, white standards. Decolonizing means disrupting this privilege in the classroom.

For English Education, pedagogical content knowledge is the foundation upon which teaching is built in ELA. However, there is recognition of a need to move away from teaching only canonical literature, limiting the range of writing genres, and emphasizing a common, standard **dialect**. High school English teachers are very aware of the changing nature of texts and youth culture, the linguistic diversity of students today, and the increasing number of struggling readers and writers in their classrooms. Transitioning that awareness into actions that will address these concerns is the future of English Education scholarship and practice.

What Is English Education in the Twenty-First Century? How Does It Connect to English Studies, More Broadly Conceived?

As the NCTE website makes clear, English Education is always looking for innovative ways to improve classroom learning. One such approach is the use of games to achieve learning outcomes. Gamification in education is the application of game playing, such as rules of play, point scoring, and competition with others, in order to engage students with problem solving. It can be an important teaching and learning strategy because it increases student motivation and engagement. For example, many high school English teachers use Kahoot!, a games-based learning platform that generates multiple-choice quizzes accessed via a Web browser or **mobile app**. The platform also creates Jumble questions that require players to place answers in a correct order rather than just selecting a single correct answer. Kahoot! can be used to review students' knowledge, for formative assessment, or to provide a change from traditional educational activities. Enough interest has been generated in gamification in education that the New York City Department of Education has partnered with the Institute for Play to establish a public school (Grades 6 to 12), Quest to Learn, that is centered around game-based learning. Backed by the MacArthur Foundation and the Bill and Melinda Gates Foundation, the school follows a curriculum created by teachers and game designers that encourages collaboration, role playing, and simulation. The goal is to encourage students to embrace active learning, problem solving, and complex challenges for a richer learning experience. Losing is just as important as winning in a game-based educational environment; failure is part of that learning experience.

Much of the current focus of English Education in ELA is on bringing greater diversity to literature and literacy in the classroom. Over the past two decades, the number of students of color and children of immigrants has increased. Consequently, English Education recognizes the need for greater diversity in the literary works taught at the high school level and for increased training of English secondary education majors to teach those texts effectively. According to the United States Census Bureau, the diversity of the population in the United States will continue to grow. However, book publication for children and teens does not reflect these changing demographics. The University of Wisconsin-Madison's Cooperative Children's Book Center (CCBC) provides a yearly report on the number of multicultural titles in print. In comparison to mainstream titles, the number of published multicultural titles by and about people of color remains low. A 2013 CCBC survey of 3,600 titles reveals that only 3.3 percent were about African Americans, 2.1 percent were about Asian-Pacific Americans, 1.5 percent were about U.S. Latinas and Latinos, and 0.6 percent were about Native Americans. High school students are not able to easily read literary works that reflect the diversity in the world around them, including possibly their own classroom.

Current scholarship in the field of English Education reflects this concern. Jamie Campbell Naidoo and Sarah Park Dahlen in *Diversity in Youth Literature: Opening Doors through Reading* (2013) and Michael Varvus in *Diversity and Education: A Critical Multicultural Approach* (2014) all note the significant absence of human, cultural, linguistic, and family diversity in children's and young adult literature. Publishers are not publishing books that accurately reflect the American life, including realities about appearance, behavior, economic circumstance, **gender**, sexual orientation, national origin, **disability**, social **class**, spiritual belief, and weight. In addition, exactly how to address issues of race, especially with respect to African American students, in the English classroom has been the focus of many recent articles in *English Education*, the journal of the Conference on English Education (CEE). Learning how to address issues of race and cultural diversity in their students' lives has become a major objective for teachers in today's high school English class. The inclusion of literary works that present such diversity in the high school curriculum reflects similar concerns with diversity in the other fields of English Studies.

Further Reading

Bell, Kevin. *Game on: Gamification, Gameful Design, and the Rise of the Gamer Educator*. Baltimore: Johns Hopkins University Press, 2017.
   Presents case studies of gamer-educators and game-derived techniques to help instructors learn effective gamification in education.

Burke, Jim. *The English Teacher's Companion.* 4th ed. Portsmouth: Heinemann, 2013.
Presents the instructional methods for ELA.

Caughlan, Samantha, et al. "How English Language Arts Teachers Are Prepared for Twenty-First-Century Classrooms: Results of a National Study." *English Education*, vol. 49, no. 3, 2017, pp. 265–97.
Analyzes a national study of English teacher preparation at universities and colleges in the United States.

Chappuis, Jan, Rick Stiggins, Steve Chappuis, and Judith Arter. *Classroom Assessment of Student Learning: Doing It Right, Using It Well.* 2nd ed. New York: Pearson, 2012.
Helps educators to conduct effective classroom assessment.

Devereaux, Michelle D., and Chris C. Palmer, eds. *Teaching Language Variation in the Classroom: Strategies and Models from Teachers and Linguists.* New York: Routledge, 2019.
Brings together teachers and linguists to present current scholarship and practical tools for teaching language and language diversity in the ELA classroom.

Foster, Harold M. "English Education: An English Educationist at Work," in *Teaching College English and English Education: Reflective Stories*, ed. H. Thomas McCracken, Richard L. Larson, and Judith Entes, pp. 260–70. Urbana: NCTE, 1998.
Presents a first-hand account of an English Education professor's experiences teaching in an English Education program in the United States.

Martinez, Danny C. "Imagining a Language of Solidarity for Black and Latinx Youth in the English Language Arts." *English Education*, vol. 49, no. 2, 2017, pp. 179–96.
Examines how English teachers can provide space in the classroom to make sense of their racialized experiences.

Orelus, Pierre, Curry Malott, and Romina Pachaco, eds. *Colonized Schooling Exposed: Progressive Voices for Transformative Educational and Social Change.* New York: Routledge, 2016.
Explores neocolonialism and its effect on student learning, especially the education of Native Americans, Latino/as, and African Americans.

Smagorinsky, Peter, and Melissa E. Whiting. *How English Teachers Get Taught: Methods of Teaching the Methods Class.* Urbana: NCTE, 1995.
Analyzes the educational experiences of preservice teachers.

Shafer, Robert E. "Out and about in English Education: How it Was!," in *Teaching College English and English Education: Reflective Stories*, ed. H. Thomas McCracken, Richard L. Larson, and Judith Entes, pp. 127–38. Urbana: NCTE, 1998.
Presents a first-hand account of an English educator's career in the United States.

Stewart, Donald C. "Becoming an English Teacher: More by Accident Than Design," in *Teaching College English and English Education: Reflective Stories*, ed. H. Thomas McCracken, Richard L. Larson, and Judith Entes, pp. 21–32. Urbana: NCTE.
Presents a first-hand account of how an English teacher in the United States was drawn to the profession.

In this Case Study, we examine how to develop a basic lesson plan in ELA for a high school English class. The specific focus is teaching the literature and language of multicultural literature in the Grade 12 English class. We offer engagement activities that you can use to help you better understand how to design a general unit plan with two assignments: a classroom activity and a formal assignment (written or oral).

Multicultural Literature Lesson Plan for ELA

Creating a Lesson Plan for an ELA Unit According to State Standards

ELA standards for a high school English class require the development of units that focus on a topic that incorporates literary works, such as those found on the CCSS reading lists. The general structure for unit lesson plans is as follows:

Overview of Unit

- Purpose
- Duration (how many classes/weeks)

Background Resources

- Reliable online background resources for the topic

National and State Standards

- CCSS (if states has adopted those standards)
- Individual State

You will find some examples on the ancillary website for the textbook.

Activities for Critical Engagement

1. *Go back to the text of this chapter and review the CCSS reading list for Grades 11 and 12. Select a text that qualifies as multicultural literature to be the focus of your Lesson Plan. If possible, choose a text you have already read or one*

of the shorter poems. Otherwise, read an online synopsis of the selected literary work. How did you determine that it is multicultural? Why did you pick it over the other options on the list?

2. Taking into consideration the length and complexity of your selected literary work, determine how many classes or weeks your high school students will spend on it. Explain your justification. Now write an overview (five to seven sentences) explaining the focus of your ELA unit and how the selected literary works fit into it.

3. Find two reliable online resources (podcast, video, visually engaging website, etc.) that will provide your students with background information on your unit. The resources may focus on the selected literary work or on the topic of the unit more broadly.

4. Now go to the state government website for ELA standards in your state. Spend some time reviewing them and try to determine three standards that your unit on multicultural literature will potentially fulfill. Briefly explain how you chose these standards. What was particularly challenging in the selection process?

Classroom Activity: Literature Circle

A group activity in the high school classroom is an excellent way to get the students engaged with and talking about a literary work. Literature circles are particularly productive in achieving these goals. Small groups of students gather together to discuss a piece of literature in depth. The discussion is guided by the students' responses (not the instructor's responses) to what they have read. They may talk about events and characters in the book, the author's craft, or personal experiences related to the story. Literature circles provide a way for students to engage in critical thinking and reflection as they read, discuss, and respond to books. Collaboration is at the heart of this approach. Students reshape and add onto their understanding as they construct meaning with other readers.

Activities for Critical Engagement

5. *Remember: you are the instructor here, not the student. How would you get students to work together in order to discuss the literary work themselves? Think back to your own English classes in high school and college. What sort of in-class activities got you engaged and talking? Design a literature circle for your students that draws on two of the activities you engaged with as a student.*

6. *In your role as a teacher, how will you assess your students in the literature circles? Come up with a grading rubric that would explain to your students how you would evaluate them.*

7. *Go back to the three state standards for your ELA unit. Which of those standards does this activity fulfill? Why?*

Formal Assignment in ELA

You may think assignments in a high school English class are designed according to the teacher's interests and expertise. In fact, they are not. Every formal assignment in the class must align with ELA standards set by the individual state. Teachers must list the standards that the assignment fulfills as part of the ELA unit. And the assignment must incorporate some of the five key components of ELA standards. Those components are as follows:

- Reading
- Writing
- Speaking and listening
- Language
- Media and technology

Alignment with the state standards is essential to creating a uniform and global learning experience for ELA across the United States.

Activities for Critical Engagement

8. *Read the selected literary work for your unit. What do you find most interesting or compelling about it as a reader? What sort*

of formal assignments did you complete in your own high school and college English courses that engaged you?

9. Create a written or oral assignment that will require your students to analyze the literary work, incorporating two of the five key components of ELA standards listed above. Your assignment might require your students to read the literary work and analyze the text in writing. Or it might require your students to read the literary work and record an oral presentation using technology.

10. In your role as a teacher, how will you assess this writing assignment? Come up with a grading rubric that would explain to your students how you would evaluate them.

11. Go back to the three state standards for your ELA unit. Which of those standards does this assignment fulfill? Why?

How Does English Studies Help Us to Understand the Teaching of ELA in the High School Classroom?

We may be surprised to learn that the teaching of ELA in the high school classroom is so highly regulated, especially in terms of the literary works that may be taught. However, English majors learn to read and analyze a broad range of literature and other texts, providing them with the ability and flexibility to draw connections across literary works, historical periods, and various cultures. As high school English teachers, they bring this expertise into their own classrooms.

Whether or not you become an English Education major, understanding something of how literature is taught in the high school classroom, the role and implementation of standards, and the design of meaningful assignments will help you to engage with and appreciate the activities and assignments in your own English classes at college.

10

English Studies in the Digital Age

If you are a fan of the *Harry Potter* books or movies, you are likely familiar with the *Daily Prophet*, the printed wizarding newspaper with "magical" images that continually change as you peruse the pages. For example, the wanted poster of Sirius Black that appears on the newspaper's magical frontpage in the film *Harry Potter and the Prisoner of Azkeban* (Alfonso Cuarón; 2004) depicts Black in action contorting his face, making him appear more villainous than his description in the written article. For many people, this dynamic visual and textual newspaper may seem the fictional creation of J. K. Rowling's imagination. However, as we move in the real world from the printed to the digital text, such imaginary publications blending print with new technologies are a reality. We are rendering text beyond print into increasingly complex digital formats with the result that technology is having a significant impact on the text forms we read and the ways we read them. Not surprisingly, digital and technological interfaces and tools are changing the ways we create and study literary works as well as practice and teach writing in the English Studies classroom.

The chapter will contextualize the "digital" in terms of more traditional approaches to English Studies, particularly creative writing, digital rhetoric, and computers and writing, as well as the digital humanities. We will explore the potential for technology to help us see texts in new ways and its related challenges.

Key Questions

1. What impact is technology having on English Studies today? Why do we need to know about it?
2. How do we use new technologies effectively in English Studies? Can only computer experts (or nerds) do it?
3. What are the conventions of digital applications and new technologies in English Studies scholarship and creative activity? What kinds of research and interpretation do such practitioners do?
4. What is the role of technology in English Studies in the twenty-first century? How does it connect to English Studies, more broadly conceived?

What Impact Is Technology Having on English Studies Today? Why Do We Need to Know about It?

Given the proliferation of technology in our lives today, we often describe ourselves as living in a digital world, one in which we are constantly engaging with our **smartphones**, **tablets**, or computers. Without question, technology is influencing how texts are produced as evidenced by the increasing number of digital books available to read online. Students today borrow **e-books** online from the library rather than pull a print copy off the bookshelf and can rent their course textbooks in e-format at a reduced cost. They conduct research using online search engines, such as Google or Google Scholar, that index information found on the internet as well as online subscription databases, such as the *Modern Language Association (MLA) International Bibliography*, *JSTOR*, *Project MUSE*, *CompPile*, and *ERIC*, that deliver articles, book reviews, and scholarly citations. New developments in technology are influencing the way we create and assimilate literary works, the way we analyze them, and even the way we teach them. It is essential that English Studies majors know how to use digital interfaces as part of the discipline and appreciate the need for proficiency with technology in order to be productive in the ever-expanding digital environments of the twenty-first century.

At the same time, we must also recognize that access to technology is not equal across the United States. Despite the fact we think that every American owns a computer or smartphone and has access to the internet, that is not true. There remains a **digital divide** based on **race**, **gender**, income, education, and geographic location. Some people do not have access to computers and other digital devices; some people do not know how to use them; and still others do not have a reliable connection to the World Wide Web. Therefore, it is equally important that students not only understand the impact of technology for English Studies as a discipline but also have access to that technology in order to learn its effective application.

How Do We Use New Technologies Effectively in English Studies? Can Only Computer Experts (or Nerds) Do It?

English Studies has generally embraced technology even if individuals choose not to use it beyond word processing and email. Computers, smart devices, and digital tools have opened up the discipline to new platforms for analyzing and producing text. In fact, the willingness of creative writing and of rhetoric and composition to become significantly more digital in recent years has encouraged the acceptance of the more specialized field of digital humanities, which promotes the application of digital tools and methods to the study of all humanities disciplines, including English Studies.

Electronic Literature

Electronic literature is a genre of literature created on digital devices, including the computer, tablet, and smartphone, that cannot be transferred from its digital space to any other format because its design and meaning are tied directly to that space. Consequently, electronic literature cannot be readily printed because it must be read and experienced in digital format. The genre employs a broad range of technologies to create such literary works as **hypertext** poetry and prose, **digital poetry**, online collaborative writing projects, **interactive fiction**, computer-generated texts, and narratives composed using email, social media, or podcasts. It may even build **chatbot** characters or narrators that are run by computer programs or **Artificial Intelligence (AI)** and conduct auditory or text communication.

Early examples of electronic literature include hypertext fiction, such as Shelley Jackson's *Patchwork Girl* (1995), published on **CD-ROM** by Eastgate Systems. Based on Mary Shelley's gothic novel *Frankenstein* (1818), *Patchwork Girl* tells the story of Mary Shelley building the creature's female companion using visual images of female body parts stitched together by text and image. The story can be entered at different points, and text and image can be clicked on to take the narrative in different directions. In 2011, Touch Press Inc. first published T. S. Eliot's *The Waste Land* (1922) as a **mobile app** for **Apple iOS**. The app includes a critical edition of the poem that scrolls vertically on the screen with a **digital facsimile** of the original manuscript with Ezra Pound's handwritten notes. In addition, there are dramatic readings of the poem by Eliot himself as well as by actors including Alec Guinness, Jeremy Irons, Ellen Atkins, and Viggo Mortensen and a visual performance of the poem by the actor Fiona Shaw. With these digital enhancements, the reading experience becomes more interactive and immersive than reading a printed book.

The argument can be made that audiobooks are also a form of electronic literature. The 2015 **podcast fiction** series *Limetown* exemplifies a new approach to the audiobook by blending it with radio theater techniques. *Limetown*'s narrative unfolds in a series of investigative reports that reveal the fictional disappearance of over three hundred people at a neuroscience research facility in Tennessee. Writers are also turning to **microblogging**, social media, and text messaging as platforms for creating and distributing their creative writing. Electronic literature and the media it employs offer the ability to publish without a press or literary agent, allowing writers greater creative control and distribution control of their own work.

Computers, Rhetoric, and Writing

As digital rhetoric demonstrates, digital media both informs and motivates the viewer to action. For this reason, students benefit from learning the practical applications and implications of writing by exploring complex concepts such as visual rhetoric, issues of access, and the social implications of online writing. Of particular interest is the role of the computer as an environment where writing can be facilitated in a variety of ways.

Practitioners often focus on the production and consumption of digital, **multimodal**, and new media texts. The majority of scholars who study the influence of computers on the writing process seem to agree that engaging students in the production of such multimodal/digital texts is crucial to the learning process for a digital world. The field encourages the use of sampling, remixing, and file sharing that invites students to conceive themselves as reproducers or coauthors of digital compositions as well as consumers of these artifacts.

Digital Humanities

The digital humanities is the academic field that actively uses computer applications and **digital technologies** for the study of the humanities, including English. It is a methodological approach more than it is a focus on specific texts and tools. Digital humanists are interested in both quantitative results, such as word frequencies or network visualizations in texts, as well as qualitative results, such as literary analysis based on those quantitative results. Even though digital tools (including MS Office, social media, blogs, wikis, websites, etc.) are used by all fields of English Studies, the digital humanities is its own distinct field: one in which computing and the humanities intentionally intersect for the purposes of practical tool development and reflection on the nature of representation. The digital humanities in English Studies not only employs technologies for the research, creation, preservation, and pedagogy of texts but also for the humanistic interrogation of these technologies as texts become increasing digitized and digital.

Digital humanities tools have broad applications in that they can analyze large quantities of text quickly and efficiently. For example, the *Oxford English Dictionary* online offers much more content than the multivolume print version ever could. The dictionary is really a large online database of all (or almost all) written words in the English language. It not only allows users to look up word definitions, pronunciations, and etymologies but also allows them to study the most frequently cited authors and texts in the dictionary, view graphical timelines of word collection for the dictionary, and access a historical thesaurus that provides a taxonomic (or classification) index of language history.

Such tools can provide statistical analyses of immense **corpora** of text and do it well, but it is essential that the practitioners understand how to read statistical results accurately if the results are going to be meaningful. One of the challenges for digital humanists is convincing others unfamiliar with the field of the accuracy of their findings: if the tools tell us something about the text that we suspected, did we really need the tools, and, if the tools tell us something new, can we really trust the results?

What Are the Conventions of Digital Applications and New Technologies in English Scholarship and Creative Activity? What Kinds of Research and Interpretation Do Such Practitioners Do?

Digital humanists in English pursue a broad range of research activities, including the critical analysis of literary works using digital tools, the creation of electronic and online editions of literature, the preservation through digitization of original literary artifacts, and the design and fabrication of digital tools for the analysis of text—all of which are valued equally as scholarly endeavors. Traditionally, computer-facilitated text analysis has been a major focus of the digital humanities. Using algorithms developed by linguists, computer scientists, and statisticians, digital humanists track word frequency, co-occurrence, and statistically generated classifications on large textual corpora, such as all the issues of *The New York Times* or all novels in British literature written by women in the nineteenth century. The results allow for **distant reading**, a type of textual analysis that finds patterns in vast quantities of text using computational tools. This approach often uses data visualization tools to create graphical representations of the **dataset**. By using such visual elements as charts, graphs, and maps, digital humanists can potentially identify trends, patterns, and outliers that have not been previously recognized.

Practitioners have also worked closely with librarians to encourage the digitization of physical texts, especially medieval manuscripts, incunabula (pre-sixteenth-century printed books), and rare print books. The creation of digital facsimiles has allowed for greater access by scholars and students to rare texts. However, with the creation of such facsimiles, the original physical artifact is seen and touched less frequently, which may seem like a good idea but actually encourages limited access to the original and the misperception that the facsimile accurately represents the physical original in every way. Such digital preservation only succeeds if scholars, students, and librarians alike recognize the distinction between the original artifact and the digital facsimile and have access to both. Equally important is the long-term curation and reliable access to digital and digitized texts. For example, the HathiTrust is a large-scale collaborative repository of and highly functional access platform to a broad digital **archive** of print material from university libraries around the world as well as copyrighted and public domain materials digitized by Google, the Internet Archive, and Microsoft. Such repositories of digital and digitized materials support emerging forms of research, teaching, and learning in the twenty-first century.

What Is the Role of Technology in English Studies in the Twenty-First Century? How Does It Connect to English Studies, More Broadly Conceived?

Technology intervenes in every field of English Studies in the twenty-first century. Philologists trace the history of the English language using such digital tools as the *Oxford English Dictionary* online. Linguists work with online linguistic corpora like the Corpus of Contemporary American English (COCA) in order to determine how words are used at a particular moment in time. Practitioners in cinema and new media studies engage with technology to create artifacts that blend text and image both in print and online. Professional writers and technical communicators employ a variety of software programs to design workplace documents both in print and online as well as write about new technologies. Even English education students must learn to engage with technology in the classroom, from smartboards to learning module systems (LMS) to online assessment tools. The **Common Core State Standards (CCSS) Initiative** also requires high school teachers teach their students digital literacy—that is, the technological skills needed for living, learning, and working in the twenty-first century.

Creative writers are also turning to new technologies to produce literary works that are more multimodal than ever before and draw on emerging technologies. Mobile apps are increasingly popular platforms for literary creation, and there is a growing interest in designing literary works for smart devices, such as Jörg Piringer's *Tiny Poems*, **minimal poetry** designed specifically for the small screens of the Apple Watch, iPhone, and iPad. Other creative writers are turning to gaming platforms to include Virtual Reality and Augmented Reality technologies.

Readers of electronic literature are participating more in the experience of the digital text. They do not merely read and view a breadth of media in a creative work but experience it by touching the screen and interacting with it. Released in 2014, the mobile app **novella** *Pry* tells the story of a veteran from the first Gulf War from his visual perspective as he goes blind. Each chapter is a different immersive experience. The reader may have to drag their fingers across lines of text so that the words are read aloud, or they may find the text expands without their control. The reader has to figure out how to read and control the content much like playing a video game, as the boundary between text and video increasingly blurs. In such a way, technology is revisioning book design and enhancing the reading experience.

Technology is also encouraging people to analyze literary works in new and often surprising ways. Given public interest in technology and its application in our society, Digital humanities scholarship and pedagogy has gained a public awareness that other fields of English Studies have not. For example, when the print novel *The Cuckoo's Calling* was published in 2013 by Sphere Books, the author Robert Galbraith was supposedly a first-time author and former member of the Royal Military Police. However, the novel was better written than expected for a new author, and questions quickly arose about authorship. A reporter from the *Sunday Times* who had been tipped off that the real author might be J. K. Rowling contacted Patrick Juola, a computer scientist and digital humanist, to find evidence to prove that Rowling was the author. Juola had developed the program JGAAP (Java Graphical Authorship Attribution Program) that mathematically analyzes the degree of similarity across a body of writing. By looking at Galbraith's language choices, the program could quantify the degree of similarity between Rowling and Galbraith. If they were completely different, this variation could effectively rule out Rowling as an author and discredit the tip. If they were very alike, especially in comparison with other authors of the same genre, it would indicate that she was the possible author. The results, while not definitive proof, revealed that the novel was likely written by Rowling or by someone who wrote in a very similar style. Public interest in the eventual identification of Rowling as the author, a fact to which she ultimately admitted, was significant.

Nevertheless, technology does not always give us the results we want and often contributes to an online culture of racism and sexism through data discrimination. Safiya Umoja Noble, a digital humanities scholar, has examined how race and gender manifest themselves on technology platforms. Much of her research has focused on how biases against people of color and women are embedded in search engines, such as Google. Despite Google's supposedly impartial algorithm, using fairly neutral language, such as "black girls," on the search engine platform used to result in sexually explicit webpages as the top hits until Google became aware of Noble's work and changed the algorithm. Unfortunately, Google has yet to make similar changes to the algorithm for the search term "asian girls" as a quick online search clearly (and unfortunately) demonstrates. In contrast, the search term "white girls" produces very different results. Similarly, online filters and social media aggregators often privilege **Standard American English (SAE)**. They are not programmed to recognize such variations of SAE as **African American English (AAE)** and will flag postings in AAE as "rude" or "toxic." To overcome the racial biases of these technologies, we need to reconsider the role of language for search terms and for digital communication. The creators of these tools must recognize that there is a diversity of speech online and develop technologies that are inclusive of language variation and can produce nonracist and nonsexist results. Otherwise, minorities will simply be further marginalized online.

The digital humanities has grown in recent decades as a field across disciplines, including English, and has become more self-reflective. Attention is turning not just to the creation and revamping of digital tools but also to the examination of the communities who produced and are producing these tools as well as to the digital humanities community itself. Not only is there a recognized need to attract more women and minorities as scholars to the field, but also there is a growing interest in examining the role that women and minorities have played historically in the execution of digital tools. For example, the first digital humanities tool, an electronic concordance of the writings of Thomas Aquinas begun in the 1950s by Fr. Roberto Busa, a Jesuit scholar, and with the help of IBM, was created largely by women (nuns), most of whose names were never associated with the project. And one of the largest and best known digital humanities projects of recent years, Google Books, has been built by the labor of anonymous African American and Latina workers who scan the books. Such efforts to identify and, if possible, address issues of diversity in the digital humanities work toward the goal of breaking down the digital divide in academia, including in English Studies.

Just as technology has, to greater and lesser degrees, changed the ways in which people live in the twenty-first century, it has changed the norms, opportunities, and possibilities for work in English Studies. Both teaching and research are being increasingly mediated through digital technology, and the skillset its practitioners learn is highly marketable in the twenty-first-century workplace. In today's world, the average person spends a good portion of the day with their eyes fixated on a digital screen—emailing, texting, using social media, and googling information. To raise and maintain public awareness of the relevance of English Studies in the digital age, students as well as scholars and teachers must engage effectively with the general public through digital media in order to present their research and creative activity, highlight their technological skills, and provide outreach in the discipline to nonspecialists. English Studies today is a rich, innovative, flexible field that reveals the ways in which technology shapes our approaches to creation, communication, and interpretation.

Further Reading

Bolter, J. D. *Remediation: Understanding New Media*. Cambridge: MIT Press, 1999.
  Examines how new media draws from and refashions old media.

Earhart, Amy E., and Andrew Jewell, eds. *The American Literature Scholar in the Digital Age*. Ann Arbor: University of Michigan Press, 2010.
  Explores the development of digital American literature scholarship.

Eyman, Daniel. *Digital Rhetoric: Theory, Method, Practice*. Ann Arbor: University of Michigan Press, 2015.
  Examines the impact of digital rhetoric on a variety of disciplines, including English Studies.

Fitzpatrick, Kathleen. "Giving It Away: Sharing and the Future of Scholarly Communication." *Planned Obsolescence: Publishing, Technology, and the Future of the Academy*. New York: New York University Press, 2011.

Discusses Open Access approaches to scholarship with new technologies.

Hayles, N. Katherine. *How We Think: Digital Media and Contemporary Technogenesis*. Chicago: University of Chicago Press, 2012.
Studies how we think through, with, and alongside media.

Hindley, Meredith. "The Rise of the Machines." *Humanities*, vol. 34, no. 4, 2013. https://www.neh.gov/humanities/2013/julyaugust/feature/the-rise-the-machines.
Addresses the development of the digital humanities from the mid-twentieth century on.

Kirshenbaum, Matthew G. "What's the Digital Humanities and What's It Doing in English Departments?" *ADE Bulletin*, vol. 150, 2010, pp. 55–61.
Explains what the digital humanities offers English Studies.

Klein, Lauren F., and Matthew K. Gold, eds. *Debates in the Digital Humanities*. Minneapolis: University of Minnesota Press, 2016.
Discusses the emerging debates in the digital humanities.

Noble, Safiya Umoja. *Algorithms of Oppression: How Search Engines Reinforce Racism*. New York: New York University Press, 2018.
Examines how search engines create a culture of racism and sexism through data discrimination.

Ryan, Marie-Laure. *Cyberspace Textuality: Computer Technology and Literary Theory*. Bloomington: Indiana University Press, 1999.
Explores texts and textuality in the context of new electronic technologies.

In this Case Study, we examine how technology can be used to produce a short narrative of creative writing as well as to analyze literary works. We offer engagement activities that you can use to help you better understand the application of technology to English Studies.

Applying Digital Tools for Creative Writing and Literary Analysis

It may seem that technology is just a tool for writing essays, finding scholarly materials, and reading text. However, all forms of technology can help writers and readers to explore literature and literary production in new and exciting ways. And you do not have to be a computer expert to do so!

Twitterature

Twitterature (Twitter + literature) is the creation of a literary work, poetry or prose, using the microblogging service of Twitter. The limited number of characters permitted for a tweet can make writing creatively for this platform challenging. Yet some writers in this genre have sent out enough text to microblog an entire novel using Twitter, Facebook, and even text messaging. You just need to be creative within the limitations of the platform.

The first part of this case study will require you to tweet, so you will need to download Twitter to your smart device (if you do not already have the mobile app). Consider creating a Twitter account just for this case study if you are concerned about who will view your tweets. When you send your tweets, be sure to use the designated hashtags for your course, college, instructor's Twitter handle, and your group's name so that everyone in your class, including your instructor, can follow each other's twitterature creation.

Activity for Creative Engagement

1. *In 2009, Alexander Aciman and Emmett Rensen came out with* Twitterature: The World's Greatest Books in Twenty Tweets or Less *(Penguin). Select a favorite novel, and try to summarize it in fewer than ten tweets without giving the title of the book. How easy is it to create such a summary? What techniques did*

you use in terms of writing style, humor, etc., to enhance (or shorten) your summary? Ask someone in the class to follow your summary on Twitter to see if they can identify the novel you summarized. How successful were they? What helped or hindered the identification? If you have access to Aciman and Rensen's book, check to see if they tweeted the novel you chose. If so, how does their summary compare to yours?

2. *Divide into groups no smaller than three students and give your group a name that you can use for a hashtag. Leave the classroom with your smart device, and walk around your college campus. As a group, create a short story that uses text in the form of ten to fifteen tweets with photos from your college campus, animations, and/or other visuals to enhance your narrative. Be sure to include one photo of all the members of your group in order to get credit for the activity.*

Word Clouds and Word Frequency

Data visualization is form of visual communication that involves the creation and analysis of visual representation in the form of statistical graphics, such as tables, graphs, and information graphics. In English Studies, we analyze text rather than numbers and, therefore, use visuals, such a word clouds and word frequency, in addition to graphs in order to visualize the results. One of the first popular online data visualization tools for text was Wordle. It classified itself as a "toy" for generating word clouds that highlight the most frequent words in text. The emphasis on its entertainment rather than scholarly purposes is significant. You may have seen such visuals generated by Wordle or other popular data visulaizations tools for text in PowerPoint slide presentations. The results are eye-catching but often do not provide the depth of detail in terms of word frequency that more scholarly data visualization tools do. For example, Voyant is a much more powerful and accurate online tool for visualizing large bodies of text, but its detailed results and generation of graphs can be intimidating to someone new to data visualization. Nevertheless, by reconfiguring literary narrative as word clouds and word frequency charts, we may be able to look at prose and poetry in ways that can generate new scholarship.

Activity for Critical Engagement

3. *You will need to find a current popular data visualization tool for analyzing text. Be aware that, as quickly as such tools appear, they just as quickly disappear as the technology evolves. Try searching online for a popular data visualization tool that is web-based or for a mobile app. You can also refer to the textbook website for several recommendations. Open the tool you select on your computer or, once installed, the mobile app on your smart device. You should have a field on screen in which you can paste text. Try writing your full name and that of each family member and/or friend. Then click on the appropriate button to generate a word cloud. Try changing colors and/or fonts if the tool you selected allows for such changes. What is the effect? Which colors and fonts do you find particularly visually appealing? Do you find any other features in the data visualization tool you selected intriguing?*

4. *Now you are going to see what results you get when creating a word cloud using the text of a long literary work. Go to Project Gutenberg (https://www.gutenberg.org/) and select a novel of your choice. Open up the novel in the Plain Text UTF-8 format, which will be the text without images or odd formatting. Select and copy the text of the entire novel. Note: You may want to avoid copying the front and back matter that provides the digitizing and edition details. Now paste all that text into the text field of your data visualization tool. Click on the appropriate button to generate a word cloud. Take some time to examine the results. Again try different colors and fonts to see if such changes highlight the word cloud differently. What words from the novel are particularly large in the word cloud? Are they character names, abstract nouns, verbs, or something else? Given what you know about the novel, are the large words significant to the narrative? What about the words in your word cloud that are small or absent? Would you have expected them to be larger or smaller? Why?*

5. *Now go to Voyant Tools (https://voyant-tools.org/) and paste the plain text of your novel into the text field on the opening webpage. Click on "Reveal" to see your results. Voyant generates a variety of data visualizations, but we will start by focusing on the*

word cloud. Does that word cloud give different results when compared to the one generated by the other date visualization tool you used? How would you explain the differences? Voyant also provides such details as vocabulary density, average words per sentence, and most frequent words. Does this information reveal anything significant about the novel? What about the other information that Voyant provides? Is it helpful? Why or why not? Given the results you see on the screen, can you determine a possible area of research for your novel that these data visualizations enhance?

How Does English Studies Incorporate the Use of Digital Tools Effectively?

Technology can help us to approach and challenge texts in new ways. However, teaching students how to use the technology efficiently and to interpret the results effectively are essential requirements if English majors are going to move forward successfully and creatively with digital tools. Many English students do not consider themselves "techies," although they have the ability to imagine new ways of seeing texts. It is tempting to simply trust the technology at the expense of propagating errors and misinterpreting results. However, technology can also encourage us to reach out beyond our discipline and work collaboratively with others in order to employ the wide of range of digital tools available productively in English Studies.

Glossary

3-D To appear three-dimensional or to appear to inhabit physical space with dimensional qualities such as width, depth, and height, providing the perception of depth. 3-D technology is used to enhance the experience of viewing a work of cinema in a movie theater.

Abbreviation A shortened form of a word or phrase that can be used in place of its full form.

Academic Writing A style of writing that is used by researchers to designate intellectual boundaries of a discipline or area of expertise. Students also use this style of writing in course assignments.

Accent A distinct pronunciation of language that is typically associated with a certain geographical location or social group.

Action Film A genre of media texts such as films or television shows, which give the characters a set of challenges. Action typically includes violence, physical altercations, and frenetic chases.

Adaptation A narrative that has been converted from one format to another. For instance, many popular books might be adapted for the screen, whether television or movie, so that fans and newcomers alike can experience the text in a new way.

Adequate Yearly Progress (AYP) The measurement of how public schools and school districts in the United States are performing based on the results of standardized testing as defined by the federal No Child Left Behind Act of 2001.

Adjunct A term applied to faculty who are hired under short-term contracts and who are not eligible for the protections of tenure.

Advertisement A written text, sound recording, or cinematic text that a company or individual uses to promote a product, a service, or event.

Aesthetic The type of response elicited by a work of art and/or the values that drive the creation of a work of art. Aesthetics connect to responses such as pleasure and revulsion and formal distinctions such as the sublime and the beautiful.

Affective Relating to a mood, emotion, or attitude.

African American English (AAE) A variety of American English spoken by some African Americans in the United States; also known as African American Vernacular English (AAVE) by linguists and commonly called Ebonics by nonlinguists.

African American Vernacular English (AAVE) A variety of American English spoken by some African Americans in the United States; also known as African American English (AAE) by linguists and commonly called Ebonics by nonlinguists.

Alliteration The repetition of the same initial sound within a phrase, line of poetry, or sentence to create emphasis or affect the tone of a piece of writing.

Alphabetism A word formed from the initials of a phrase that must be spelled out, such as BFF (Best Friends Forever).

American Sign Language (ASL) The primary sign language used by deaf communities in the United States and most of Anglophone Canada.

Analog Game Games that are played without the use of technology; board games are a primary example.

Analogy (1) The linguistic process by which a word form, often deemed irregular, is changed according to a recognizable, regular pattern governed by rules. (2) The process of transferring meaning or information from one subject to another.

Analysis A detailed examination of the elements of a text.

Animation A type of media that uses illustration or modeling to convey visual messages, often by having an artist draw a collection of successive drawings that portray a single movement or gesture. Animation includes an array of techniques from stop motion to CGI.

Annotated Bibliography A bibliography of cited works, in which each citation is followed by a short descriptive and evaluative paragraph that summarizes the source and analyzes its usefulness, relevance, and accuracy.

Anthology A published collection of written works, such as poems or short stories.

Apple iOS The mobile operating system for Apple smart devices.

Applied Research Research that seeks solutions to problems and that results in practical applications as opposed to publication in scholarly, peer-reviewed venues.

Archival Materials Primary source materials that document the heritage of a particular person, group, or organization.

Archival Research Research that involves the study of unedited primary sources, which are held in an archive, special collections library, or other repository.

Archive (1) A collection of unedited primary sources, historical documents, or other important records. (2) The physical space where such sources are located.

Argument A practice in written or oral communication in which the writer or speaker attempts to persuade their audience of something. Academic writing is often structured around persuasive arguments.

Argumentation The style or form speakers or writers use to convey their ideas and to present evidence in order to persuade an audience.

Aristotle's Rhetorical Appeals The three categories of persuasive rhetoric introduced by the philosopher Aristotle: ethos (the credibility of the author), logos (facts or reason), and pathos (emotions).

Art Creative or imaginative works (painting, sculpture, writing, etc.) that give their audience aesthetic pleasure because of the relationship between their elements.

Arthouse Cinema Cinema produced for the purpose of advancing or pushing the boundaries of creativity in the form. Aimed at niche markets rather than the mass market, arthouse films focus on the artistic process of filmmaking and screenwriting, and they are often described as having a serious tone. Arthouse films typically only see a limited release or a showing at a film festival.

Artificial Intelligence (AI) Computer systems that can perform tasks that typically only humans can perform.

Artist's Statement An artist's written description of their inspiration, creative process, and message of their work.

Audience The spectators, listeners, or readers of a piece of communication or artwork.

Augmented Reality A computer-generated interactive experience in which the real world is digitally enhanced to create a partially immersive environment in real time.

Auteur Theory or Auteurism The theory that a film is an extension and portrayal of a director's unique perspective and that the film should explicitly appear to be so.

Author The creator of any written work, such as a novel, short story, play, or nonfiction work.

Autobiography A written work that an individual composes to tell the story of their own life in its entirety.

Avant-Garde A term used to describe art that is ahead of its time or experimental.

Banking Concept of Education The idea that educators possess all power and knowledge and deposit information in students to be stored and then returned to the instructor without question or modification.

Basic Cable Television A service that allows viewers to pay to access television programming from a large number of available channels without an antenna. They can also add packages to supplement their basic service for an additional fee.

BCE Before Common Era or previous to year one CE (common era). This term is now preferred to BC (Before Christ) to place ancient texts, people, objects, or time periods.

Big Data Extremely large, complex datasets that are too voluminous for traditional data-processing software to manage and analyze.

Bildungsroman A type of novel that details a protagonist's development from childhood to adulthood; also called a "coming of age novel."

Biography A written work in which the author details the life of another person.

Biolinguistics The study of biology and the evolution of language.

Black American Sign Language (BASL) A dialect of American Sign Language (ASL) used most commonly by deaf African Americans in the United States; also known as Black Sign Variation (BSV).

Black Sign Variation (BSV) A dialect of American Sign Language (ASL) used most commonly by deaf African Americans in the United States; more commonly known as Black American Sign Language (BASL).

Blog Originally weblog, a webpage or website that can act as a journal, an ideological platform, a record, and more. Typically, blogs are run by individuals or small groups and are regularly updated for their audience.

Blu-Ray A disk format that stores a much larger amount of high-definition data and video than regular DVD formats.

Board Games A set of objects including a playing surface, pieces and/or cards, and rules that people use for entertainment purposes. Board games may include a narrative component. Examples include chess, *Monopoly*, and *Ticket to Ride*.

Brainstorming A common technique of idea generation in which a group or individual spontaneously generates words or phrases that pertain to a particular purpose.

Cable Television A system through which consumers gain access to television programs by cable wiring rather than broadcast signals.

Capstone A culminating project such as a paper, presentation, or research experience, or clinical experience that synthesizes the skills of a student's major. Also referred to as a senior exposition, portfolio, or thesis.

Case A grammatical category that is determined by the syntactic function of a noun or pronoun.

CD-ROM Popular in the 1990s, a pre-pressed optical compact disc containing data that can be read by a computer.

CE Common Era or following the period now referred to as Before Common Era (BCE). This term is now preferred to AD (*Anno Domini*) to place ancient texts, people, objects, or time periods.

CGI Computer-generated images or imagery. CGI has become somewhat synonymous with special effects created with computer technology. A particularly well-known use of CGI would be the dinosaurs in 1993 movie Jurassic Park.

Chapbook A very small published written work (usually poetry) that typically consists of up to forty pages.

Characterization The description of the distinctive nature of a character within a work of Literature.

Chatbot A computer program or Artificial Intelligence (AI) that converses via auditory or textual methods.

Cinema (1) The production of films or television, (2) a theater at which these films are shown, or (3) the film industry as a whole.

Citation Style The method in which sources are given credit in a written text, which varies by academic discipline. The most common citation styles that undergraduates will encounter in English Studies are those of the Modern Language Association (MLA) and the American Psychological Association (APA).

Class A social hierarchy based on socioeconomic status and other markers such as education and professional occupation.

Classical Education A form of education developed during the Middle Ages based off of the traditions of Western culture. A classical education would typically include education in mathematics, philosophy, history, art, music, literature, Greek, and Latin.

Classical Rhetoric A type of rhetoric that emphasizes the contributions of Greek and Roman philosophers, including special attention to the Sophists and Roman rhetoricians.

Clause A unit of grammatical construction that includes a verb and sometimes a subject and can function as a simple sentence or part of a sentence.

Clinical Experience An authentic teaching experience in which an Education student near the end of their program is given control of a classroom and works with real high school students to ensure that they are ready to become a teacher.

Clinical Linguistics The study of language disorders and their treatment from the context of linguistic theories and methods.

Close Reading An analytical method in which the critic examines formal details or patterns in a text and then uses those details or patterns as a key to deeply engaging with the text's content or meaning. Proponents of Close Reading believe that the text alone—without reference to the author, historical knowledge, or other information external to the text—provides all that readers need to understand or interpret it.

Close-Up A shot used in visual media wherein the subject is tightly framed, using zoom technology or filming at a short distance.

Cloud Storage A platform available to users over a network such as the internet on which data is managed, maintained, and stored.

Clustering A common technique of idea generation in which a group or individual links related ideas and concepts. This also might be called mapping or webbing.

Cognition The mental process of acquiring knowledge and meaning.

Cognitive Approach A psychological approach that assumes our way of thinking affects our patterns of behavior. In literary studies, cognitive approaches integrate the scientific understanding of the brain with the analysis of literary works.

College and Career Ready (CCR) Students who graduate from high school prepared to succeed in postsecondary opportunities, such as college or career paths.

Comic Book Films The cinematic adaptation of a comic book, usually that of a superhero. These films often hinge on action such as high-energy fight scenes, car chases, or shootouts and sometimes fall into the science fiction category when characters gain superpowers.

Comics A narrative that is illustrated and told in the form of a sequential arrangement of images and words, comics are often printed in magazine format and sold separately and collected. More and more comics are converting to digital and offering subscriptions for consumers to download and read the issues using their devices.

Commentary An expression of opinions or explanations about an event or situation.

Commercial A television or radio segment created to advertise something such as a product, service, or event, which is interspersed between content intended to entertain or inform the audience.

Common Core State Standards (CCSS) Initiative Appearing first in 2010, the CCSS sets a precedent for the academic progression of students K-12, specifically in what they should know of English Language Arts (ELA) and mathematics.

Communication The act of connecting between individuals or groups, through verbal or nonverbal means, in order to exchange information.

Communication Studies An academic discipline that studies how humans communicate with one another, from conversations that occur in real time to how companies advertise their products.

Comparative Analysis Analysis that involves looking at the original object of study alongside other related objects to trace similarities and differences.

Composition The full range of practices involved in the writing process from its initial stages to a finished product.

Computational Linguistics The study of language that applies the techniques of computer science.

Computer-Assisted Textual Analysis The use of a computer to scan a specific text for analytical purposes.

Computing Technology The equipment associated with computers, such as hardware and software, which allows for digital processing to take place.

Connotation (Connotative Meaning) The implicit feeling, association, or idea that is suggested from a word in addition to its explicit meaning.

Console Equipment that users connect to a television or screen to play video games or access online content to stream.

Consumer Culture Under capitalism, consumer culture is the economic strategy through which the processes of commercial exchange (buying and selling) are rendered as important features of identity, community, and society in general.

Content The information, ideas, meaning, or story of a text.

Context (1) The events, information, ideas, or culture through which one situates an object of study or understands something. (2) The words and sentences that surround any part of a discourse and help determine its meaning.

Contingent Faculty University instructors on part-time, temporary, or full-time contracts who are not eligible for tenure or promotion to assistant, associate, or full professor rank. These instructors teach for lower pay and often do not have comprehensive benefits packages for health care or retirement. This term is sometimes used interchangeably with adjunct.

Continuity Editing The process in cinema that focuses on maintaining a fluid visual narrative for the viewer.

Copyediting The step in the writing process where the process of reviewing and correcting is implemented in order to improve readability and correctness, ensuring that the text is free of error and that the text communicates clearly to its audience.

Core or General Education Requirements The set of courses or competencies required by a university for all students; these introductory courses generally include breadth across liberal arts disciplines, which provides a foundation upon which students can build in their more specialized major coursework.

Corpora (singular Corpus) (1) Large or complete sets of works of writing. (2) Large bodies of text stores in electronic databases.

Cosplay The practice by fans of creating costumes of their favorite characters from movies, television, video games, or books and wearing those costumes to signal their membership in their particular fandom and to connect with others who share their interests.

Counterculture A community within a larger culture, which has values that defy the conventions of the larger culture from which they emerge. Countercultures tend to be quite large and challenge the status quo to effect broad social change.

Craft The way an author uses skills and techniques that they observe in what they read as a model for their own creative writing.

Creative Genre The type of writing in which a creative writer chooses to specialize, such as poetry, fiction, or creative nonfiction.

Creative Nonfiction A form of prose writing that draws on facts and real events and is written in an aesthetically pleasing style. Sometimes referred to as CNF.

Creative Process The process that writers follow when constructing poems, plays, short stories, novels, and more.

Credential Proof of qualification in a profession, which might include a certificate or a degree.

Creole A language developed from a mixture of different languages that is used in a community and acquired by children as their native language.

Critical Race Theory A theoretical framework that examines the society and culture in a written work as they relate to elements of race, law, and power.

Criticism The analysis and judgment of a literary or artistic work, which may take a positive, neutral, or negative view and relies on evidence to substantiate its claims.

Critique (1) In creative writing, the term to describe the feedback offered to authors in writing workshops. (2) In critical theory, the term used to specify criticism that uses a theoretical apparatus and methodology to organize its inquiry.

Crunched The processing of large amounts of data or performance of very complex procedures, usually done with the assistance of a computer.

Cultural Hegemony A theory of power, which emerges out of the Marxist theories of Antonio Gramsci, that explores the ways in which those who are oppressed by the dominant culture or who lack power within that culture participate in the institutions, social norms, and value systems that oppress them.

Cultural Studies A theoretical framework that emerges out of Marxism to account for the influence of social class on the production and consumption of arts or culture.

Culture Industry A theory spearheaded by Theodor Adorno and Max Horkheimer, the culture industry describes how popular culture under capitalism functions like an industry. This works in two ways: the industry creates the products the people need, and the products available create the need in the people. The culture then maintains this idea that people need products that are unimportant to health, survival, or happiness, such as expensive cars, clothes, and homes.

Data A set of informative quantitative or qualitative values.

Database A collected set of data that is stored and organized, usually on a computer, for easy and quick access.

Dataset A collection of related information that can be manipulated individually or analyzed as a whole by a computer.

Declension The linguistic inflection pattern of nouns, pronouns, and adjectives indicating case, number, and gender.

Decolonizing the English Curriculum The effort to de-emphasize privileged white canonical authors and include a greater number of marginalized minority authors in the English Studies classroom.

Deconstruction Analysis that centers on the instability and ambiguity of language, asserting that meanings are unstable due to their dependence on arbitrary signifiers. By assessing language and how a text might unravel itself, deconstruction seeks ways to discover the text's internal contradictions and to destabilize the text's meaning.

Deep Reading The active process of thoughtful and deliberate reading for the purpose of enhancing the understanding and enjoyment of a text; term coined by Sven Birkerts in *The Gutenberg Elegies* (1994).

Demystify To make a difficult topic easier to understand. This term is often deployed in Marxist theory to discuss the ways in which consumer culture mystifies the ways in which individuals are oppressed by socioeconomic class. In this context, theory helps to expose hidden meanings and agendas.

Denotation (Denotative Meaning) The straightforward definition of a word or phrase, absent any associations or values that speakers, writers, listeners, or readers might assign.

Deposition The testimony of a witness in a civil or criminal proceeding taken before trial.

Description A spoken or written representation of something or someone.

Descriptivism The objective analysis and description of how language is actually used by a group of people in a speech community.

Descriptivist A person who focuses on how a language, such as English, is really used rather than giving rules for that language on what is correct and not correct.

Diachrony (Diachronic Analysis) An approach to the analysis of language by focusing on the development and evolution of language throughout history.

Dialect A regional or societal form of language that is distinguished by features of grammar, vocabulary, and pronunciation.

Dialectical Logical discussion of sometimes opposing or different ideas and opinions. The "dialectic" is a term introduced to philosophy by Georg Wilhelm Friedrich Hegel, and it orients analysis through the interrogations of binary oppositions (weak/strong, woman/man, passive/aggressive, etc.).

Dialogic Meaning is generated by the ongoing dialogue between interlocutors and does not exist in static isolation.

Dialogue Communication between two or more individuals or groups within a text such as a book, movie, or play.

Diaspora The forced migration of a people from their homeland. Examples of diaspora include the Jewish diaspora in the aftermath of anti-Semitic violence such as the Holocaust and South Asian, African, and Caribbean diasporas in the aftermath of British colonialism.

Diction Word choice in a text.

Dictionary A reference book or tool that lists words alphabetically and gives their definition, pronunciation, etymology, and usage.

Digital Divide The economic and social inequality of access to technology, computers, and the internet.

Digital Facsimile A photographic copy of a text in digitized form.

Digital Game A game played using technology; video games are a primary example.

Digital Media Content that is digitized and can be transmitted easily over the internet or other computerized networks.

Digital Poetry Poetry that employs computer programming or processes in the composition, generation, and presentation of the text.

Digital Rhetoric Rhetoric that focuses on the ways in which digital media are used to inform, persuade, and motivate action.

Digital Scholarship The use of digital technologies and tools to find evidence to achieve scholarly research goals.

Digital Storytelling The presentation of a narrative through multimedia, such as text, images, video, audio, social media, and/or interactive elements.

Digital Technologies Electronic tools, systems, devices, and resources that generate, store, and/or process data; examples include computers, smart devices, social media, and online games.

Digital Tools Various digital applications that assist people in their everyday lives, such as cell phone apps, word processing software, slideshow presentation programs, and more.

Direct Analysis Analysis that involves focused attention on a primary source or text.

Direct Object The noun or pronoun that receives the action of the verb in a sentence..

Disability A condition connected to mental or physical health that affects movement, cognition, or sensory perception and that may create differences in an individual's approach to tasks, thinking, knowing, or feeling.

Discipline A particular branch of knowledge with normative habits of thought, methods, terminology, and areas of inquiry.

Discourse Continuous text (written or spoken) longer than a single sentence. Fields outside of linguistics, such as rhetoric and composition or critical theory, sometimes attach additional connotations to the word "discourse" that emphasize motivated speech and the connections between discourse and the communities of which we are a part.

Discourse Analysis The study of the ways in which language is used between people in written, spoken, or sign language use.

Discourse Community A group of people with shared values or interests and agreed upon conventions for communicating.

Discourse Marker A word or a phrase that plays a role in managing the flow and structure of discourse.

Discourse Theory A theoretical framework that focuses on power relationships and the ways in which they are initiated, preserved, and expanded in written and oral communication.

Distant Reading A term coined by the scholar Franco Moretti to describe a technique for analyzing vast numbers of texts with the assistance of digital tools and technology; the opposite of Close Reading.

Document Design The use of layout and visual elements to create a unified document that effectively communicates information and meets audience needs.

Dolby Surround Sound A recording technology in which four channels of audio are encoded onto two different audio tracks, which are then put into stereo program sources such as DVDs or television broadcasts. The use of two separate tracks gives the illusion of sound that encompasses the audience.

Drafting The step in the writing process where one prepares a preliminary version of a text that will later be revised. Polished pieces of writing typically require multiple drafts and revisions.

Drama A composition in prose or verse that uses dialogue or pantomime to portray a story involving conflict usually intended to be acted on the stage; a play.

Dramaturgy The process of composition and representation of theatrical or dramatic works.

DVD Meaning digital versatile disc, a DVD is a compact disc that stores large amounts of data, typically used for audiovisual materials such as movies or television seasons.

DVR Meaning digital video recorder, this piece of equipment allows people to digitally capture broadcast television programs to be viewed at their convenience, rather than at the time when they originally air.

Early Modern English A variant of English used primarily from about 1500 to 1700, specifically represented by written documents from 1476 to 1700. Examples of Early Modern English include Shakespeare's *Hamlet* and Milton's *Areopagitica*.

Ebonics The term used by nonlinguists to refer to a variety of American English spoken by some African Americans in the United States; linguists refer to it as African American English (AAE)) or African American Vernacular English (AAVE).

E-book The electronic version of a book that can be read on a digital device.

Ecocriticism A theoretical approach that uses issues connected to the environment, nature, and ecology as the analytical framework through which to understand cultural texts such as literature.

Ecolinguistics The study of language in the context of the ecology and environment in which language groups are embedded.

Editor A professional employed by a periodical or publisher who is responsible for shepherding writing toward publication. Editors identify promising projects, secure feedback to improve the final product, and coordinate copyediting, production, and marketing of publications.

Education Licensure or Certification The certification process by which prospective teachers become licensed to teach within a given area after completing required coursework, degrees, tests, and other specified criteria; an English major with Education Licensure or Certification is completing a double major in English and Education.

Elective A course that is not made mandatory for a student's core, major, or minor requirements but which a student can "elect" to take and continue to make progress toward their degree.

Electronic Literature A genre of literature created on digital devices that cannot be transferred from its digital space to any other format because its design and meaning are tied directly to that space.

Emoji A digital icon used to express emotion within electronic communication.

Empathy The ability to pick up on, understand, and share the feelings of another person.

English as a Second Language (ESL) The teaching of English to individuals whose native language(s) are not English.

English Language Arts (ELA) The subjects in K-12 education that include reading, writing, listening, speaking, and viewing for the purpose of developing a student's ability to comprehend and use the English language correctly and effectively.

English Methods Course A course that specifically focuses on the techniques and process of pedagogical English.

English Secondary Education Major An English major pursuing training to teach English Language Arts (ELA) at the high school level in the United States.

Episode A single installment of a television or radio series. An episode of a series is comparable to a chapter in a novel.

Epistemology The branch of philosophy that is concerned with the theory of knowledge.

Essay An argument-driven prose composition that explores a focused theme or topic.

Ethos The credibility or reputation of the writer; one of Aristotle's three rhetorical appeals.

Euphemism An inoffensive word or phrase that is substituted for one considered to be offensive or unpleasant.

Evidence The facts and information provided to support a particular claim or stance.

Evolutionary Biology A subfield of biology that focuses on the evolutionary processes of different species over time.

Evolutionary Linguistics The study of the origin and development of language through human evolution.

Explainers Short videos or blog posts that make sense of what happens in a cinematic, popular culture, or new media work, often connecting what happens to "canonical" or written source material.

Explicit Knowledge Knowledge that can be easily transferred to others because it has been recorded in a format that allows for such transfer.

Exposition The part of a piece of writing in which the background information necessary to understand the content is given to readers.

Fairy Tale A children's story that usually contains aspects of fantasy and magic and ultimately teaches a life lesson of some sort.

Fan Art Works of art created by fans of movies, television shows, books, comics, or video games. The artwork may contain one or more characters from the source text, but it may also include other characters that have been created by the fan themselves.

Fan Fiction A written work created by a fan of, and featuring characters from, a piece of media such as a movie, television show, book, comic, video game, or television show. Typically, this work either satisfies a problem the fan had with the original content, continues the story of a particular episode or plot, or just allows the creator to explore the characters further. Fan fiction may correspond to "canon," which means keeping faithful to the original source text, or it may diverge from the source text to create scenarios that would not work within "canon."

Fan Theory A prediction that a fan makes about what will happen in films, television, video games, or books based on exhaustive analysis of material that has already appeared as well as media connected to their object of interest.

Fandom A collective of fans, which is usually regarded as a community.

Fantasy A genre of writing that usually involves magical elements of some kind.

Feature Writing In depth reporting on an event or topic of interest that is typically published in newspapers, journals, magazines, or other similar formats.

Feminism A belief system that advocates for the political, cultural, social, and economic equality of the sexes and opposes patriarchy, which it perceives as oppressive.

Fiction A form of prose narrative that uses imagined events and characters to create a story.

Field A specialized area of inquiry in an academic discipline. Each chapter in this textbook covers one or more fields within the larger discipline of English Studies.

Field Research The collection of research data outside of traditional research spaces such as in natural settings or social environments.

Figure of Speech A word or phrase that is used in a nonliteral sense to enhance the beauty of a piece of writing. Some of these include similes, metaphors, hyperbole, and personification.

Film Festivals Events designed to present multiple films over a series of days at indoor and/or outdoor screening venues. These festivals usually take place in a single city or region and typically showcase mainly arthouse or indie films. They also include networking events for industry professionals, press conferences, and talk-back sessions for audiences. Famous film festivals include the Sundance Film Festival and the Toronto Film Festival, among others.

Film Noir Typically describing American thriller or detective films from the 1940s and 1950s, a cinematic style is characterized as being gritty, fatalistic, pessimistic.

Fluency The ability to understand a language and communicate in it as well as, or almost as well as, a native speaker.

Folklore Traditional beliefs, values, and customs of a culture that is passed through generations by oral storytelling.

Folktale A story that connects to a specific culture and is typically passed down over time by word of mouth.

Font Style A set of displayable text characters of the same specific style and design.

Forensic Linguistics The application of linguistic methodology to the forensic context of language, law, criminal investigation, trial, and judicial procedure.

Formal Report A professionally written statement of facts related to a business matter.

Free Verse A form of poetry that does not follow a set rhyme scheme or meter.

Freewriting A common technique of idea generation in which a person will continuously write without formal regards to spelling, grammar, or topic.

Game Narrative The storyline and events that take place within a game.

Gaze Theory A theory focusing on sightlines in works of cinema, which argues that the character who is doing the looking has power over what or who they look at. By analyzing the sightlines in a work of cinema, viewers can find a key to its interpretation.

Gender The characteristics connected to emotions, behavior, preferences, and more that we typically associate with people based on their biological sex. Individuals may have a gender identity that does not match their biological sex, or they may inhabit a gender identity outside of the binary categories of masculinity and femininity; for gender in grammar, see **Grammatical Gender**.

Genre A category that a piece of writing or cinema fits into based on its formal characteristics.

Genre Fiction or Cinema Plot-driven works of fiction or cinema that align with an established type or interest area in order to appeal to existing fans. Some examples of these include mystery, science fiction, and romance.

Global Literature Literature from around the world, spanning different cultures, languages, and ethnicities.

Golden Age of Cinema or Hollywood Spanning the years between the 1920s and 1960s, a period of innovation and excellence in cinema, which was fostered by the studio system that controlled the industry at the time.

Grammar The whole system and structure of a language that includes syntax and morphology.

Grammar Book A reference book outlining the grammatical structure of a language.

Grammatical Gender In Old English, a classification of nouns as masculine, feminine, or neuter and, in a sentence, the required agreement of words related to those nouns; nouns in Present-Day English use only gender largely based on animateness and biology.

Graphic Novel A book-length work that uses both images and words to create its narrative.

Graphics The production or products of digital art.

Great Vowel Shift A series of major changes in the pronunciation of vowels in the English language from the fourteenth to eighteenth centuries that influenced all dialects of English; the Shift primarily affected the long vowels of Middle English.

High Culture Aspects of a culture, or of cultural products, which are considered elite and are often associated with upper-class individuals.

Hippie A counterculture group of the 1960s characterized as youth movement that protested war and violence.

Historical Linguistics The study language change over time.

Horror (1) A type of genre fiction or genre cinema that creates scenarios and characters designed to scare, disgust, startle, or terrorize its audience in some way. (2) As an emotion, horror refers to extreme shock, fear, and disgust.

Hybridity The making of a new identity as a result of competing cultural influences.

Hypermediated Imbedded in a number of different formats, each of which influences a person's understanding of the information at hand.

Hypertext Text displayed on a computer or other technological device that links to other text that can be read progressively.

Idea Generation The initial step in the writing process in which the writer narrows focus and considers options for what to write.

Identity The conditions that make someone or something who or what they are; can include features of personality, social status, cultural background, physical appearance, history, and more.

Ideology A system of ideas and ideals that are pervasive among a group of people that are often connected to politics or economics and may reflect unconscious biases, mystifications, or philosophies.

Imagery A figure of speech that uses descriptive words to paint an image of a scene in a reader's mind.

Impact A text's effect or influence on its audience, other texts, or the world.

Inclusion The practice of involving and empowering individuals from diverse intellectual, disability, gender, sexual, class, racial, and ethnic backgrounds in order to promote and sustain a culture of respect and belonging for all members of a community.

Independent Film Also called an indie film, a work of cinema that typically has no ties to major film studios and is distributed by independent entertainment companies. Often, these films are premiered at film festivals and never see widespread theater release.

Inflection (Linguistic) The change in the form of a word in a language to express a grammatical function or linguistic attribute such as tense, mood, person, number, case, and gender.

Inkhorn Terms A foreign borrowing of a word into English that is deemed unnecessary or overly pretentious.

Inspiration Feeling mentally or emotionally stimulated to do something; an especially important concept in the fields of literature, cinema, and creative writing.

Interactive Fiction A story that allows the reader to choose how the narrative will proceed.

Interactivity The ability to engage directly with a media technology to customize one's individual user experience.

Interdisciplinary Research or education that combines two or more academic disciplines.

Interlocutor A person who partakes in dialogue.

International Phonetic Alphabet (IPA) A system of phonetic symbols created to represent in writing the sounds of all world languages.

Internet of Things The interconnection via the internet of computing devices embedded in everyday objects, enabling them to send and receive data.

Internet Subcultures Groups that are deeply embedded in online connectivity and are formed, maintained, and disseminated through the internet on various websites, apps, gaming platforms, or webpages.

Internet Technology The infrastructure specific to the internet and which allows the internet to function.

Interpretation The act of examining and describing the meaning of something.

Intonation The rise and fall of the voice when speaking.

Investigative Reporting A form of journalism in which a reporter spends months or years investigating one important event, crime, or controversy and then creates a long, detailed report with their findings.

Invited Readings Public events where established authors are invited to read their work and engage with their readers by answering questions or signing books for them.

Irregular Verb A verb that uses an internal vowel change rather than the addition of *-d* or *-ed* to the verb stem in order to indicate the past tense.

Ivory Tower Referring to a person or place as being sheltered from the practical problems of reality.

Jargon The specialized terminology or language associated with a specific social or professional group.

Journalism The activity or profession of reporting for news organizations; journalistic writing typically aims to communicates facts quickly and succinctly to keep readers informed.

Jump Cut A technique in video editing that consists of an sudden transition from one shot, or one scene, to another. Usually, this type of cut signifies the passage of time.

Knowledge Data, information, skills, or facts that an individual gains through education or experience.

Language of Wider Communication (LCW) A language used by people as a medium of communication across language or cultural barriers.

Language A method of human communication that can be spoken, written, or visually represented (as with ASL), which consists of a structured and conventional use of words.

Language Poetry Poetry that emphasizes the reader's role in finding the true meaning of a written work.

Lexical Categories Parts of speech in a language.

Lexicon A reference book or tool that is very similar to a dictionary but includes both bound and unbound morphemes..

LGBTQ An acronym that stands for Lesbian, Gay, Bisexual, Transgender, Queer that is used to describe individuals and communities that inhabit often marginalized sexual identities.

Life Writing A form of personal narrative that records the memories and experiences of the author or of another person.

Limited Release Media that only reaches a small or restricted audience. For film, limited releases open in fewer than 599 theaters, though if it gains popularity it might open in more.

Link Also known as a hyperlink, data on a webpage or website that a user can follow by clicking, usually which takes them to a new webpage or website.

LinkedIn A social networking site that is business-oriented and designed to connect employers, job seekers, and colleagues within a profession.

Literacy The aptitude to read and write.

Literary Agent A professional who is hired by an author for the purposes of dealing with publishers and others involved in the publishing of the author's work. Authors secure literary agents through a competitive process through which agents select authors based on the quality of their writing.

Literary Canon The group of texts that literary experts agree that educated people should have read.

Literary Criticism Commentary on the quality and character of written works, particularly those works that are included in the literary canon.

Literary Fiction Works of fiction that are deemed as worthy of being a part of the literary canon because of their formal qualities and attention to revealing important truths or reflecting significant issues in society. This category is opposed to genre fiction.

Literary Magazines Publications that feature creative writing and that target niche audiences of writers and teachers of writing.

Literature Review An evaluative report of the findings from secondary scholarly and critical sources about a topic to contextualize one's own research.

Logos The evidence, logic, and facts of the information contained in a piece's content. Logos is one of Aristotle's three rhetorical appeals.

Long Vowels Vowels that have a perceived extended duration of sound.

Low Vision Visual impairment that is not correctible through glasses, contact lenses, medication, or surgery.

Lyric Poetry Verse compositions that take personal emotions as their central subject.

Mainstream Commercial Publishing The industry of producing and selling books to a mass market audience for profit.

Marxism The political and economic theory spearheaded by Karl Marx and Friedrich Engels, which asserts that social and class conflict and oppression is the direct consequence of capitalism. Capitalism, by Marxist definition, depends on the exploitation of the working class for capital gain among the elite. Marxism, as a theory of analysis, examines social difference and the tensions created among a society under capitalism.

Mass Audience The large general public of consumers.

Mass Consumption The purchase or use of capital (goods and services) by a large number of individuals.

Mass Culture The values, mores, ideas, and beliefs that are developed from a common exposure to the same culture over time, such as music, art, or cinema. This is specifically media that is mass-produced for mass audiences.

Mass Media Any means of communication that reaches a large number of people or a mass audience.

Materialist Approaches A way of studying works of writing through using physical evidence to draw conclusions about the histories and cultures that created them.

Mechanics The rules of written language.

Media Ecology The environment of competing sources of information that shapes our understanding of the world and the information we consume.

Medium The form by which something is created, communicated, or expressed.

Melodrama A work of drama meant to appeal to the emotions of a viewer, which is characterized by exaggerated characters and exciting events.

Meme Media that is copied, spread, and modified over the internet at a rapid pace, going viral, usually in the form of humorous images, videos, or texts.

Memo A brief, written message, usually connected to workplace communications.

Memoir A form of personal narrative that details certain events in one's life but that does not necessarily offer a comprehensive portrayal of the author's entire life story, as autobiography does.

Metaphor A figure of speech that uses direct comparison to insinuate a deeper meaning. The line, "The world is a vampire," from the Smashing Pumpkins song "Bullet with Butterfly Wings" is a metaphor.

Metathesis The transposition of letters, sounds, or syllables in a word, such as "aks" for "ask."

Meter The rhythm of a piece of poetry, which is produced by the pattern of stressed and unstressed syllables, known as feet, and the number of feet per line.

Method Acting (The Method) A range of training and rehearsal techniques emphasizes sincere and emotionally expressive performances, which depend on improvisation, drawing on one's own emotional present or past, and inhabiting the emotional and psychological reality of one's role.

Methodology A set of rules and procedures for conducting a task or executing a project, such as the rules and procedures for conducting or executing a research project in a given discipline or field of a discipline.

Metrical Poetry that is composed with a set number and pattern of stressed and unstressed beats per line.

Microblogging A blog that only allows for short text updates.

Middle English The form of the English language spoken and written after the Norman Conquest (1066) until the late fifteenth century.

Minimal Poetry Short poems designed for viewing on digital devices with small screens, such as smartphones and Apple watch.

Mixed-Genre Writing A written work that blends elements and themes from two or more genres of writing.

Mobile App A mobile application designed to run on a smart device.

Montage A filmmaking technique of splicing images or video and editing them together sequentially to create a continuous scene.

Mood The atmosphere or tone of a text.

Morphemes The smallest units of meaning in a word.

Morphology The study of word formation.

Motion Pictures Synonymous with movie or film: a feature-length recorded cinematic production that is released in movie theaters or on television.

Movable Type Printing type made up of individual pieces with a single letter or other character that can be assembled to print any desired combination or line.

Movie Synonymous with motion picture or film: a feature-length recorded cinematic production that is released in movie theaters or on television.

Movie Theater A building in which films are shown for public consumption, usually which charge a fee for attendance.

Multimedia The use of multiple forms of media, such as video, sound, or text, in one presentation or production.

Multimodal Any text that engages multiple modes of communication. While multimodal texts may include digital formats, they need not do so.

Multiple-Author Text A text that is written and published by multiple individuals, such as a journal or research paper.

Music Videos Short-form cinematic works produced to accompany popular music.

Narrative A story detailing events that occur to real or fictional people, written to entertain, inform, or educate the reader. This could be written, spoken, illustrated, acted out, or utilize other forms of media to convey its message.

Narrative Point-of-View or Perspective The vantage point from which a work of poetry, fiction, or nonfiction tells its story. Typical examples are first person, third-person limited, and third-person omniscient.

Neologism A newly coined word or phrase that is in the process of entering common use but that has yet to be accepted fully into mainstream language.

Network Television A telecommunications company that distributes television programming that is paid for by commercials and broadcast over the airwaves by local broadcasting stations into consumer's homes by means of an antenna. The "Big Three" television networks in the United States are ABC, NBC, and CBS.

Networking The cultivation of personal and productive relationships for employment or business purposes.

Neurolinguistics The study of the relationship between language and the structure and functioning of the brain.

Neuroscience A subfield of science that deals with the structure and function of the brain and the nervous system.

New Criticism A twentieth-century formalist approach to interpreting literature that relies on the technique of close reading to marshal evidence.

New Formalism In the late-twentieth and early-twenty-first centuries, a movement in English Studies away from highly politicized theoretical approaches to criticism and back toward approaches focused on formal analysis. This movement corresponds to the new formalism in American poetry, which promotes a return to metrical and rhymed verse.

New Historicism A theoretical approach that draws upon material culture and historical artifacts to situate interpretations of artistic, literary, and cultural texts.

Nickelodeon An early venue for watching cinema that charged one nickel as an admission fee.

Nonfiction A form of prose writing that creates a narrative from facts and real events, emotions, and experiences using the techniques of literary representation usually reserved for fiction.

Nonliterary Expository Essay An organized piece of prose that explains a specific topic or set of ideas not related to literature with less depth of argument and research than is found in a persuasive or research essay.

Novel A long-form prose narrative that uses fictitious events and people to tell a story.

Novella A very long short story or a very short novel.

Nuyorican A combination of the terms "New Yorker" and "Puerto Rican," which refers to the people and culture of the Puerto Rican diaspora located in or around New York City.

Objectified To have had one's status reduced to that of an object without autonomy.

Objective Unbiased when observing and forming conclusions.

Occasional Writing A written work composed for a particular occasion or event.

Ode A form of lyric poem meant to be sung, which addresses a specific person, object, or emotion.

Official Language A language given legal standing within a country or region, used by the government and courts and taught in school.

Old English Earliest form of the English language spoken and later written in England by the Anglo-Saxons during the early Middle Ages until the Norman Conquest in 1066.

Online Linguistic Corpora (singular Corpus) An online database of real-world text samples from a language.

Ontology The philosophical study of being.

Open-Mic Nights Informal events held in public spaces like cafes or bars that invite writers to share their work in front of a live audience.

Organization The act of arranging a text in a particular manner.

Organizationally Situated Authors The professional writer who serves as a knowledge creator and information collaborator rather than simply as an information manager, packager, and publisher.

Original Pronunciation The production and performance of literary works from an earlier period of English spoken in the accent in use at the time they were written.

Oscar Movie A film that is made with the express purpose or hope of earning an Academy Award nomination. The Academy Award, or "Oscar," is given by the Academy of Motion Picture Arts and Sciences in recognition of excellence and cinematic achievement in many different categories, including acting, directing, cinematography, costuming, and more.

Oxford Comma (Serial Comma) An optional comma before "and" used within a list of three or more items for clarity.

Panning A technique of filming that incorporates a camera's movement from one viewpoint to another, simulating a moving gaze.

Pantoum A Malaysian form of poetry that is composed of three stanzas following the rhyme scheme ABAB and where the second and fourth lines of a stanza are repeated as the first and third lines of the following stanza.

Parody An imitation of the style or content of a text with exaggeration for comedic or satirical effect.

Participatory Culture A culture in which individuals act as prosumers (contributors or producers) rather than simply as consumers.

Pathos The effort to persuade an audience through an appeal to the emotions. Pathos is one of Aristotle's three rhetorical appeals.

Patriarchy The organizing principle that puts men in positions of power in social institutions.

Pausing The filler or hesitation marker, such as "um" or "ah" or "like," in spoken language.

PC Personal Computer.

Peak Television Contemporary (2000–present) television, in which the options of shows, movies, or channels for the viewer to choose from are so innumerable and exhaustive that it can seem overwhelming.

Pedagogy The methods, practice, and profession of teaching.

Peer-Reviewed Articles Articles that have been evaluated by several researchers or subject experts in the academic community prior to accepting it for publication in a scholarly journal.

Peer-Reviewed Journals Scholarly journals that published articles that have been evaluated by several researchers or subject experts in the academic community.

Performativity A concept that critical theory borrows from linguistics to describe the ways in which language, representation, and embodiment can constitute actions in the world. For theorist Judith Butler, gender is performative.

Personal Computer (PC) A device that allows an individual to access documents, the internet, or video games.

Philology The study of the structure and historical development of oral and written language in historical sources.

Phoneme The smallest distinctive unit of sound in a language.

Phonetics The study and classification of sound in spoken language.

Phonology The study of sound patterns and meaning in a language.

Photographic Image An image that is captured and recorded by a camera either on film or digitally. The process of taking and developing a photographic image is called photography, which records light and radiation to produce a chemical reproduction of a real-time scene.

Phrase A sequence of two or more words that stand together and form a component of a clause.

Platform In English Studies, a program or system on a computer used to generate a particular file or an environment that encourages certain types of communication.

Play A form of Literature designed to be acted out on a stage in front of a live audience.

Playwright An individual who writes plays.

Playwriting The act of writing a play designed to be acted out on a stage for a live audience.

Plot The events or action of the narrative in a written or cinematic work.

Podcast Fiction A podcast that presents a fictional story as episodic, online audio recordings.

Poem or Poetry A form of writing that eschews the typical grammatical constructions of everyday speech and writing in favor of a stylized composition that emphasizes rhythm and figures of speech to convey its content and to give its audience aesthetic pleasure.

Poetic Devices Tools meant to enhance a poem's meaning and intensify the mood and feeling. Poetic devices can be used to enrich other genres of writing as well.

Poetic Form The classification of a poem, which can be derived from elements such as the poem's structure, meter, rhyme scheme, and rhythm.

Poetry Slams Competitions in which poets share their work and are judged by the audience and eliminated until there is only one poet remaining.

Point-of-View Shots A filmmaking technique and camera angle that substitutes or emulates a character's viewpoint, allowing the viewer to see things as though they are themselves the character.

Possessive In grammar, the form of a noun or pronoun that indicates the belonging of one thing or person to something or someone else.

Postcolonial Theory An approach that investigates the cultural legacy of colonialism, focusing on the impact of colonialism on various cultures and societies as well as areas of land.

Postmodernism A twentieth-century movement that represents a departure from the ideas of modernism and brings about an attitude of skepticism, cynicism, and overall distrust of ideologies and theories, especially in relation to art.

Poststructuralism A system of thought that argues that structural analysis, by its logical extension, creates additional structures that must be endlessly unraveled.

Poststructuralist Film Theory An approach that sees deconstruction as a necessary tool in unravelling the infinite meanings that cinematic works might convey.

Praxis An accepted practice or custom.

Premium Cable Television An add-on to basic cable television service that allows viewers to subscribe to a channel or package of channels for a subscription fee in order to access programming that does not include commercial interruptions. An example of premium cable television is HBO.

Prepositional Phrase A modifying phrase that includes a preposition and its object.

Prescriptivism The attempt to set rules defining the preferred or "correct" use of language.

Prescriptivist A person who emphasizes the rules for a language, such as English, on what is correct and not correct rather than focusing on how that language is really used.

Present-Day English Any variety of English in use by speakers today.

Presentation Software A computer program, such as PowerPoint or Prezi, used to create a sequence of text, graphics, and audio that usually accompanies a speech or presentation.

Pride A term for annual events that happen around the world to celebrate LGBTQ identity and raise awareness about important issues in LGBTQ communities. The first Pride events were organized to commemorate the June 1969 Stonewall Riots in New York City.

Primary Source The primary object of analysis for a scholar in English Studies, such as an unedited, original manuscript. This term can also be used for published texts that are the object of criticism.

Print Media Communication that appears in written or illustrated form, such as newspapers or books.

Printing Press A mechanical device for applying pressure to an inked surface resting upon a print medium, thereby transferring the ink.

Problem-Posing Method of Education A theory of education that gives students ownership over their learning by encouraging them to identify problems, determine research questions, and work independently or collaboratively to discover solutions to the problems that engage them.

Program In this case, an electronic set of instructions used to generate a particular file.

Proofreading The step near the end of the writing process reserved for identifying and correcting errors in spelling, grammar, and punctuation.

Proposal (1) In business, a written document designed to persuade a prospective client to buy a service or product. (2) In academic writing, composition in which the author identifies a topic, states research questions, explains methodology, and suggests a workplan.

Prose Narrative A piece of writing that tells a story using a style and structure that mirrors the patterns and grammatical tendencies of everyday speech.

Prose A form of writing that uses the natural rhythms of speech and grammatical structures of spoken language to convey its message.

Prose Poetry A poetic form that avoids using lines and stanzas to organize its content but that does use poetic devices and other features typical to poetry.

Prosumer A customer who is not just a consumer but also directly involved in the design and manufacture of a product.

Psychoanalysis A set of theories and therapeutic techniques that focus on the unconscious mind and which forms the basis for treatment of mental health disorders. In English Studies, psychoanalytic approaches encourage readers to interrogate and analyze texts by investigating unconscious or repressed desires that are evident in the text.

Psycholinguistics The study of language in the context of psychology and neurobiology.

Psychology The scientific study of the mind and its functions, particularly focused on effects on behavior.

Publisher A person or company that prepares written works for sale.

Punk A subculture that emerged in the 1970s characterized as anti-establishment.

Purpose The motivation for producing a piece of writing, including the objectives that the writer would like to achieve.

Qualitative Method Research and data collection, such as interviews, images, videos, or soundbites, that is non-numerical.

Quantitative Method Research and data collected through polls, questionnaires, surveys, etc. for statistical, mathematical, or numerical analysis.

Queer Theory An approach that developed out of the fields of women's studies and gay and lesbian studies that appropriates the pejorative term "queer" to signify an expansive approach that considers the writing produced by LGBTQ authors, the representation of LGBTQ identities, the values of queer communities, and the very definition of "queer."

Race A category of identity established through the creation of social hierarchies based on the color of a person's skin.

Reader Response Theory A theoretical framework that focuses on the readers' reactions to a text as the fundamental evidence for interpretation.

Realism A style of writing in which fictional characters and events purport to mirror the way that people behave or events unfold in everyday life.

Recording Technology Devices that allow for the documentation and display of auditory or visual media. Used for informational, educational, entertainment, and casual purposes, these devices include things such as microphones and video cameras.

Register (of Language) Referring to a scale of formality in language, including informal registers that are typically more conversational and formal ones that are more academic or professional.

Regular Verb A verb that adds –d or –ed to the verb stem in order to indicate the past tense.

Research Question The central question that a research project or paper is focused on answering.

Résumé A document that summarizes the personal, educational, and professional qualifications and experience of a job applicant.

Reverse-Chronology Résumé The standard format of the common résumé in which education and work experience are presented from most recent to furthest in the past.

Revision The step in the writing process where a text is changed, expanded, clarified, corrected, and improved from an earlier version.

Rhetoric The art of persuasion in speaking and writing. Rhetoric focuses on the techniques communicators use to reach their audience.

Rhetorical Analysis An analysis that identifies an author's strategies used to persuade their audience.

Rhetorical Situation The event or situation that gives rise to the use of rhetoric. The rhetorical situation includes the social, historical, or personal context, the speaker's motivations, and the audience being addressed.

Rhetorical Theory An analytical approach that focuses interpretation through a consideration of a text's rhetoric.

Rhetorical Triangle The three components of rhetorical communication: writer/speaker, content, and audience.

Rhetorician An expert in the field of rhetoric.

Rhyme In terms of words, lines, or syllables, to rhyme is to end with a sound that corresponds with another.

Romance A type of genre fiction that is focused on the relationship and romantic love of two people and that usually has an optimistic ending.

Romantic Comedy A genre of cinema that focuses on relationships between characters and portrays the ups and downs of love in a humorous, light-hearted way.

Russian Formalism A theoretical framework that focuses on poetic techniques, language, and the structure of literature.

Sans Serif Font A type of font that does not use serifs, or "tails," at the end of text characters.

Sapir-Whorf Hypothesis (Theory of Linguistic Relativity) A theory in sociolinguistics that argues that the structure of a language determines or greatly influences cognition and behavior in the culture in which it is spoken.

Science Fiction A type of genre cinema or genre fiction that focuses on the impact of current or possible future technology on society; stories of this genre typically take place in the future or outer space and deal with extraterrestrials or robots.

Scopophilic Desire To seek pleasure from looking or watching. An important concept in cinema studies.

Screen Refers to an electronic screen on which television shows, movies, or other videos can be played.

Screenplay The script of a cinematic work.

Screwball Comedy A genre of cinema that became popular in the 1930s and 1940s, usually focusing on a heterosexual relationship in which the male's masculinity is challenged, leading to a "battle of the sexes." In the face of the Great Depression, screwball comedies focused on escapism and light-hearted, hopeful themes, while still criticizing social class tensions. Screwball comedies are a precursor of today's romantic comedies..

Script The written text for a play, which includes character dialogue, blocking directions, and stage directions.

Secondary Source A work of criticism or scholarship that provides context, evidence, or a contrary viewpoint about the topic of research or interpretation.

Semantics The meaning or relationship of meanings of a word, phrase, sentence, or text.

Semiotics The study of signs and symbols as elements of communicative behavior; has a significant influence on the development of critical theory, especially the poststructuralist analytical technique deconstruction.

Sentence A set of words that expresses a thought and contains a subject and predicate.

Serial Consisting of short segments at regular intervals, with each making up part of a larger whole. Many novels in the nineteenth century were originally published in serial format in magazines, and much television programing uses a serial format, with individual episodes of a given program airing daily or weekly.

Setting The location, or locations, where a narrative or an event takes place.

Sexuality A category of identity connected to an individual's sexual orientation, desire, and/or experiences. Sexuality, or sexual identity, can be broken down into a number of categories, including lesbian, gay, bisexual, queer, straight, asexual, and more.

Short Story A story that has a fully developed plot and theme but is considerably shorter than a novel.

Showrunner The person with creative control and responsibility over a television series. Sometimes the showrunner is the person or team who created the concept for the television series, but sometimes the showrunner, who has creative control from day to day, did not actually create the show's concept.

Simile A comparison using like or as that is commonly found in poetry.

Simulation A virtual representation of reality.

Simulacrum/a From Jean Baudrillard's theory, a term that indicates a "copy" of a thing that never really existed. Baudrillard points to Disney World to exemplify this theory.

Single-Author Research or Publication Research conducted by one person, eventually resulting with a written scholarly work by one author. Some fields of English studies (e.g., literary studies) value single-author research more highly than others (e.g., professional writing and technical communication).

Skills-Based Résumé A document that lists a person's job qualifications in skill categories rather than in reverse-chronological work-experience categories.

Slang An informal register of language that is typically restricted to a particular context or group of people.

Slash Fiction A genre of fan fiction that focuses on the interpersonal relationships and sexual relationships between fictional characters of the same sex.

Smart Device An electronic device, such as a smartphone, iPad, or Android tablet, that is cordless, mobile, and always connected.

Smartphone A mobile phone that performs the functions of a computer and usually has a touchscreen interface, built-in camera, music player, and internet access.

Social Action Organized interaction with individuals or groups with the goal of social reform.

Social Media Apps, webpages, or websites that give users a platform to connect with one another, share their thoughts and content, and communicate.

Social Robotics A form of Artificial Intelligence that is designed to interact with humans and other robots.

Sociolinguistics The study of language that explores the relationship between language and culture.

Sonnet A poem composed of fourteen lines, with ten syllables in each line, and which usually follows one of two rhyme schemes: ABBAABBA CDECDE (Italian Sonnet) or ABAB CDCD EFEF GG (English Sonnet).

Sound Vibrations that travel through the air and into an organism's ear, which allows them to "hear."

Sound Effects Sound created, both artificially using technology or practically using real-life equipment, for use in a play, movie, or other media productions.

Sound Recording The technological recording, storing, and replaying of sound waves such as singing, music, sound effects, or spoken words.

Soviet Montage Theory A methodology that seeks to understand and create visual art or cinema through heavily edited montage or splicing together a sequence of film to create a whole. The theory itself focuses on the idea that a series of connected images could portray a set of complex ideas and therefore represent the entirety of a film's ideology and intellect.

Speech A form of discourse that is delivered orally to an audience.

Speech Act Theory A theoretical approach that explores the way verbal utterances can be used not only to present information but also to carry out actions.

Spoiler When important plot information of a book, movie, television show, or other media is shared with someone, which effectively ruins the suspense or surprise of the narrative.

Spoken Word A form of poetry that is meant to be performed.

Stadium Seating A seating arrangement, also known as theater seating, which is historically associated with and used by performing arts and sports venues. This is the type of seating in many movie theaters.

Standard American English (SAE) The variety of American English used in professional communication and taught in school that is perceived by Americans to be lacking any distinctly regional, ethnic, or socioeconomic characteristics.

Standardized Test A form of testing that provides the same questions, answers, and prompts to a collection of test takers and is then scored in a "standard" manner as to compare the relative performances of the test takers.

563

Story A narrative detailing events that occur to real or fictional people, written to entertain, inform, or educate the reader. This could be written, spoken, illustrated, acted out, or utilize other forms of media to convey its message.

Storytelling Traditions Conventional approaches to passing on knowledge from one generation to the next in a given culture or community by telling stories, often orally and many times in a group setting.

Streaming Services An online source for entertainment media, such as television shows, movies, or videos, that provides an alternative to cable television. These networks often require monthly paid subscriptions (Netflix or Hulu) or payment to "rent" streaming material for view (Amazon Prime Video or YouTube).

Structural or Structuralist Linguistics The branch of linguistics that deals with language as a system of interrelated structures, originating from the ideas of Swiss linguist Ferdinand de Saussure.

Structuralism A theoretical framework in which elements of human culture must be understood through the analysis of their relationship to a broader system or structure in that culture. By applying a structure to the object of study, the theory argues, and by analyzing the structure as it contains the object of study, we can discover the object of study's meaning.

Students' Right to Their Own Language First introduced in 1974, this statement made by the CCCC asserts that the individual has an inherent right to be taught and to learn in a language that matches their own patterns and dialects.

Studio Arts Fine arts disciplines such as music, theater, or painting in which students receive practical training from mentors who themselves are artists and creative practitioners.

Studio System The method of filmmaking and distribution that dominated the Golden Age of Hollywood. Major studios (primarily Paramount Pictures, Metro Goldwyn Mayer, Warner Brothers Pictures, 20th Century Fox, and RKO) produced movies on their own film lots with a creative team locked into long-term contracts and notably took power over exhibition by way of vertical integration, which meant that the studios had ownership of every part of the filmmaking and showing process, thus capitalizing on their revenue. The studio system thrived from 1927 to 1948.

Style Guide A manual that presents a set of standards for the writing and the design of documents for either general use or for a more specific publication, organization, or field, used to improve communication; also called a manual of style.

Stylistics The study and interpretation of written and spoken texts through the close examination of language.

Subculture A social group whose values and norms differ from those of the majority. These groups may be influenced or may be formed by specific beliefs or a common shared interest, such as people who hold particular political views, share a similar fashion sense, or participate in fandoms of certain television shows. Subcultures tend to be smaller groups than countercultures, and they do not challenge the status quo of mainstream culture in widespread ways.

Subject The noun or pronoun in a sentence that performs the action of the verb.

Subject-Matter Methods Courses An Education course that focuses on the conditions, processes, and results of teaching, learning, and education in relation to content.

Subjective Having been influenced by personal opinions when forming a conclusion.

Survey Courses Foundational introductory courses that are sometimes intended to be taken in a sequence with other courses in order to prepare students for more specialized upper-level course offerings.

Symbolic Action Expression that conveys beliefs and desires so strong that they count as a kind of action in themselves.

Synchrony or Synchronic Analysis An approach to the analysis of language by examining language at a specific point of time, usually the present, without taking history into account.

Syntax The set of rules, principles, and processes that govern the structure of sentences in a language.

Tablet A small portable computer with a touchscreen interface and internet access.

Tacit Knowledge Knowledge that cannot be easily transferred to others because it has not been recorded in a format that allows for such transfer.

Talkies A term used in the 1920s to identify movies that had synchronized sound to accompany the visual recorded narrative of motion pictures. This term marked the transition from silent films to films with recorded sound.

Telegraphic Narrative A technique for telling stories that relies on the audience's ability to process brief visual or verbal messages, understand their connotations, and put together a story based on those communications.

Television A device or system that receives signals and transmits video from stations and produces those signals on a screen. The term might also refer to a television program, which ranges from short skits to commercials to full movies or documentaries.

Temporality The state of existing within the passage of time.

Text A general term referring to the artifacts that English Studies practitioners create or interpret. Works of language, literature, rhetoric, cinema, professional writing, and more may be referred to as "texts."

Text Mining The process of scanning a written work to pull out significant information.

The Kuleshov Effect A technique of filmmaking and montage, the Kuleshov effect was created by Lev Kuleshov in the 1910s and is described as the phenomenon in which viewers of a film derive meaning from two shots as they interact instead of from one shot in isolation. Kuleshov's own creation of this showed a man's face, spliced with three separate images. Depending on what those images showed, the audience understood the emotions and motivations of the man a different way.

The Musical During the Golden Age of Hollywood and following the introduction of sound to filmmaking, a genre of feature film in which dialogue between characters is interspersed with song breaks that apply directly to the narrative.

The Sophists Itinerant teachers of primarily philosophy and rhetoric in ancient Greece.

The Western Fiction or Cinema that focuses on cowboys in the western United States, usually set in the late nineteenth to early twentieth centuries. Characteristics of this genre include a focus on the harshness of life on the western frontier, specifically the often desolate landscape and sociopolitical tensions within small towns, saloons, railways, or military forts.

The Workshop Method or Model A method of writing instruction originating in the creative writing classroom in which writers share their creations by reading them aloud and then get feedback from their peers in the workshop.

Thesis Statement Usually a one-sentence assertion that summarizes the main claim of a text and why it matters; typically an essay or research paper.

Tone In writing, the attitude of the writer to the subject or audience, typically conveyed through word choice or viewpoint of the writer.

Transatlantic African Slave Trade The segment of the global slave trade that forcibly transported around 10 to 12 million enslaved African people to the Americas from across the Atlantic in the sixteenth to nineteenth centuries.

Transhistorical An approach to literary study that cuts across the temporal boundaries through which literary periods are formed in order to draw comparisons, synthesize, and contrast texts that typically are not put into conversation with each other.

Transitions A passage, phrase, or word in a text that seamlessly connects two topics or ideas to each other.

Transmedia Experience The intentional encouragement by a business to involve the customer in active collaboration and storytelling across multiple traditional and digital delivery platforms.

Transnational An approach to literary study that cuts across the geographical boundaries through which national literary canons are formed in order to draw comparisons, synthesize, and contrast texts that typically are not put into conversation with each other.

Tweet A short post made on Twitter.

Typeface A set of text characters that all share similar design; similar to font.

Usability In document design, the measure of effectiveness, efficiency, and satisfaction by the user of a document or multimedia presentation.

Usage Guide A reference work that explains how written and spoken English is used in terms of grammar, style, syntax, and word choice.

Value Something's worth; in this case, a text's importance and usefulness.

VCR An acronym meaning videocassette recorder, a machine that can record or play video and audio on a television. The first VCR was developed in Japan in 1976, and they quickly became antiquated in the face of DVD technology, leading to their discontinuation in the late 2000s.

Verse Poetry.

Video Game An interactive piece of digital media in which the player controls what appears on the screen. The very first video game is thought to be a 1958 creation similar to Pong, coded by physicist William Higinbotham.

Video Game Narrative The story that is portrayed through scenes, dialogue, and visual elements in a video game, which are often activated by the player's decisions. While some games have very little narrative, such as Pong or Tetris, there are many in-depth, open-world games that hinge on a player's understanding of the narrative and how it is being told, such as *Horizon: Zero Dawn* or *Skyrim*.

Video Rental Business Brick-and-mortar businesses that emerged after the development of VCRs that allowed customers to rent videos to watch in their homes, such as Blockbuster. With the emergence of the internet, these entities closed their doors because they could not compete with the convenience of mail order services, automated kiosks, or streaming services that provided the same or better content with more convenience.

Villanelle A form of poetry consisting of nineteen lines and six stanzas, where the first five stanzas are tercets, followed by a singular quatrain. The first and third lines of the first stanza are alternately repeated as the last line of each consecutive stanza.

Viral When a piece of media, usually a picture or a video, gets widely circulated very quickly on various internet platforms such as Twitter or Facebook. Examples of viral media might be an amusing picture of an animal, a video or sound recording of a well performed song cover, or a politically charged tweetstorm.

Virtual Reality A computer-generated, immersive simulation of a three-dimensional environment that can be interacted with in a seemingly real or physical way by a person using special electronic equipment, such as a headset.

Visual Narrative A story conveyed through visual media and mediums such as photography, film, or illustration.

Visual Rhetoric A method of communication and persuasion by using visual images and texts. Visual rhetoric might involve both placement of images in relationship to each other on the page as well as the use of particular colors or visual styles to create a particular response in the audience. As with verbal rhetoric, visual rhetoric engages audiences through the emotions (pathos), credibility (ethos), and facts and information (logos).

Vlog A video diary that is popular among celebrities, especially those who have gained their fame through the internet. The style of the video lends to a feeling of inclusion and rapport, as the vlogger speaks directly to the camera lens and the viewers. The word is a blend word, or a term that uses blending, of the terms "video" and "blog."

Voice The distinctive style of an author of a text.

Web Technology The technology that allows computers and other devices to communicate and share resources using something called markup language, which is the specific code that informs a website's formatting from within a text, such as HTML.

Website A digital publication accessible through the internet that may include multiple pages to organize content.

Webtexts Pieces that have been composed with the intention of disseminating them on websites or other platforms accessible to the public through the internet.

White Paper In business, an authorative report or guide that combines expert research and experience in order to argue for a specific solution or recommendation.

White Space Also known a negative space, the area on a document or other form of media that remains unmarked and typically white.

Wide Release A movie that is shown in theaters nationally, specifically in six hundred theaters or more throughout the United States and Canada, so that it might reach as many viewers as possible during its run.

Wide Shot Also known as a long shot or a full shot, this is an element in filmmaking, photography, or video production that frames an image so that an entire subject is within frame; often used to establish scenery and space.

Wiki An online encyclopedia that allows public editing and collaboration by its users, often leading to pages that offer information on very niche interests.

Word A single component of language that has a distinct meaning both on its own and within a phrase.

Word Processing Software A computer program that is used to manipulate a text document by inputting, editing, formatting, or outputting.

Writing Process The various steps that bring writers from the blank page to a polished final draft including idea generation, drafting, revision, copyediting, proofreading, and formatting for submission.

Young Adult Fiction A category of fiction that is intended for teenage audiences and usually follows problems and scenarios that readers of this age range would also be facing during this time of their life.

Zine A homemade, noncommercial magazine-style publication devoted to specialized or unconventional subject matter and that targets a niche audience.

Index

Printed in the USA
CPSIA information can be obtained
at www.ICGtesting.com
LVHW050305101224
798756LV00001B/64

* 9 7 8 1 3 5 0 0 5 5 4 0 7 *